The SUPER–SYSTEM

World's No. 1 New and Improved Ultimate Nihilist Theory of All Social Reality

by

Martin Josef White

ACKNOWLEDGMENTS

Since evading the clutches of education, I have never written for anything other than personal enjoyment. This work is, then, a departure, a shout unto the void.

I thank forever and above anything else my beautiful wife Christine Nevada Michael. Because of her I saw not much reason to sequester myself away to write books, for I became much too stimulated living a life I could not have imagined as a lonely boy. Our life has been our own separate and unimpeachable wonderworld. The other, far lesser thanks go to every author of pop culture, the music, the books, the movies, the sports, the television, the magazines, in appreciation for your talent and drive, the cavalcade of popular spirit that permitted me to bring a heightened sense of fun to join my more troubled psychic inclinations.

NOTE1: Unlike all "Acknowledgments" pages, this one cannot feature a socially bounteous roster of selfless individuals who collectively wiped the brow of the creator, placing him to bed nightly in communal under-support with saintly understanding and feathery encouragement. No one is to blame here, but that was just not the case.

NOTE2: There were no agents, editors, grants, professors, mentors, foundations, readers, colleagues, think tanks, blog sites, or publishing houses in, around, or within the pages of the book. As such, the errors, and errors of style of formal thought, will have troubled, and will trouble, no one but myself.

NOTE 3: The sentences are not in the tightest formation. There is repetition, restatement, tangent-hopping, maddening leaps – sometimes all in one paragraph. B and C and D do not always flow smoothly, effortlessly, painlessly from A in these paragraphs - at times, there are chasms of discontinuity, but this was simply a function of the climb. There is yet an animate sense to all of the constructions, or else I would have hit the delete key eventually. The task and the edifice was enormous, and I used only natural tools in my free climb.

November 2011

Chapter ONE
DEFINITION OF TERMS

DT1.-   **One**

The *supersystem* is the encompassing network of networks intersecting, reinforcing, supporting institutions and structures and organizations and corporations and laws and regulations and cultures that operate each moment above and in our individual actions and destinies.

DT2.-   **TSS**

The operating principle behind the *theory of the Supersystem* (hereafter referred to as tSS) is that all that we encounter as sentient beings is only fathomable as belonging to the enormous complexity of governed time, space, history, tradition. We are short-lived human beings, bound by our environments, our limitations, our minor dimensions, yet we continue to imagine ourselves as individuals of immense natural favor. We imbue all of our inherited social realities with great validity, as if there is an animate soundness to all the institutions that have somehow come along with our singular profound arrival on terra firma. However, the tSS presupposes that in this society built upon generations of settled civilization, there is now a *logical corruption* (LC) that is in virtual control of our existing social institutions.

DT3 -   **SR**

As a species, we retain limited self-governance, able to restrain our impulses towards destruction and injury in tenuous ways, but we are often incapable of seeing obvious tendencies towards deleterious or delusional actions that result in self-harm. We as Americans are extremely poor in *social regulation* (SR). In our nearly mindless devotions to "God"; the "Invisible Hand"; the sainthood of Mom, Dad, or the Family; Money; Art or Literature; Machines; Drugs; Nature; or whatever cultural artifact diverts us from the pointlessness of over-articulated society, we become inured to the absurd conditions of social reality. The gaze back to history gives us the superior position to scoff at Nazi Germany's obtuseness, the bestiality of genocidal European conquerors, the ignorance of haruspiscencers, the idiocies of flat–earthers, the ignorant lives of our misbegotten ancestors, but at our own feet lie terrible global economic inequality, warfare, poverty, and environmental degradation. Every existing institution in our social reality is devolving from within, afflicted by the dimensions of unalterable largeness and logical corruption (LC).

DT4 -   **HOPE**

You will wonder if such anger at the supersystem and despair at its correction implies withering anger and suicidal inclinations. I am not trying to give you a loaded gun, nor do I want to place one at my temple. I understand that I am not giving you immense hope, nor I am filled to the beatific brim with it. If we as a species cannot learn to provide for own social regulation, we will deserve the extinction that is rushing towards us. I would like to augment my chosen methods of escaping the dangerous, immoral, immovable supersystem with some convivial effective social protest, but I haven't found those good-time union halls yet. Those who do not have in the supersystem would gladly change places with us who do have, so they can try the breast-beating and guilt-mongering and liberal wishings-upon-a-star

Logical corruption is the operation by actors within large institutions that is necessarily inhumane, lying, deceitful, evasive, cumbersome, unproductive, or criminal. Our human social world could not function, given our limited capacity for self- and other-directed criticism, if higher levels of power were not awash in the poison of LC. Great rivers of effluvia of print have been wasted over the use of the terms "good vs. evil" and "conscience," as if humans do not conform their working and public selves to the dictates of imposed social conditions. We do have functioning cognitive powers of opposition and self-restraint, but we will die off as a species if we wait for humans to outgrow the corrosive effects of their social stations and positions. Once we first appreciate the real dimensions of the supersystem, we can then undertake a massive campaign to govern it, subdue it in places, or we can just marvel in our moral squalor at the over-large task of conquering our inherited predicaments – even of the good kind. Since the supersystem commands great allegiance to its dominance of its social reality, as well as its over-supply of electronic consumer goods and command of individual aspiration and anxiety, there is no move to eradicate its nature. The goods move, the money courses though its tributaries, the imperatives of the day-to-day reign o'er the land.

DT6 -   EVIL OR PROCESS

There is surely so little we can do about all, of this, now. Were all corruption the product of evil, were evil unknowable, was death and despair and violence the province of only the dark side, we would be able to summon forth religious awakening and call for gatherings on the hill to pass around the Coke and sing songs of coruscating goodness. That will never be, because all of our social institutions are governed by processes that spring from our common myths, our common folk pathways, our common honed human instincts. Each of our grand social institutions (GSIs) are subject to intense social erosion (SE- bring the acronym total to five, out of a self-imposed allotment of ten for this unsanctioned project). The judge in his chambers is as constrained by the reigning ethos of American exceptionalism as the punk teen, albeit in far different contexts, within different rules of engagement, with other traditions to contend with, but connected by many strands of cultural mythos. Detailing the social psychology of our GCI's takes great effort, deep inside penetration, heedless whistle-blowing, nursed inter-personal rage, and though exposes of our diseased GCI's have dotted our best-seller lists, they are more typically scorned and consigned to the remainder bins of disgruntlement.

DT 7 -   THE BANALITY Of THE "Banality of Evil"

Evil is not "banal" when it shoots a bullet into a head, drives a tank into a protester, cancels a life, massacres a community., drives species into extinction. A health care dys-system that needlessly plunges people into bankruptcy, early death, or ceaseless financial anxiety may be many adjectives, but surely not one of them is "banal." The perpetrators of our dubious and deleterious social systems may be perfectly fine burghers in others situations, as was Adolf Hitler when gardening, Paul Anka when given enough shirts for his crew, George W. when seated in a luxury box with a gay friend, technowarriors when pitching batting Little League batting practice, but these mundane pursuits have no impingement upon the acts of destruction that are occasioned by the champions of colonial imperial power. Our actions are not mitigated by any compensatory acts of kindness, but must stand, each in their totality, each in record of associations and effects. Social process is the human métier, yet we have so little contact with the conditions that adjust all social reality. Whether scarce or in surplus, the distribution of social goods is according to a sorry warehouse schedule that has lost all its receipts, its staff, its vehicles, and is in a self-looting stage.

DT 8 - **CONSPIRACY**

In perverse strengthening of the supersystem, any opposition to it that attempts to access its dimensions has become conspiracy-theory tinfoil mad speculation. Lizard rulers hiding aliens and the cure for AIDS – easily marginalized comic-book fantasies of unfathomable "evil" that make social awareness seem like lunacy. In fact, the supersystem does work through stealth and duplicity, through murderous conspiracy and genocidal war, through official lies and successful global cover-ups – but that's just for breakfast. And it quite easily runs on a second track of normal, every-day bureaucratic competence and instinctual honest professionalism – all of its reaches and methods and buttressing layers are observable, rational, right outside the door. What precisely happens in the corridors of power is known in detail only to its real purveyors, who have every reason to evade clear scrutiny and immediate revelation, and who must have acquired some capacity to dodge and weave through business-like non-discovery. The equally powerful charge of immorality can be lodged against American liberals, who pay taxes to an enormous military and spy industry, incarcerate more of their fellows than any other country, place profit and its calamitous inducements to corruption above all human values, and then pretend that all this consequential power is obtained through innocent, laudable means. Whoever killed JFK and dropped the Twin Towers and denied your medical claim and deliquesced your kids , it was a human being or number of them, all enmeshed in a social system that breathes and acts with overt human agency. Why exhume the bodies to celebrate once again the killers?

DT 9 - **INFO-OVERLOAD**

Unfortunately for the purposes of this book, the tSS is the product of reading during an age of Information Overload (IO), causing its sources and structures to be temporal and fragmentary. All knowledge, in the face of such global historical enormity as the Supersystem, is tentative, subject to comment, dispute, and necessarily incomplete. Further damning this project is the stipulation that all human knowledge is social, without value unless it causes direct effects in society as a whole. Within western civilization, the reduction of thought to an individual avatar, or savant, or genius, or artiste, has created an *autological culture*. Within this atomized construct, books are written by self-referential poets and dreamers, lectures given by professors hiding fractious personal crises, politics driven by ego-blasted "leaders" of universal duplicity, families headed by over-stressed parents, cars operated by solitary warriors of the rain-slickened clogged highway.

In an *autological culture*, the drone/auteur goes on and on, without surcease, without the loving intervention of his or fellow human cognitive peer individuals. The deluge of print since the Gutenberg has threatened the choking of our oceanic currents, in great part because readers expect to gaze rapturously upon the sacrosanct works of their solitary deities. Our brains are inclined to veneration, linked in one experiment to rats peering at pictures of their alphas rather than getting hits of sweet red juice, but our hypothalamus should recognize that this is often counter-productive. Not one more *book*, the IO world says, not one more stirring call for global social transformation from one First World merit-class dropout typist with a buying and driving history. All of our "authors" have fashioned *unitexts*, reflective of only one individual's arrangement of the 100 million cranial neurons. How many of them look upon their once-cherished texts later with loathing, seeing the folly of devoting so much bubbled-in time to the sound of their brain on auto-repeat? How could symbols on lines in ordered pages give them that *satisfied longing for purpose* that the world of living creatures so clearly could not? Who wishes never to hear their own predilections and habituated phraseology be recorded publicly, for mockery, even of the self- kind? An honest reader of non-fiction will be beset by the *whipsaw effect*, crashing between ideological contradictions that seep out separately from the well-researched, vetted, semi-persuasive, glossy books. In an age of Information Overload, the discontinuities between talk and action and between irresolvable sides leave the reader an one-person hung jury, unable to commit in necessary degree to either side. Never having to match an action to talk, our age is is simply a near-fight, radically discontinuous but unable to bring the issues to any cleansing airing, so the Big Boys rule the playground with only the chaos below them to manage.

DT 10 -   POWER GRAB

Our established social institutions interlock at many foundational junctions. The reasons for our mountainous frustrations with our society's operations are because of how reinforced our enemies are within their bureaucratic fortresses. This is true all across the political spectrum, but of course the weight of history is with the powerful entrenched structures. In our human pre-history, there were no churches, no expense-account hedge fund tax write-offs, no apathetic denizens of the anti-intellectual couch, but were instead bands of hunter-gatherers with enough of their own problems of food and shelter to shame we inheritors of civilization's benefits. National myths and religious delusions can wax and wane, there is always evolution or devolution within the natural order, but when there is such monumental reinforcement of unearned assumptions of blessedness in the imperial America of today, there are incredible bulwarks of support for militarist, wealth-hoarding, and unconscionable social reality. This has been the **Power Grab,** the relentless, omnidirectional, non-systemized usurpation of social processes by rich elites. After the WWII was won with the civilian dead buried by the millions overseas, American power set about to put a $ sign on every epiphenomenon of time and space and fantasy and reality and the oceans in between, and all of our human institutions became corrupted with this invisible command to monetize away, monetize tomorrow, seek the ground and make it pay.

DT 11 -   THE OUTLOOK

All humans possess individual temperaments and genetic dispositions that condition their accommodations to the supersystem. Not one life is guaranteed by specific circumstances, but broad and general influences are remarkably powerful and consistent in their effects. To see the world from the perspective of the individual is to miss the larger tendencies, the ones that enforce our social outcomes. The human animal is scared of the practice of social regulation, so we suffer in the darkness and chaos that this abhorrence brings – beset by an absurd world of mountebanks on the nightly news, specious lying political theater, faith-based sociology, lunatic business predation. In this laissez faire farce of supported myth, the profound and joyous spaces of the electronic playsphere oppose the bumptious invidium of human social degradation.

DT12 -   THE OCEAN AND THE LAND

Every year the supersystem still stands, a few will be doing well, the mass will be in a state of anxious fluxion, and the competing mass of poor will be left to suffer and die. As long as there is a social reality, a larger concept of global political status, there will be a hierarchical system that will be fed by the imposition of specious control upon the lower tranches. There will be numbers, goods, outlays and price-fixing, outlaw economics beyond rational understanding, a finite and concrete supersystem that will not be much besides feared and loathed. An ocean of talk and writing and roundelay of comment will always be seen from this land, and its massivity will depend on no one force or person or nefarious group, but on secondary sub-sections of inaction and elite convergence of controlling interest. The leaders of this will be drawn from the more immoral or moronic elements of the established conduits for upward mobility, the fully decrepit higher academic system, the fully corrupt judicial system, and the cretinous inherited wealth class.   There is, at present, not the slightest power to capsize these marvelous instruments for the transmission of criminal bequests.

DT 13-   HUMAN HISTORY

Because of the supersystem's immensity, we will all be but minute in relation to it. We are phantasms of interstellar dust, fated to live in abject contemplation of the illusions of consequence we can never be. And that's a charitable view, let alone placing the infinitesimal size of our decaying DNA against the massed global fortress of the social redoubt, and the unapproachable forces of history, and the limitations of time, space, and the scientific continuum yet to come. Back in our early human history, when hunting and gathering in bands, we were truly dependent on the workings of the group, and were of immense benefit to each other in our desperate functioning to survive. In this late stage of atomization the human race is split between a televisual bubble for half and a desperate struggle to eat for the other half. For neither side of current humanity is there a "meaning," a "purpose," that can override the supermassive weight of the supersystem, which will deny any popular uprising of political resistance, will contort any technological innovation towards the benefit of the elite, will bend all lives towards false justifications. This work is not call for a revolution – there have been plenty made in the last three to four to five decades, and no revolution has occurred. No uprising from disaffected young people, no altering of the colossus, no political responses to fevered book clarions, no bright openings into the once-darkening sky. Extremely large, massively powerful, fully invested social forces do not dissipate once the enlightenment of reasoned opposition hits them - they may shape-shift, co-opt, mutate into separate colossus, but they will not accede to superior regulation just because a majority of sane folk think they should.

DT 14 -   THE REAL

The Supersystem is the total field in which these arrayed institutions support each other and deny you your sense of effect and change. There can be no list of the supersystem's particular variables that approaches scientific rigor, but they are destiny's vexations nonetheless. Where are the archaic myths still in full spectrum effect? What atavistic urges govern the petty bureaucrat? What historical weight impels the authoritarian sycophant to the upper levels of political power? What fears keep the servile judge from intervening in state oppression? What psychological evasions permit a privileged caste to promulgate false doctrines of earned superiority? What makes a functional idiot with an advanced degree? What constitutes human dignity and human integrity? The answers are beyond our capacity for discerning metaphysical truth, but we should always seek greater heights of appreciation. We can always laugh at new ways of seeing how ridiculous we are, and in our uncovering of larger sheet of our cognitive delusions, we advance yet further beyond the shore we so recently crept up upon.

DT 15 –   DISALIGNMENT

No words can convey the nonsensicality of so much global wealth and 24-7 stock tickers producing Haitians running of mud biscuits to quell hunger pangs because they have no food 90 miles off the Florida coast, where retiree golfers complain about the Mexican help. To combat this, humanity must become *disaligned*, but no society has ever rejected its established institutions of courts, religious indoctrination centers, legislatures, commercial enterprises, transportation venues, or methods of animal slaughter. Better than to throw all of civilization's shackles off is to begin to implement enforcement of *social regulation*, a state of Scandinavian legal sanctions on social institutions and personal consumption. However, the immediate legacy of our heedless pursuit of imperial profit will head off movement to this liberal wonderworld fortwith, and we will forever bemoan what could have become of our better world. To sum up the epochal irony, within our innocence was the malevolence of our own extended violence.

DT 16 -   PUERILITY

In detailing the intractable mess of the supersystem, we can search and find data and statistics, from each of the universe back through the middle and out into the stratosphere. In exposing the logical depredations of the large institutions controlling our social universe, the testimony to the power of the supersystem is so plainly evident as to be hidden. No one can or should defend burgeoning economic inequality except first-rank mountebanks, but American social discourse has kept the conversational focus on easily manipulated digressions on sports, weather, how Caitlin is doing in her classes, and the rising cost of gas. As with so many of our observable social phenomena, the causes blend into the effects, with the people's inane politics and straitened psyches both a contribution to and extraction from the supersystem.

DT 17 -   FUTILITY

The foremost danger is seeing any piece of the Supersystem than can be located and grabbed as somehow constituting the whole of it. The veneration of the individual libertine intellectual must cease – all that matters is large-scale effect, and no one, not the dead ghosts that liberals chase nor the new counterfeit credential strivers of the classroom, not last year's new "next greatest novelist" nor tech billionaire, has done a damn thing to stop the tide of erumpent fascism. We can play a little music, raise a damn cool Jesus kid, be a good backroom attorney for a lesser state department, tell a good story at the family picnic, do better in two or more life areas than our parents, keep it together better than our siblings, be the green god of torts, or be any other variety of modern-day hero, but we can never, never, contend with the stupidity that constitutes our social reality. Shooting crimes among the underclass, mass death across the planet in faraway places, squabbling politicians, fortunate rich, technological fixes for our endemic boredom, sports stand-ins for our waning military bloodlust – that'll be your News at Ten, every night unto infinity, if you still are above a comatose level of postprandial functioning. .

DT 18 -   MORNING IN AMERICA

Humanity lives every day now under the supersystem. Children grow up in houses punished by the warping of humanity wrought by economic deprivation and ethical corruption. Adult men and women wonder why they did so little with their lives compared to their youthful televisual dreams. Vain hopes placed in existing institutions like the supernatural religions, the profit-beholden corporations, the power-contorted schools and courts, the ad-infested main media, are extinguished as the jobs go begging, the existing workplace gets meaner and tighter, the bills mount, the neurotoxins increase. These supersystem stories, however, these great American novels and Pushcart short stories and indie dramas and animated documentaries and concept CDs, are dead on cultural arrival because in all of them there is neither a happy ending nor a singular arch-villain. Who wants to see, up close and personal, how we are enmeshed in the invisible and impenetrable supersystem, fated to hope for institutional help and institutional reform that will never arrive? What code could write us out of this story of supersystemic entrapment? What on the Web was curing atomization and its attendant diseases of loneliness, stupefaction, mental incapacity, and specious non-communication? Human psychology prefers to tinker with what is at hand, not focus on what has been lost or destroyed or is fated to never appear. If bad thoughts obtrude, they get diverted into apocalyptic fatalism, seeing the ultimate nonsense of "end-times" where there is only decline. The beer is still cold in America, heavy metal heroes still walk stooped among us, every gas station will open tomorrow, the credit card company is waiting patiently for the next swipe...

DT 19 -   PERSPECTIVE

Why are we, as human individuals, so awful at recognizing our powerlessness as acting human individuals? Why have we failed so utterly in assessing the limitations of our individual molecular consequence upon the movements and courses of the known world? First, we do see the world from an adept perspective, where our minds and perceptions are active, yet the world is static and composed of familiar elements. We see, and think, exert, and maneuver in synchronized, dynamic motion while the world appears in its familiar forms of other people, recurring obligations, safe transportation, familiar food. We hum with electric energy, while the world is encapsulated by our vision and reduced in threat and disturbance, so we imagine ourselves the actor and the world the canvas. That is an illusory perspective – our atoms belong to the universe, and have no great function within our temporary housing of self. A force that cannot be moved, except in the most unusual of circumstances, becomes awesome, beyond reach, and then without existence. Our supersystem is such an entity, beyond our touch, thus worthy of dismissal. The supersystem does loom over us, does operate with a detectable decibel level of white noise, but it has mastery, and thus is not connected to us. We matter, to ourselves and our kin, and that which cannot be connected to us, ceases to be mentioned. Without the basic need to hunt and gather, humans have become unable to find communal understanding, and have lived without a clue as to how to construct a meaningful life that balances technology, money, knowledge, violence, and sex. Disdain, celebration, avoidance, immersion, distance, mania: what could possibly constitute the proper mixture for the proper life? Who does not fail to exploit, misunderstand, over-value, get wrong, neglect?

DT 20 -   POWER AND OPPORTUNITY

Without being sure, there should be a *calculus of power* (C-P) in political philosophy. It is not enough to dream of a better world; nor is the personal political. We stand not on the shoulders of giants, but on toxic pavement. A butterfly beats its wings in Kinshasa, and then dies. We now leave no legacy to our children, let alone the seventh generation. Need more rejections of messiah complex liberalism? There are good and nice thoughts that are necessary for the foundation of the sauce of movement politics, but only back in the 60s, and not now, once they have curdled so long ago, getting rancid the moment Ronald Reagan became president. There will be hierarchies, and there will be a state, for as long we foresee human breath. Utopian fantasies of marzipan ladders and puppy parks are not entirely without purpose, but the supersystem has kicked out hundreds of millions of tragic avoidable deaths, *in our lifetime*, is heading foursquare for the death of the human-supporting ecosphere, and we need to construct navigable roads into its operational core. New-time charlatans and scurrilous opiners of self-anointed goodness are not going to disappear, but they cannot be given any room to further the cause of elite control and mass subservience. Are we on the right track if we do nothing? A true calculus of power would see the vanity behind every forced smile, and be ready to bolt at the merest opportunity. We have lost every opportunity ever granted to us, but there are more to come.

DT 21-   SOCIAL BRAIN

The social brain functions in a tripartite system: 1) *awareness of quotidian self* (AQS). 2) *knowledge of unrelievable suffering of others* (USO). 3) *struggles with grander purpose to self* (SGP). As we come to exist in adult physical form with a functioning consciousness, we are steeped in the irreconcilable antagonisms between these great reservoirs of thought. Who cannot think of what we cannot do for others that we never seem to be able to do for ourselves? The gift of our incessant drive to *understand* our curious position of multi-faceted cognitive dynamism coupled with brute animal doom is too much for the limited personal ambit. What constitutes the optimal adult ratio of AQS to USO to SGP? For every situation that the adult human visits inside the supersystem, the tripartite social brain adjusts the self, moving around barriers of lack of equity and misperformance and failure. There being no objective standard for human morality, the individual's social brain finds holes within the conscience that permit dumping of all manner of disconnections and reservations. For many who have never cultivated their powers of self-criticism, the AQS-USO reservoir is all but dry, at least in its close-to-the-surface wells.

DT 22 -   ONE TARGET

Against reduction, the tSS does not set up a "Triple Crisis," or a Ten-Point plan, or find any numbers other than 1 (the Supersystem) and much higher (the nearly infinite number that identifies all the social institutional representatives of the supersystem). Major areas of trouble are evident, across the economy, the courts, the schools, the workplaces, families, that roster of bourgeois destiny, but they all are controlled by the animating prejudices of the governing ethos. Getting at one area without locating the heart of darkness and performing major surgery upon it, is most likely a good life's work, but not sufficient to heal the body politic. Pointing out vast monoliths of corruption is a form of tourism, a good precursor to a well-researched restaurant meal, but not a form of situated living, nor good doctoring

DT 23-   **AGAINST THEORY**

There is no –ism associated with the tSS, since neither Mao, nor Friedrich Hayek, nor Deepak Chopra provide the terms or the layout of the theory. The tSS does not advance a party, not a program, not a society, not a ten-point program, not a revisionist history, not a school, nor does it call for broad-based collective social action. The theory is not meant to be adopted, nor disregarded, nor venerated – it simply is a presence, an approach. If there were better times in history, if there are moments of intense socially-derived happiness, if the future shall be monorails and communal singalongs, then none of that is the totality of today, and nothing will be the wasted opportunities of yesterday. We are fated to share the planet with loathsome people, with intractable human-run social problems, and are not likely to find the cures for what ails us. False idols and spendthrift clowns are going to lead the human way, and if there may be yet side parades that have rational actors and evidence-based loathing, invitations to them will be hard to come by.

DT 24 -   **SCOPE**

In the theory of the Supersystem, calls for voluntary reform are absent. Social policy is not dictated by books delineating ten-point plans, nor by appeals to our better natures, nor by realizations of consumerist excess. The supersystem will grind on, powered by uncontained mass following of mass-produced desires, until the supports for its destruction of resources or equity break, suddenly. Bombs and agribusiness and corporate manufacturing and every other multinational institution filled the spaces for the expansion of Big Business across the globe, visiting electricity, indoor plumbing, and beyond-family living along with the toxic despoilation and dead peasants. The social world of humans has become a mess, ungoverned except by these mean precepts of profit through miasmatic control. . Do you really want to sort out the ethics of how the new world order or new world disorder shall operate? High-minded rhetoric is a human propensity, yet our blueprints for social change are such shoddy, curled disasters. How do we know that our late-stage call for "sustainable relocalization via renewable energy equity from carbon reduction quota achievement" is within the bounds of human social action? We can look to Third World cooperative societies for models, but the human social world has never gone back to the past and found its future. The bonds and associations that constitute the current supersystem are cross-global, epic and precisely networked, so that our operations within it in are, at best minute shifting. Nothing we wear, nothing we eat, nothing that we dream or aspire to, does not contain improvident histories that can never be rectified.

DT 25 -   **BY WEDNESDAY**

The global legal framework for protecting the remaining environment while restoring social justice to human economic and cultural activity will need to be in place by Wednesday, with a worldwide enforcement team, redesigned detention centers, tribunals of astounding sensitivity to communication of circumstance, and community centers for flautists and bongo surf rock to invigorate the upsurge of leisure time. If that "progressive" fantasy is out of reach, then all social theory must be a lamentation of how much is lost, how much is run by the forces of unrestrainable venality. Look back – we have been, each on our own, offering liberal proscriptivism since the Enlightenment, and we must see the forces of power as happily unengaged with the torrents of tear-stained paper and ginger-snap entreaty to a fallen world.

DT 26-   THE   HYPER-ARTIFICIAL

To the Manichean dualism of the *artificial* versus the *real* there is the third criterion of the *hyper-artificial*. Nature is a world of stench and decay, obliteration and furtive escape, alongside the birth and social uplift good parts. This natural state of anti-meaning and terrible loss can be modified with deodorant, hair color, penicillin, and sexual deviance. However, this modern world should have been limited from its passage into the hyper-artificial, where technology becomes the master of individual aspirations, resulting in 50 year-old multiple birth mothers, anti-democratic elections in alleged democracies, cell-phone wanderings, steroidal food, and extreme sport suicides. In all systems, the real (blood, emotional intensity, species individuation) becomes transmuted over time into the artificial, wherein adaptation surpasses need as the driving force. In the supersystem, the artificial becomes the hyper-artificial, turning against real needs through the processes of enforced corruption. Try getting a good seat at a waterfront table when you come in with that line of talk, though – most folks will slide quite easily into the hyper-artificial, buying oceanic supertankers of corporate toy junk for their little tyrants who stumble into an adult stupor bereft of inquisitiveness.

DT 27 -   THE SCENE

Each of the major social institutions are fundamentally and irreparably flawed. The courts; medical care; global commerce; higher education; literature; popular culture; labor; scientific research; politics; travel; food; religion; and a thousand other satellite endeavors, all dedicated to deleterious practices, myths, and corrupt internal governance. The reforms and the revolutions are at the ready: proven disasters, pipe dreams, destined re-creations, or non-starters. Small-bore changes and incremental upswings and piecemeal benefits could be rustling down the pike in any one of these venues, but minor inclinations towards justice were the refuge of the privileged, not the major domain of humanity. Time has run out on the liberal dream of collective betterment, leaving endless chattering as the building suffered internal structural collapse in room after room. Here was yet another clean-up crew, from the same parasitic enterprises, mouthing yet another round of pieties and pronouncements. Humanity had to begin a massive repair, but the shovels and hammers were in the hands of those who had caused the deteriorations to accelerate. Their recompensed salvage operations were bound to fail, some even in the short term, and they were only capable of operating in small corners of the building.

DT28 -   THE   REALITY

The Industrial Revolution has come and gone, to other shores, yet the consumer commuting world is its unregenerate spawn. The skyscrapers are in place, the energy needed provided by decayed carbon lifeforms formed over millions of years, the concomitant social myths ever-supported by our collective actions. No need to sound the alarums: the process has been like the explosion of a dying star:

irreversible and brilliant. If we clean up a corner of the environmental destruction here, we will be off-loading them to an unfortunate hinterland, most likely in the stricken Third World. Cloak ourselves in the garment of green purity, awake to a fantasy of harmonious, "sustainable" living, even in that unrealizable ideal state, we cannot undo the legacy of the heedless, marvelous engineering of the resource-exploitation generations. They gave us our world, and we were powerless to switch course.

DT 29 -   **DAUNTING**

The mind will devour itself. With no social outlets for cognition, the mind becomes a thicket of recombinations, interpolations, abstruse meanderings, and intransigent expansiveness. Other humans are expected to sit rapt before the gibbering monologue merchant, but no physical construction ever happened through the mind alone. Our critical faculties are unrivaled, capable of the utmost refined discernment, resulting in the presence within every mind of a professional censor, evaluator, and antagonist. Yet we destroy our animal gifts by failing to examine our own propensities for self-overvaluation, our limitless indecisions, our bountiful errors of social misunderstanding. No society should tolerate a failing, devastating supersystem, yet we persist in allowing the tattered overlay of the past (outmoded precepts, distorted stereotypes, religion, baseless authority, hollow myths, and the antediluvian exercise of social violence upon lowered orders) to dominate the glorious tomorrow. We grow, only slowly, only in minor patches, only with the most rare of fortunate sunlight.

DT 30 -   **THE MOVEMENT OF ELITE POWER**

There is no primary covert insidious force fomenting corruption, as humanity has commonly seen the depraved workings of the elite, as through Satan, Babylon, the infidels, the Jews, the WASPs, the evil or the wicked, angry gods, displeased supernatural vortexes, or irredeemable alien Others. Instead of this mysterious unfathomable affliction, the workings of the human social world are controlled by identifiable, constitutive processes. However, most humans can stand but only so much awareness of individual ineffectuality and the smallness of human consequence, so they overvalue their leaders, grant higher status to pathetic social traditions, trust in rhetorical promises of triumph, and construct fetid pools of antagonism to contain enemies. They disdain the ruling influences that guide their actions, such as fear, the accumulation of wealth, the flattery of superiors, the displacements of anger, the vanity of moral worth, the protection of social standing. In America, doctors dispense research-deprived anti-depressants; judges sentence selectively prosecuted unfortunates; soldiers shoot unarmed foreign civilians; CEOs invade politically unprotected shores for evangelical product-selling; robber baron banks are recapitalized by taxpayer-stolen funds; according to established social norms that grow in reach and distortion as powerful entities aggregate.

DT 31 -   **THE STRUCTURE**

The superstructure lies beneath, fans out in all direction around, arches overhead, and is transmuted into the ether above each of us. Another system of supports and   construction could well have been built, but the public space has been appropriated by the continuously expanding design, all built on an unworthy bedrock of various irrationalisms known as "religion" and "individualism" and "corporate capitalism."   This supersystem is the product of thousands of years of social evolution, conditioning its adaptions, however perverse and detrimental, to withstand alleged crises. Every individual makes decisions to commit actions of at least some perceptible effect, but unless there is a collective regulatory structure, the haphazard rule will reward the powerful. The needs to make a living, the desires to purchase goods, the constructions of shelter, and the intangibility of individual lives in a technology-centered environment, send the masses across the deficient structure, one foot at a time. Social science can string out game theory and place genetics into the Petri dish, but our heavily mortgaged politics keeps policies threadbare and in the control of commercial interests. For a society that has no great need for its human inhabitants, its children grow without any trellises, searching in vain for purpose, doing senseless jobs that become corrupt and loathsome to great numbers, but pay the bills and thus are sacrosanct. In such a tremulous social world, sex and love are five different things.

DT 32 -   TERMS AND CONDITIONS

In the supersystem, humanity has met the match of its own creation. There is a common set of assumptions and fears and directed thinking that suffuses the actions of our authorities, the ones whose amplified decisions constitute our benighted or bejeweled social reality. In almost all of the power exercises that mankind has performed, design plans have infiltrated the cognitive biases of the judge or supervisor or torturer. No one has the intellectual time to unearth these real determinants of social command in their substantiality for a given situation, but a forensic anthropology could stand to improve its detective method, before we all perish from misappreciated power relations. To assess the supersytem will necessitate the invention of metrics and terms and angles we have not been able to fashion. Contemporary social reality cannot be approached using the fully discredited terms like "equality," "equity," "justice," "North-South," "sustainable," and their diaphanous like. Where have we earned the right to speak so confidently of the brighter days of reform when we have no track record? Through established economic policies of discrimination in favor of the rich such as the mortgage deduction, the refusal to tax financialization schemes, non-existent regulation of corporate-military procurement, stocks and bond insider trading and computer manipulation, a thousand other incremental weights

Chapter TWO
RECENT BACKGROUND

There can only be *inconsequentiality* to the intellectual efforts of one nictitating mind in the face of the overmassive enormity of the American military-corporate-governmental colossus. We have gone very, very wrong, to the tune of tens of trillions, the greatest fear-based waste of our human heritage that humankind could ever imagine, right here in the U.S. of A., and we are but the living witnesses outside the gates to this history-breaking destruction of opportunity. Engineers with a similar passport went to the moon, created cell-phone networks almost overnight, constructed international cities of epic everyday commerce. Music is now short typing away from instant availability, but we have a nearly impenetrable governing supersystem that is not allocating social goods in an even remotely defensible way. Technology has given us our latest modern selves, but continues to rob us of the last vestiges of social purpose. Humans have an instinct to be set to work that is useful and productive, and there may be a few "jobs" in the supersystem that offer those rewards to the quixotic, but the truth of our times is that the flock has dispersed, and grazes only where it can.

In 1965, SDS president Paul Potter gave an antiwar speech in Washington, including the following prophetic call:

What kind of system is it that allows good men to make those kinds of decisions? What kind of system is it that justifies the United States or any country seizing the destinies of the Vietnamese people and using them callously for its own purposes? What kind of system is it that disenfranchises people in the South, leaves millions upon millions throughout the country impoverished and excluded from the mainstream and promise of American society, that creates faceless and terrible bureaucracies and makes those the place where people spend their lives and do their work, that consistently puts material values before human values and still persists in calling itself free and still persists in finding itself fit to police the world? What place is there for ordinary men in that system and how are they to control it, make it bend itself to their wills rather than bending them to its?

We must name that system. We must name it, describe it, analyze it, understand it and change it. For it is only when that system is changed and brought under control that there can be any hope for stopping the forces that create a war in Vietnam today or a murder in the South tomorrow or all the incalculable, innumerable more subtle atrocities that are worked on people all over- all the time.

The system that was named, partially described, and somewhat analyzed became the supersystem, and it was neither understood nor changed. The Left, right, and center became workers and managers of that system, which moved, after great time and devastation, from Vietnam to Grenada to Panama to Mexico to Nigeria to Iraq to the farthest reaches of outer space and deep water. The protests became a counter-culture, but then the counter-culture became an adjunct to the dominant culture, supplying the taxes, the mortgages, the teachers and professors, the music and video businesses that entered into the main currents of the American imperium. No protest of the 60s, 70s, 80, 90, or 00s interrupted the reign of profit-central corporate military fascism, a protean and reinforced beast. Thanks, more protests, said the last wave of ninja-clad stormtroopers at Pittsburgh's G20 summit - we only get paid if you *demonstrators* get together and make a *protest* and we get hired for wages and mileage to bust your heads using super-sophisticated state-of-the-corporate art death rays.

RecBack 1 -   STASIS

You cannot make waves in a stagnant pond. Nothing moves, the muck is too great, the ripples stop at your feet. The supersystem is, of course, the *stagnant pond*, and you, the hopeful individual of thought and remorse, is the protoplasm wanting to *make waves*, but to reiterate, you can not, and will not, make waves in a stagnant pond. History has not ended here, nor is there any lack of *development*, though the overall picture is one of a terrible stasis, a momentous loss of purpose and hope and change and justice and outlook and action and nice folk. Our on-the-ground institutions of social restraint and intimidation function with refined regimentation, giving thugs and scions alike the curious mixture of mass conformity-through-specious-individualism that sends dull schooling into prisons and prison rule into mass schooling. Lacking any invigoration from the outside, the institutions become hollow inside and decayed outside, like abandoned water hose.

RecBack 2 -   60's and PRINCIPLE

If the battle is always fought according the rules of engagement of the last war, the current opposition must concede the faulty generalship of the 60s. Foremost among the colossal blunders was the the inability to see the dominant power of the corporate capitalist state enterprise, which would make dentists out of autonomists, war criminal presidents out of minority community organizers, militarists out of pot-smoking layabouts, punitive neo-con judges out of milquetoast lickspittles. Pabulum should never again mark the words of the would-be reformer – we are not going to solve the energy crisis by harnessing the static electricity generated from riding our sparkleponies. Declamatory self-ennoblement is not a politics, not when the other side has centuries of global encirclement. No ghosts are going to re-enter the scene to cleanse the newly fallen world – no Cesar, no MLK, no Bolivar, no Che, no Karl or Friedrich, no Jesus nor Mohammed nor the Mahatma nor some hookah artist. There is a stand to made, but it has great requirements for intellectual integrity, which so far has only meant principled opponents making gestures of resistance, staying in dumb jobs, leaving those below them relatively unmolested, stopping the flow of bullshit at their doors, or facing insistent truths.

RecBack 3 -   PRIOR "CHANGE"

To allow for criticism of this stance, the Berlin Wall did come down, the French Revolution did place a few leftists in charge of the guillotine for once, the soviets placed the worker as rock star in white Russia, the Zapatistas command their territory, good intentions surround the anti-imperial left. Yet each situation of a social reality that was or is antithetical to the supersystem is of no practical use today, when the specious elite command of both culture and politics is so bordering on that totemic term "totalitarian." . Being so very recently rodents, humans are given to variations only upon the hallowed experiment: we push the bar for hits of that sweet red juice, and will return to that bar again and again if the delivery system becomes clogged or unreliable, capable of being diverted only if presented with a picture of the alpha leader we are commanded by nature to follow. No human leader can take on the supersystem, however, not with the forces of surveillance, harassment, demonization, frustration, and sorting available in ever-buttressed means. If the red juice (in the form of chosen cultural entertainment) does come sluicing towards us, as it must in this technologic age, we become anxious that there will be *something we will do that will cause the backup of the delivery system*. Our political reality has become an incipient terror in this recurrent stimulus response, permitting only the obviously corrupt and fraudulent hoax of corporate media "democracy" and corporate pressure groups and witless corporate commentary. The "People" are a fiction lost to a few moments of distant history, now a herded, self-lacerating, focus-grouped manipulable concept of activated tastes and inconsequential predilections. Whatever flavor "people" come in, and there are observable distinguishing features among a few set groups, there is no capability for a concentrated action against the enormity of the reinforced supersystem. Large scale events, such as nuclear attack and consequent world war in that holiday resort known as the Middlle East, may yet mock this depiction of stasis within the supersystem, but horrific geo-political megawar would only be confirmation of the concept of the on-going degradation and usurpation of existing social institutions. Will bureaucratic insanity prompt the pushing of the nuclear button? We have been so near before, and those incidents were not at a time of recognized global economic and ecological existential crisis.

RecBack4 - **FAILURE OF SOCIAL INSTITUTIONS DURING BUSH/CHENEY**

For a large substratum of Americans, the recent political era can be summed in the fear-inspiring names of Bush/Cheney, and the continuation of Obama reprising Clinton. The Bush/Cheney cabal will be viewed by many as arch-fiends, the twin figureheads of the worst Presidency in American history. However, far greater problem for the future is the collapse of the nominally bulwark institutions against these sophomoric fantasists. For all of the Bush-hating, the multiplex of anti-Bushisms spread across the global mall, the rejoinder should be: how then did he come into power? Do you want to absolve all other institutions for responsibility for allowing the neocons such wide and fantastic sway? Not one element of civil society, not the churches; the courts; higher or lower education; scientific research; social activism; literary artistic expression; investment of venture capital; the "free-market" principles of corporate capitalism; international NGO's or the United Nations music; sports; prayer; local politics; the Internet; familial devotion; or any other, stopped the visible arrival, rise, and dominion of Bush/Cheney. Not one bomb-destroyed baby will be returned to life from these thriving institutions. To say they collapsed is too charitable, implying that any one of these has delayed the onset of this militaristic supersystem in the past. These institutions have none a glorious history, though there have been moments of genuine rebellion in American history. No historical re-enactments can be envisioned, precisely because not one movement in history forestalled the ascension of these tinpots managers, lickspittle law school clerks, and cafeteria gangsters. Our social institutions were traduced by the forces of agglomerating profit-seeking recalcitrance, operating in that little moral region of fearful self-assurance that activates our latent desire for tough intransigent violence.

Progressives may yearn for the halcyon 60's, when college kids stopped a war, got blacks to like them, let gays come out, made going to college a universal rite, got women to work like men, and put TV's, computers, and video in every home. The war, however, was an American production from the early 50's onward, and was stopped only after the dogs of war bred generation after generation, a maddening sponsorship of mass murder and terror across the regimes of Eisenhower, Kennedy, Johnson, and Nixon, with the deaths of millions of Vietnamese a far greater legacy than the empire's temporary suspension of faraway bombing.

RecBack5 -   LOST OPPORTUNITIES

There was no new dawn, no New Age, no speaking truth to power that power did not slough off instantly. Books were written, drugs were taken, classes were held, identity politics found their pockets of triumph, families were formed by now-working flower children, and essentials truths about vacuity and ill-health were deepened as the culture staggered into fast-food joints, high-tech bombings, antidepressants, and divorce. It matters not whose consciousness was raised, or how much of an improvement the tone and liberality the 90's culture marked over preceding generations of bibulous cranks. What was the total carbon consumption? What was the Gini coefficient? What was the technological achievement of instantaneous computer communication? Did a consumption-based leisure economy up the happiness quotient? Did the bombs get disassembled? Did global poverty reduce? If the numbers are negative, then we suffered through a loss of planetary dimensions. Through religion, myth, intransigence, in-aptitude, and massed- gnorance, we let all the opportunities get squandered on a prosperous few and a marginal, failing middle. And that story continues unabated today.

RecBack6 -   THE FOREGROUND

A state of meaninglessness is reached when two dominant options provide no opening for a third. The Republicans were a mutant species, of interest only to entomologists, but the Democrats were the tragedy of the times, nice liberal rockstars and dope-smokers and presidents of colleges and brilliant engineers and smart teachers and MacArthur geniuses and gorgeous waitresses and well-read city folk, all fully incapable of contending with the power dynamics of the supersystem. The corporate command of the commons was to thwart their every good intention. The arrogation of cultural superiority by these boomers and Gen Xers was tedious, as they pursued cretinous ends of financial supremacy that invariably turned toxic. The boredom inspired by the awfulness of those two social outcomes, of wolverine Republicans and hapless self-advancing Democrats, could fill ten lifetimes, and yet there seems to be no end to the supply of the two-bit con artists that become the shock troops for both sides. On every American campus, the next level of bullshit compost is formulated and manufactured to be spread over the generational fields. The smell is awful, but the green lawns will entice the next round of captive fortune-owing parents.

RecBack7 -   RECENT   AMERICA

America itself has been the product of the supersystem. The scourges, the parsons, the ascetics, the folk left, the fundamentalist Mormons, your Mommy and Daddy, the corporate advertisers, the apostates from neo-con orthodoxy, impenitent novelists, your boss, your God or gods – not one entity restrained the establishment of this overflow of effluvia and plastic packaging. No one stopped you, nor your

18

neighbor. There were ways to have done so, to have performed a level of social regulation that could have placed straps upon the runaway machine of Manifest Destiny, but only the lonely look back and see openings. You can agree that it can and may get worse, much worse, but that is not why we humans are in business, to concede that this was all a great mistake.. Better to find some points of agreement with other fortified humans that admit a minimum daily allotment of truth, and start capitulating to your inner demons. You and I know it went wrong, all wrong, and if we can extricate ourselves from the downward arc of this lifetime with some signs of "progress," it will be a miracle. For many, this truth must be rejected because it calls forth inaction, a pessimism that denigrates any "progressive" action as inconsequential, frivolous, vain, doomed, fraudulent. What *actions* should have been taken to head off the supersystem from 1960-2020? The direct actions were scattered and relentlessly beaten. No cities were taken over, no police repulsed, no transnational global corporations placed into receivership. The Battle for Seattle, Chiapas, Cuba, Venezuela, the World Social Forum, Greenpeace – what was the grand and total sum of the chants, the declaiming into megaphones, the decentralized planning committees, the T-shirts, the Garden Gnome Lbieration committee – a thoroughgoing rout, but not a problem for the Left. Losses; jail terms; brain contusions; no-protest zones; torture, solitary confinement, and decades-long imprisonment for animal liberators; paid and rewarded informants; governmental harassment and private assassinations- there was no defeat that did not seem ennobling and acceptable to the traduced, marginal royal left opposition. History and righteousness was always on their side, so a pathetic ineffectiveness was just another invitation to continue offering victimhood. The ninja Taser-deploying police were even polite as they herded, smashed, denied, and exercised "restraint" as they bound the hapless trespassers. If more of us could have joined, the fines and fees imposed by the happy courts could have paid for even more training exercises and mobile headquarters.

RecBack 8-   NO   DEMOCRACY

All of our political philosophies have failed miserably, and now we stand condemned to extinction because of our static ignorance. Democracy is an invitation to the criminal usurpation of the public sphere by capitalized corporations, and works only in its initial, illusory incarnation of granting of influence to the newly enfranchised electorate. The people's access to self-government becomes steadily eroded as burgeoning enterprises of substantial wealth gain control of the courts, the commercial markets, the press and the arts, the educational support apparatus, and history. Bigots and strivers erupt in well-coiffed splendor on election day as democracy becomes an arranged match of induced ignorance against the plebeian forces of principle.   What is the dollar cost of the US elections since its industrialization? How many polls, focus groups, media ownership buys, artificial events, and corporate propaganda has passed through our alleged "democracy"? Why can "democracy" be accorded such veneration when it has never existed, and has such obvious shortcomings?. Like the horrific faith in the "unseen hand" of the market, like the malevolent faith in either some omnipotent deity or in the cherished salvation of a beatific afterlife, this unreflective devotion to some abstraction of the collective goodness of "the people" is a useful tenet that promotes passive acceptance of elite manipulation. If I want my plumbing fixed, I don't ask every able-bodied resident of the town for their input – I ask for the expert. People who've never studied plumbing, who don't know how to solder – their suggestions and decisions are not as equally valued as the licensed master plumber. So why do we present the most important of social tasks, that of electing the powers the will be, to some fantastical chicanery of money, advertising suasion, xenophobic sloganeering, prostitution, and corporate scientific propaganda? Democracy is not the least worst political system – in puffing up vacuous tribalism and superstitious lockstepping, it has insurmountable deficits. Far better would be to construct an ideal of managerial hybrid regulatory socialism/capitalism, governed by open processes of debate and rigorous inspection, but not subject to the ultimate approval by disinterested, incompetent voters. However, don't look for that model coming to a theater near you anytime soon – stopping the mud slide of electoral politics with a garden hose is foolish.

This is said after millennia of practice and theory of "democracy," constant thought and debate and tenure on this subject, and 10,000 books written in the current year that concern that very subject. Degrees of hierarchy and power rule the social worlds of my experience, from birth to what will be my death, none of which I created. I have never seen democracy, would not know it if came in and took ownership of my house. All of the decisions that I have ever participated in, from the smallest to the largest, were worked out without a full equality between all interested parties. Unless a mighty wind comes through the known world to smooth out all peaks and valleys of registered power, we will continue to live within social institutions that are undemocratic. A regulatory managerialism would be my vote for a better political system, with eligible voters needing to pass a test of competency, a sure upgrade from this irrelevant marionette show, but without an upfront fee, I cannot do the work for this grand solution.

RecBack9 - POPULAR NASTINESS

Every sentient adult spends slices of thought in bitching, a phantasmorgia of recriminations, bemoanings, observations of endemic spuriousness, and blatant caustic hatefulness. In our time, when the confluence of mass education, affluence, and cowboy mythology led every second college student to imagine a destiny of hierarchical superiority, the perpetuation of a system without an organizing purpose has left suburbs full of frustrated would-be punjabs. This psychic eruption of individualist aspiration overflowed every barrier, and can no sooner emerge into a cohesive stream of social action than lava can clean a swimming pool. We are done, with only the blather of unheedful barkers to accompany our demise. What one issue could such a deluded, fantasizing populace gather round? If America, in the form of an NSA/Halliburton/Keebler consortium, announced that it blew up the moon, the majority of the populace would be fine as long as satellite reception was not affected.

RecBack 10 - OFF-SHORING

After the manufacturing boom of World War II, the masters of the great American industrial system were headlong purveyors of the soot, grime, effluent, and morose corpses of their lightly regulated factories, but the risks of opprobrium became too great - off-shore went the presses and the belts, the casts and the smelters, to operated by unseen unfortunates in invisible lands who had no unions, no identity, no reality. Why would an empire of production and consumption have continued to actually make its trinkets in its own environs, where the stink and the horror and the pestilence could become such an obvious rebuke to the entire operation? Economic realities do not happen in the supersystem because of rational planning, not in this bizarre fear-based acceleration of massive financial criminality, but from logical corruption meeting ineluctable needs.

RecBack 11 -   **MARXISM**

The Theory of Supersystem (tSS) is not a Marxist concept, nor is there is a communism or a socialism lurkig around its precepts? Folks across the world want to work hard, get ahead, buy something, get a place – commonplace imperatives. Power accrues despite our egalitarian instincts, leaving every social reality countermanded by a supersystem. Every society is going to be governed by interlocked structures, from hunter-gatherer clans riven by petty enmity to socialist utopias beset by dictatorial militarists. The problem is that socialist analysis is proving to win the intellectual battle while its precepts lose, spectacularly, the real economic war. Any social critic worth a dime has seen the *commodification* of all that exists by the corporate order, from air to space to water to a baby's health to gambling upon gambling. Like wood charred by smoke, there is no way to get back an economy sold to these interests. Who gives up advantage? Why see inevitable decline in that which rules through enormous accretion?

RecBack 12 -   **CLIMATE CHANGE**

Dangerous climate change is the new backdrop to the human condition, as the planet enters its febrile convulsions from the heedless employment of fossil fuel technology. Notions of global justice pervade the proffered solutions of carbon taxes or carbon banks or carbon trading, though there are no historical precedents to draw on, not even the CFC treaty, to illustrate how extremely powerful states willingly give up spoils completely integrated into institutional reality. CFCs could be replaced by equally-performing propellants – there is no lie-performing substitutes for coal, oil, or natural gas. The hot planet will bake its supersystemic faults into disappearance, death, disintegration, violations of all moral principles, with the only question of how bad matters get before the supersystem itself is threatened, though by then, the cause of "sustainable" living will be foregone. Without any evidence of reduction of carbon dioxide concentrations across the globe, and with the evidence of gain and incipient gain, we can only conclude one direction of outcome

RecBack 13 -   **DEBT TO THE 60S**

The present supersystem has had enormous success in proffering popular culture to the masses, in ways that that built upon the Great Leap Forward of the American 60's. There is no part of my cultural being that does not owe its vitality to that minority of disaffected youth, who blew away the puritanical 50's horrors of no pornography, anti-sex crusades, Pat Boone, patriarchal dinner seating, three network channels of nursing home entertainment, overt segregation, and crypt-keeper politicians. Within the present supersystem are interstices where the great truths of personal uplift reside, where the remnants of anti-authoritarianism, intellectual honesty, laughter, and propulsive beats open up this hidebound world. Those illustrious forebears are living healthier and more engaged lives than their parents, but in their selling-out and retreats into discarded traditionalism, they betrayed the instincts of their youth. Others fell into the netherworlds of loopy spiritualism and drug damage, and none articulated a view of the enormous growth of the supersystem during their halcyon anti-establishment collegiate days. These generational archetypes will never end their presence in our culture, and the divide will remain great between the Yippies and the hardhats, even if subsequent history has blurred and confused the former line between drug-taking refuseniks (now the semi-working proletariat) and establishment Pecksniffs (now the college-educated, rock fan, corporate managers). Yesterday's worries have been canceled with the arrival of today, but it would be nice to have a cause to join, a movement to glory in, a development to admire.

RecBack14- 60s STARS

The supersystem is staffed and maintained by working adults, who are thoroughly invested in the perpetuation of their station, their avenues of financial supply, the maintenance of their gods, the support of the imprisoning police. No one "radical" escaped the coruscating allure of stardom that the culture of the 60's promised, not one is today without the taint of irrelevance from overweening ego. The imbeciles of the reactionary right appropriated the music, the sex, and the language, leaving a detritus of a faltering improvement in the civil lives of formerly abused, lynched, denigrated, tortured, intimidated groups. In the shadow of this historical legacy, inheritors of principled opposition have found no model for protest, action, or initiative. What from the 60's succeeded? In what area of the supersystem was there a gaining of ground?

RecBack15 - KNOWLEDGE

"Resistance is Futile." It was to the American Way, to the John Foster Dulles, Nelson Rockefeller, Eugenics, Oliver Wendell Holmes,, Henry Luce East Coast Establishment of the war hegemony. Obviously, the supersystem did not just happen, as some accidental virus, inchoate and ineluctable; it was, rather, manipulated by extremely rich men and their minions to benefit them, sweeping all intermediary forces along in a planned, operated, massive sequence of related extensions of their titanic powers. They, the lords and dukes, killed and usurped, overtook and overcame, in starts and sinister campaigns, all across their fair globe, and they were the winners. Rather than being cranky about their depredations, which have all happened and are yet burgeoning into new areas, we need to concede that round to them, and get busy on the next assault on global order. As a literate person, you will have been told many, many ideas and facts and factoids and all manner of ephemera and cultural textings, and so what will be one more questionable paragraph to your busy life? Most of all what you will learn from here on out in your life will be just a deepening confirmation of that which you *know*, what your experience has taught you to feel almost completely, what your neural pathways have ground into a fine quicksilver.

RecBack 16 – APPARATCHIKS

In dealing with epic structures and global events, the theory of the supersystem cannot lose sight of the elemental psychology that drives the human actors performing its dictates. Taking their places in great colossal enterprises, apparatchiks are always, always anxious that they will be found out to not be "tough." Donning their suits-and-ties, kissing the wife and scratching the cat, these masters of faraway doom and unobserved robbery set off every day to protect the world from knowing the secrets of their inner incompetence. We will never be able to reproduce the bureaucratic lies and deceptions that took America to war a time and time again in Iraq, in Afghanistan, in Grenada, in Latin America, but at least as much as those factors is the terrible insecurity of striving, stunted positional players, the millions of minions who process insanity into consequence for a living. Nothing is remarkable about these men and women, who have organized war, theft, intimidation, and expropriation as it has been throughout our human history, and we may well do small versions of this work in our work and daily lives. However, self-examination can be performed well, not at all, or insubstantially, and only the most damaged refuse to allow others to see the weakness of doubt within themselves.

RecBack 17 -   NEOCON FANTASY

To go deep into the workings of the supersystem would require the monomania of our finest madmen, those relics of earlier pre-popular cultural times when mental illness, dyspepsia, and norms of study produced abbeys of lunatic monks. At the outer margins of our concrete highways exist a few latter-day obsessive reader/writers like Noanm Chomsky, Peter Dale Scott, William T. Vollman, and a ring below them of functionally anonymous blog proprietors with enormous burrowing instincts and intact certitudes. I cannot command a overarching knowledge of criminal conspiracies great and small that these stalwarts have pinpointed in the halls of government and corporate offices and global   Although American neo-cons have gravitated to Zionist operators because of the clarity of purpose of the ethnic warriors, who are motivated to mass killing and apartheid devastation because of their perceived ethnic victimhood, the pull of history and religion may account for more of the folly. America, with no rational reason for its war surround of the Israeli cause, has become managerially infatuated with the elite Israeli commandos, the state justification of ethnic killing, the sense of embattled national purpose.   Money, weapons, official corruption, and a sense of national illegality are endemic products to both states, but the bizarre alliance is one that humans of differing power stations are prone to, the larger bully developing hard-to-undo ties to an over-heated acolyte.

RecBack 18 -   DEMOCRACY AND WAR

How much do we blame "the people" for all this? Are they blind, happy, indifferent, mindless, evil, dumb, transfixed, insensate, callous, immoral, spineless, vapid, hypocritical, murderous, venomous, willing executioners? Or are they all good at heart, humane, salt o' the earth once ya get to know 'em, repositories of untapped radical wisdom, plain-spoken sages of the secret tear inside, beings of consummate love and understanding? Of course humans are neither extreme to the exclusion of the other, but conglomerates, subject to inchoate social controls that make them serfs to the conditions of their place and time. As the supersystem gained in strength after Vietnam, it removed the conditions of its greatest threat, but incorporated its great systems of social command into war. Youth were no longer subject to an arbitrary draft, but could choose to serve the military sacrifice machine because of a lack of economic alternatives, an intact culture of aggressive violence subsidized by corporate academic billions, and geo-political imperialism. Polls may show a majority of "The People" against this or that war or bomb run or terror crackdown, but each of those polled holds exactly zero political weight upon the governing levers of security power. The forces of democratic justice   have no cultural weight, no advertising presence, no legal backing, no realistic demand to make of individuals to demonstrate, no capacity to generate figureheads, no way to counteract virulent jingoism against it, no way out, no record of effective repression, no way forward.

RecBack 19 -   ALTERNATIVES

There was not a major institution left untouched in the destructive descent of the supersystem, in comprehensive cataclysm of industry that afflicted all major sectors with terrible common pressures, yet there was not a "revolution" in sight. Though individuals can lead chose any number of anti-imperial courses, from veganism to no child to bike transport to re-purposing worn sweaters to backyard onion gardens, the globe-crossing supertankers bringing hideous figurines to the indebted stand athwart any private renunciation. Could there be an alternate supersystem? There are finer versions of our social institutions available in other lands, a more secular polity in Europe; a better medical system across broad swaths of the other continents; better food; a slower pace of life; better family care for elders; an actual community in Chiapas; smart clubs in Denmark; green energy in a more equitable economy. Yet these minor marvels are only piecemeal, always under attack, and wholly non-transferable to the American colossus. No new day will bring the cleansing of every irrational founding myth that undergirds the exceptionalist narrative of America – quite the opposite, these delirious, poisonous errata are producing more fervent judges, solons, and allied hoi polloi.

RecBack 20 -   RECENT FOLLY

No recent *crisis* illustrates the command of the supersystem as much as the Great Bail-Out of the Bush/Obama handover. With the Great Lie of the "free market" in such quadrillion-dollar relief, the People fumed for more "free markets," as if they walked around with their feet in the air and hands propelling them o the convenience store. Dumb people with advanced degrees were let loose with computer models all over the globe in the purest example of the folly of "deregulation," , and yet, since the supersystem is so shot through with lunatic myths and unsupportable inducements to perilous greed, there will be only halting recovery, which, is producing stunning and fabulous inequities of bonuses for convicted kleptocrats and debt peonage for the falsely un-accusatory. When all the computer models for unregulated trading flew into meaningless orbit, the crisis of humanity became front-page news – but what was going on? What was a quadrillion of derivatives or collateralized debt obligations but the nonsense of our species bare? Who had the money? What was money that was not there? "Smart" people had made all this money disappear, and weren't they disappointed in themselves? Weren't the masters of the universe now beyond broke? Was there an actual crisis if the banks stayed open? Why did it feel like global capitalism wasn't in the least inconvenienced? The "investors" were still in their vacation homes while companies went belly-up, gas prices went down, a Fort Knox a day was siphoned from some vast reservoir of untouchable wealth to "inject liquidity," or do some other fantastical crapshoot while the poor and sick of the world lived under a hotter sun. Pro-Reagan apologia issued forth from the formerly liberal political magazines and political pulpits; shout-outs were made to the formerly embalmed; the corporate news lead with a cavalcade of absurd fraud   - one day's swarm of maggots feasting upon the open necrosis of the supersystem. Do you want me to shout down the swarm? What good would that do – the body is obviously dead, the process of festering and decomposing is apace. I would be adjudged a lunatic for berating a carcass. I am sorry that this has become the reality, the death of an unhealthy, old being, so unable to be resuscitated, advanced in its senility, yet now so finally, clearly dead. May its expiring tissue be of some use to the extant universe. Long will we grieve, but we must move on, must look to our fight for survival with diminished resources. Heaven forbid the possibility of no rescue, now that we alone stand.

RecBack 21 -   CONSOLIDATION

After this evaporation of a quarter-plus of the human world's financial wealth, the governing economic system was said by some on the left to be a "zombie." How could any sane critic attach any vitality of life to the cliché of the "evil dead"? Capitalism and the free market, the Fed and multinational banks, Wall Street and the academic economic orthodoxy: dead at last. What could come next as a rebirth? Socialism, nationalizing the banks, a green economy, trials for the white-collar perps, no more military Keynesianism, congressional panels skewering CEO's for having the audacity to fly first-class, a new dawn necessitated by the fires of economic destruction. Yet these zombies held on, re-organized, owned the president and his zombie cabinet, escaped all manner of prosecution, invented zombie acronyms, traded trillions between or to themselves, held onto their every real, flesh-and-blood advantage – not at all the work of zombies, mutants incapable of purposeful action, but of real, collusive, rewarded perpetrators. What were a few complex and unseen and retrograde repairs when the building and the above-ground structure was a wholly-owned enterprise of the mortgage-free owners of the global elite? Crisis capitalism had come to the modern world, and there more global ones in store, but each would be a consolidation of power, control, and living space for the socially favored.

RecBack 22 -   THE LAUGHING PIT

Social reality does not need one more catalog of its endless ills. With a dead politics of God, family, guns, war, and business-friendly populism, attended by plethora of unaccountable experts, the thriving destruction of all and sundry needs its disruptions. How could there be more to this known world than dislike for its foolishness and cherishment of its riches? Mainstream, enfranchised pundits and assayers saw worth in the "bipartisanship," in the "post" this or that, in "tremendous openings" amidst "crisis" and enduring liberalisms in the corpus delecti. Far too much was too far gone for lectures and Powerpoints, footnoted Borders'-bound books or bar debates. The "problems" were not unforeseen, nor mysterious, nor irrational, nor insusceptible, but were instead due to reigning orthodoxy. The faith placed in "regulation" was as lunatic as the faith in a male sky-god, and as resistant to direct criticism. State capitalism had placed a monumentally minor and nearly unstaffed agency of the SEC in alleged oversight of the financial colossus of investment banking, and when the great undoing of 2008 blasted untold trillions of monetary wealth into nothing, the proprietors shook themselves off, concocted a ridiculous cover story, and went back to the laughing pit.

RecBack 23 -   SRI

During this period of no alteration, companies accorded some fake "green" status were beneficiaries of greenwashing, with some company-wide recycling initiative fronting for horrific business practices of destruction through extraction. Titans of deceit and hubris (Google, Novartis, Staples) were rammed through "social equity" screens to permit a froth of morality over the usual swill of business pollution. To be precise, mutual fund "investing" was not direct venture capital investing, but more betting on a horse race, of only the slightest relationship to the nature of the horse or the jockey. For good and practical reasons, none of us were going to reconfigure the predations of corporate capitalism with our pile of pennies and trite pleadings. Bugs in the continental swamp of business could imagine the beating of wings as consequential to those operations of massive decay and carnage, but the water of commerce would always remain fetid.

RecBack 24 -   NEO -COLONIALISM

You will have committed many errors, proffered many judgments in need of serious alteration, ignored many superior avenues, and been shamed by ridiculous notions of intellectual superiority. Yet, despite this debilitating notion of a better man you or I could have been, we will soldier on, resolute in our cause, protective of the elite campaigns that swirl above us, stalwart with our wounds and intact aggression. Who is an acknowledged disappointment to his interior self? We may have made no *contribution* to the widening of the aperture of human consciousness, have designated no forces akin to the van der Waals forces, are not well versed in the rudiments of our spectacular universe, and have made precious few people happy with our immediate personal presences, but we can remake this conundrum of enlightened frustration if the given the good company and some cessation of violent threat. . Only through knowing ignorance can the wise shape the cause of human social action. Because of the unrestrained acquisitive genius of the capitalist forward arm of the supersystem, the mass of humanity faces its daily life decisions with the dangers and tremors of self-delusion, interpersonal fear, and recalcitrant awe. None of us has the slightest idea what to do with the disconnect between our pieces of knowledge and our benign intent. What part of the adornments and the entertainments of the average westerner is derived from the violent intimidation and destruction of the people and biosphere of Africa – what on the western feet, in their ears, in the cabinets, in their pockets, down the road, up in the sky? Neoliberalism has been a further exploration of the western curse upon that region, as greater and greater amounts of the natural resources and humans from Africa are subjected to providing the west with its now semi-cleansed appetites.

RecBack 25 -   VOTING AND INDUSTRY

The "American people" are now bits and bytes on corporate spreadsheets, so that voting in America has all the moral weight of stopping at a 7-11 and getting a Slim-Jim instead of a Twizty-Goo. How many apparatchiks and employed mandarins are needed for a campaign? What is the dollar cost of this charade of speeches, meetings, debates, greetings? There is no tangible connection between voting and political economy, only a decayed, wrongful system of empty rhetoric, advertising, and unaccountable posturing. How much can you wish for and not get before you walk away? The questions are trifles to the supersystem, for it traffics in 24/7 instantaneity and intra-penetrativity, nano-observations hurtling like electrons through the collapsing void. To be a cultural observer, let alone a cultural critic, let alone a cultural theorist, now demands an impersonation of command – who can cope as one prefrontal cortex with such a surround of cacophony and electrical disturb? Atomized resistors sleep alone at night, warmed only by the glows of their disembodied entertainments, while the hyper-reality of industrial production is someone's workplace assignment in the morning.

RecBack 26 -   RECENT HISTORY

What were we arguing about? How much more "history" can we stand? In any epoch of humanity, there are wars of surpassing horror, with the day carried by furious and unrepentant racists and morons. Do you want to know how deep our own US economy is in military research, procurement, and delivery? It is not we who are doing the killing, it is the others, the ones we have given the lit fuse to, the ones in whose guaranteed misery we see profit. With the blood dripping from our hands, fresh on top off the coagulated old, what we do we want to talk about – how "peace" and "love" are our true desires, but there is a time for strength, a time for hunting down the unlucky foreigners or unfortunates with the massed obliterations of our war apparatus. The necessary conspiracies gained their murders and cover-ups, the public and the intelligentsia were mollified through the accomplices of the media, "education," taxes, the "system" that was never quite understood. There are great errors of continuity and credulousness that bedevil our stupefied epoch of multinational global corporate techno-global war and industrial dominance, but the errors have been driven into place, deep and everywhere.

RecBack 27 -   MASTER PLANS

What will bring down the forces of ignorance, hate, and evil in this world? Who has the master plan to combat the Master Plan? That delirious hope we drove ourselves with, that consumerist and pre-bill-paying demand that the world shower us, instantly, with pirate treasure, still reverberates in the adult mind, in our sacramental clicks on Amazon and our haggles at the urban bazaar. Should we stop our pretensions of unearned sagacity and become the cloddish though placid idiot our available avocations of televisual veneration and sexual pheremone hunting have bequeathed to our corporeal self? This surrender would leave the stage to the rigid historians and professional antisepticians, the unreflective purveyors of deterministic jargonalia – exactly what has happened, and the precursor of tomorrow's greater fall. Lines on a screen can never be the fantastic bloodstream of social action, where human social reality is constructed far, far above each of us.

RecBack 28 -   NEW DEAL TO 2008

Others can diagnose the economic system as good doctors, seeing the lack of regulation and crisis capitalism colliding with the great unwashed as the crash point. Then, from the doctors, comes the prescription: "democracy," "collective decision-making," "empowerment," not without merits as medicine, but not likely to restore vigorous life, not even close. Although regulation of business was a part of the New Deal, this restraint upon capital (though corporations and banks and financial dynasties survived this minor threat quite well) was systematically attacked and raided and stripped of its never-strong innards until it was revealed as DOA in 2008. Good position papers from the newly-alive radical left economists covered the funeral, explaining derivatives, credit default swaps, the hideous Alan Greenspan, the abortive $700 Paulson 3-page bailout, Hyman Minsky, Obama, Marx's theory of value, econobloggers, the Japanese Nisei, and a thousand other new discrete variables. What was the next line in the equation? Where was the solution set – in the next column, the next book, the next fake Nobel? Amidst the babble and the profundity, as trillions of wealth evaporated across the globe, the computers froze on the next line. The only great consolation for living in this age of the supersystem is the reveal of supersystemic maraud. Revisionist history has obliterated the ur-texts of the credulous 20th century – even tenured liberal professors write about the propaganda and the murderous racism that drove the imperialism of the American century, but we all, critic and Daddy Warbucks alike, dine on its efforts and conquest every night.

RecBack 29 -   US WAR

Tomorrow, we invite all foreign armies to gear up and have a whack at us on our shores. We've been parading and genuflecting before the battle flag and the drum corps since that little stateside war 230 years, and we can't handle the paucity of war here. The Civil War killed the requisite of hundreds of thousands of Americans, and yes it was conducted here, but it only lives on as a war should in the deepest pockets way down south, and is all but irrelevant to the northern victors. 3.5 million Vietnamese and southeast Asians died at American hands in our recent past, and we have gone on to generate multiples in Middle East deaths, to add to the totals of foreign engagements by the U.S. of A. military machine and its killer operatives. Overweight suburban monsters are tired of playing simulated video games and leading simulated paintball and NASCAR and Cowboys lives – they seem to be crying for war to come to them, to their homes, to their very selves. This time, we could do Keynesian economics right, a sustainable great War "right here" that will be directly before our red-white-and-blue eyes. Think of the "authentic" comradeship and historical celebration, the CNN ratings when "Enemy Bombs Hit Cleveland!" "Bring it on," one departed abjured leader cried early in his recent misbegotten rule – but that battle cry was incomplete, because it was not brought to us. "Bring it on HERE," is what the American psyche seems to cry for, where we can all get in battle gear and pop-pop-pop at bad guys as they swarm our backyards. Since "America is no. 1" we are guaranteed to win no matter or what invades our shores, commie or jihadi or perils of any hue except white, so we should get ready with some bigger Memorial Day to July 4th parades, along with some choice battle re-enactments, this time with up-date- clothing and food.

RecBack 30 -   MASS REALITY

From secular, deist beginnings as a constitutional republic of white propertied men, America is now a pluralistic society of massive supported enfranchised religions. The missing tax dollars; the hours spent seated before charlatans; the intimidation of free-thought in their offspring by their parents; the specious cover for sexual panic and sexual abuse by church leaders and acolytes alike; the corruptions of politics and academia by stultified theists; the appropriation of the social commons by faith-healing lunatics; the inculcation of violence and killing by separatist religious sectarians – what's the running total on all this chosen death and destruction and denigration of thought? In the marketplace of ideas, the sellers are con artists, and the gewgaws are chintzy, but the suckers keep buying. The worker/manager knows that the economics and politics of daily living depend on controlled subservience to bosses, rules, obligations, and the general public, and though this may be furtive at times, most often it is a sense of rewarded deception. The underlying myths of the supersystem do not have to reign in plain sight for the power of the institutions to continue. The citizens of Nazi Germany, the rich of contemporary America, the killers of colonial subjects, the high priests and ministers of the dominant religious right: all need not have any solid *belief* in the philosophies underlying their horrors, but all are sustained by available systemic reward. Humans do not need to think about their actions, nor about their conditions and can operate with wholly incorrect knowledge, but will chase whatever benefits have been set out for them, beset by fears along the way.

RecBack 31 -　　　COMMON TARGETS

Details of collusions and endemic cross-satisfactions between institutional actors like the courts, the religions, the politicians, the academies, the police, the corporations would prove conclusive, but exhaust a tired populace. Our bureaucracies work as partners in innumerable, insuperable ways. The illusion that some major miracle may prove the undoing of the conservative superstructure has defined the chattering of our post-nuclear age, but the time has come for a surcease. Reactionary backlashes promoting right-wing charlatans have been the only political issuance of the supersystem when threatened, delivering us faith-based lunatics of the darkest mind that drag better-intended liberals into similar pits of official destructiveness. The common singling-out of the a) evil of the political class or a) the stupidity/laziness of the common man becomes a tired evasion of the far greater danger posed by the supersystem above all else, to crush all initiatives, to lead the elites into the gravest off-loading of responsibility. All levels of the supersystem reflect the overall workings of the supersystem, products of its larger command.

RecBack 32 -　　　SYSTEMS

The "systemic" critical formulation has been in sociology for decades, and while the word does point to the inter-relatedness and multidimensionality of social problems, the word is also a millstone, most often followed by nothing, no concrete or specific analysis of the individual "system." Moreover, the word itself should be superseded by "super-," which signifies that social problems do not exist in discrete, walled-off social arenas, but are made up of strands, influences, and forces that cut across many institutions. Human social conditions are sustained by a multiplicity of factors, and though they may change according to crises and shifting imperial demands, the realities of our common lives need thorough investigation and cross-institutional intervention. And what do we get? Ad hoc committees; interest groups; religions; disciplines; books on one topic; legal precedence. There is no guarantee that a redesign of society will not lead us down well-rutted paths to destruction, similar to where we are today, but we could do worse than be true to our principles, and talk as if they meant something. The beauty of our human constructions, from our societies to our most awesome buildings and parks, the lore of poetry and the lure of romantics since the dawn of civilization, are now revealed as heedless folly, wasteful of the fossil fuel energy now percolating above our lonely coil, but they were made strong, our Easter Island statues. Humans are going to inhabit their social reality, are going to leave the useless hand-wringing for the true sports, and seek advantage in accentuated illusions.

RecBack 33 -　　　THE HUMAN PLANTING

The point of reading should not be to receive support for preconceived positions, but in this over-saturated infoworld, the mind's tendencies to seek out familiar subjects leads to further lengths of footnotes for a single topic, rather than the shock of confrontational newness. Pay too much attention to the small stuff, and you get throbbing paralysis, although the nation as a whole is not paying attention to much of anything besides the Screen: the computer-, video-, cell-, or televisual screen of the cosmos (TSC), and that is and will be our fate. We reject the material

29

we have rejected in the past, feel minor shifts in the same areas of liberal weakness as before. The modern intellect must be a whipsaw, subject to movements from one side, then another, then back from the other, a constant transition of focus that narrows with age and opportunity, but never begins the real job of cutting without distorting pressure. Since none of us have prepared for our work in any true facsimile of apprentice artisanship, we will never be suitable for the management imperatives we may fall into, yet we could have been more than our McShit jobs. Humanity's grasp of the balance between risk and reward got lost in the change from the bow to the plow, and "science" has brought us dangerously far down both paths, rewarding us with even higher levels of species extinction risk and expansive state military violence. Our job as life forms is to grow no matter what the soil nor what the weather or the cover, and we will continue to establish our stressed roots, extend towards whatever light, adapt to the seasons, avoid predators, twist towards height.

RecBack 34 -   SOCIAL NUMBERS

Give the US military industrial complex a number, a value. Call it: .71. This number/value becomes a representation, whose value is determined by the computer-assorted investigative sociology. The number has a plus or minus degree of certainty, but before this effort is derided as haruspiscence, the social reality is that the military industrial is a real and incredibly dominant force across swaths of the US economy. It has metastasized, it is fed by diverse budgetary streams, it has command and control – as a social force, it is not supernatural., but fully operational across the globe. If that .71 is not a rational number, it still can be a number that move up or down depending on entrenched social forces, and this MI complex will cause suffering, death, and privilege for vast numbers of people. We confront the world with trivial numbers by the bucket-loader, but are in the numerological blindness of oblivion when assessing profound and large forces. All of our large institutional powers have a number, all are in the danger zone of profound corruption heading for terminal decrepitude , yet we approach them with flyswatters and faint hearts. These numbers can be made to decline, and a few may well, but our global community needs low 20's from all of them.

RecBack 35 –   SIGNS

Unlike in the Cultural Studies realm, we have no need to discover talismans, hidden meanings, overlays, simulacra, recapitulations, or whatever new term erupts to signify sitting-productivity. The supersystem is real, current, and over-large, so it needs no subtle miniaturizations. In the human social time before the Supersystem, an antiquity of competing but bordered nation states and empires, local powers dominated discrete societies, and power had not become diffused so far across and up and down the human area. Elites have garnered outsized power since the beginnings of domestic civilization, but the overlays of religion and secular political myths have obscured the dark controls from around and slightly above, permitting minor liberal democratic upsurges, but encasing the massive project. The operations run not on mysterious signs or significations, but on the honed career path, the well-understood pressures, the ever-widening construction of walls between elites and victims, the shaping of cocktail-party chatter and the sinuous breaches between corporate law and actual regulation.

RecBack 36 –   MUTENESS

In the face of on-going war, circa today, technowar, made in the U.S. of A and delivered in the Middle East, where does the quotidian western consumer culture meet the horror? Would you like to register your outrage, – how, to whom, for what effect? Writing should not be a forum to express, over and over, the pitiful objections of the removed and healthy and untouched citizen at the latest iteration of human-wrought carnage – what matter is our "concern" or our "understanding" when the accomplishments of the administrators are in ever-greater insulation from public disapproval? Does each new expression of outrage supersede earlier condemnations of crimes?   Entire zip codes have been "against" every last American war since the Great One, establishing a pulsing skepticism about overseas technowar and corporate black ops, but this academic "concern" has been without effect, suburban disaffection with no consequence or consequences. How many unheeded calls for this or that signify the existential muteness of the caller?

Rec Back 37 -   BEFORE THE GATES

With the theory of the Supersystem (tSS), the drawbridge is up before the entrance is attempted: how can the actions of powerful elites, so shrouded in official state secrets, official public relations dissembling, and official disinterest in discovery, be described from way outside? If we are claiming monolithic status for the great institutional actor of covert foreign diplomatic action, then can how can its operations be defined, spread out on sheets, and probed with dissector's acuity? Great obsessed amateur outsiders would say that the Information Age yields all its secrets eventually to the discerning detective, but even Sam Spade was hired at a working wage. With the Internet, speculation runs rampant over every last inroad of the Empire, but where is the one stop shopping for the Grand Unified Theory of all political action? Were any social institutions still standing, there would be less room for interrogations of the fairly obvious, but the Bush Years were the demonstration of the full collapse of our social institutions, led by the sad capitulations of the academy.   Americans had no political involvement with their own communities, and were left with peevishness and sullen disinterest that suited the elites as they fashioned their fortified command. Where was civic engagement supposed to come from – nightly blatherings of fake reporters outside Capitol meetings?   DPW meetings? Interns?

RecBack 38 -   WISH FULFILLMENT

The Supersystem does not respect junctures or spectacles, so the allure of a diversity figurehead worked to solidify rather than disturb essential processes at the top. The naked power grab of the neocons during the Bush junta years advanced the limits of possible public discourse and practice (global war, "entitlement reform" of privatization, undemocratic "leadership," "faith-based" governance, the Department of "Homeland Security," and you can fill in the rest of Orwell's prophesy if you wish from the wonderful years of 00-09). Corporate dominance of all was functionally unchallenged, as a retread crew re-occupied the corridors of power temporarily ceded to outright lunatics and born-again fascistii. Even in the most radical calls for "economic transformation" from anti-globalization radicals was applause for the rhetoric of green capitalism from select corporations, as if that strangulation sector was most in the need of apologia and comfort. Raptures of "progressive change" after the McCain rejection were the cries of a despised minority dreaming of cultural power after so long in the desert, but where could they find the waking proof? Were they going to trust in Clintonianism again, or the neoliberal Harvard aesthetic of empire? Did they, in their "progressive" easy chair, imagine a hotline to the President that would over-ride the moneyed sector's? How much wish fulfillment could grown men and women luxuriate in – and then feel superior in confessing as mild "disappointment" as they pulled the diversity figurehead lever once again in 4?

RecBack 39 -   **SOCIAL POLICY**

Human unhappiness has as its majority shareholder social policy. The dashed hopes of workers, fired worker, and unhired workers; the count of cultural loneliness across the atomized wilderness; the unredeemed longings of those betting on a whim and a prayer for their unearned fortune to appear from a cross, a lottery ticket, a business proposition, a song, a book, a drug deal; flooded and blighted communities asked to provide social amenities and education on a level with their cross-state rich brethren. Social policy, based on hundreds of years of discrimination and repeated dis-accumulation, continues the Great Failures, condemning the poor to early death and fateful suffering, distorting the rich to greed machines and spiteful inebriates. There are also enlightened and lasting accomplishments that were borne of social policy, but the rationality of rights won and safeguards imposed is a minor washed-over barrier against the waves of the battering supersystem. The astonishing 2008 collapse of the global finance system was foreseen by disaffected former Wall Street capitalists, but the supersystem never asks for public input, nor is subject to daily audit The taxpayers somehow ponied up "taxpayer bailouts" of the buccaneering investment banks who perpetrated the criminal conspiracies without ever voting a single penny to their robbers. Trillions came and went and never reappeared in public without a single observation of the heists. Yet the great charade of "pulbic opinion" was so far poisoned in the noxious swill of libertarian corporate lying that a few Orwellian terms turned the heist back upon the victims: "socialism" did it; "the government" duped the bankers; the "free market" needed to become more "free" through more state-sanctioned giveaway of the public treasury to the rich; the stupid "buyers" through their venal default on legal loans had sunk the economy of the righteous corporate shareholders; the inferior "poor" countries of the world were incapable of standing the American-dispensed "freedom" to privatize their way to religious reclamation. In such a debased mass political culture, the knobs were given a slight twisting and the pathetic collapse of a globalized market imperialism became another rejection of the strictures against plunder. What other outcome other than the enfranchised lying of the Obama PR machine to blunt or co-opt or reject or infantilize the opposition to this criminal oppression could there have been? Without a countervailing force within a thousand miles of the financialization ranch, who was going to lead what kind of charge into the compound of suicides and health-care deprived carcasses and foreclosed sheetrock manses? A rescue of the imperiled global financial system was needed - that had the unexpressed consent of the huddled masses – but of what kind and with what conditions and to what end, only the forgotten fates shall ever yield the lost secrets.

RecBack40 -   **2008**

The great financialization flame-out of 2008/9 occasioned much work from the suits-and-ties, business not as usual. Amidst the dire warnings and the traded trillions from the bottomless treasuries of every conceivable origination, the concepts of wealth and money became speculative fictions. With all the heroic numbers and elemental disorganization at the top, the few contrarian economists were mapping the debris as never before, but the established tribunals and mouthpieces of the moneyed classes rotated their chairs and simply adopted a new, somewhat chastened but functionally untouchable new language. Borrowing the Skinnerian reduction of "the stimulus" while leaving out the necessary "response," knowing that there would never be one, the solons delighted in a new piratical focus. In some towns, all that stood next to the Dollar stores were empty buildings, but crime keeps many cultures alive with each new generational spinning of the proceeds.   With incipient ecological collapse blocking the reindustrialization of the decrepit American economy, elites could consolidate and knock over sectors with impunity, undeterred by the former needs to gain cooperation from labor or regulatory compliance with the government.

RecBack 41 -   PIGS AND PIES

There can be no undoing of the conspiracy of gross international theft of value perpetrated by the elite. Do you want to contemplate the enormity? Can you register the bill of attainder against these malefactors? On the more practical level, what can possibly be done with the squalor of ill-gained currencies? Take it all back, "redistribute" it, leave a few to operate the gates, tax them to a fare-thee-well, expropriate, garnishee? How? Where has that ever been done? The money needs to come back, the houses need to be down-sized to a livable space, off-shore companies need to be smashed, the derivatives and commodities robbery needs to be prosecuted to the demolition of the industry, the reins and restraints need to applied, all in the service of containing the destructive impulse of aggrandizement that is all too human and historical. Pigs are flying all around the pies in the sky on this imperative, but the recognition must be that all of us are prone to think we are better and more worthy than we really are, and need to have limits to ourselves as well as to the fat-cats we so habitually deride as "evil." Good intentions fostered in sylvan colleges meet the heat of practical necessity in the upper funnel tube of the grand beer blast of power – fermenting even the most innocent of nascent "reformers" into swill.

RecBack 42 -   SOUND

The cacophony of the Information Age is the air, the sound: all voices, some far more mellifluous than others, all in the service only of blasts of errant molecules, since we do not have any working socio-political outlets. We lack the structure, the capacity for productive talk, and are subsumed under the putrescent husks of legal protection for multinationals, torture justifications, aberrant health care, and lackluster task forces. History is going to be no guide for us: no global empire had the means to infiltrate the daily social and economic lives of all human beings and animal and plant species the way this carbon-suffused global corporate delivery supersystem has gathered unto its being.

RecBack 43 -   AMERICA IN RERUNS

How low have we gone? Are there statistics that can encapsulate unnecessary pain? Can we measure the chasm between what is and what should have been? The micrometer Left has hewed to a decidedly authoritarian veneration of Names, inviting the rabble in to sit at their feet as they intoned theoretical musings about this or that *observation*, always with a reverend around to summon forth the call-and-response of the doomed outcast. If we suffer and plead and remonstrate and bleed to no avail, to no earthly purpose except for blind circumstance, then we should get up off the floor, excuse the "religious left" out the door never to be invited back. The craving for meaning crowds self-pity into the room, but down the hall there is a party. A long and happy life should have been ours, supported by a decent and capable supersystem, but if we had been left to forage and build on our own, very few of us would have made it out of childhood. We are built on the salutary efforts of earlier humanity, from the working plumbing in our pipes to the electrons that bring us reliable comedy shows. There should be the sense that we have somehow *arrived*, have seen how the various scenes resolve themselves, watched the street competitions and the avoidances play themselves out to a generic outcome, where the folly of youth and the derangement of age give us marginal yet lasting wisdom. However, given the level of stupidity that occupies official discourse and private contact alike, there seems no need to wait for the DVD commentary on our recent history – reruns will be plaing until we that last off button.

RecBack 44 -   **BANKING**

The awful grandeur of the supersystem lies in its repetitive structural destruction. The S&L crisis of the 1980s was more than a foreshadowing, a precise presagement of the "Epic Recession" caused by the sup-prime housing bubble's explosion in 2008. In the intentional stripping of regulatory power of the government, in the corrupt collusion between criminal politicians and criminal bank owners, in the determined avoidance of reform even after the thousand felony cases of control fraud, the S&L crisis was a warm-up for the world-wide criminal enterprise of financialization that brought dystopia into the forefront of social thought. Bankers in the 21st century supersystem were working off the successful criminal blueprints that rewarded the economic elite of the late stage of the prior century. The forces of large-scale investment were directed towards global openings of supply and monetary capitulation, and there has been no end of the upward numbers for this specious chasing of fictitious capital. Could there have been less accomplishment?

RecBack 45 -   **THE OBAMA ERA**

What is the value of a dead ancestor compared to the value of a living fellow human? There are no dead bones speaking to us, no spirit world of land-inhabiting guiding memories. Instead, we have the functioning available world of common humans, each advancing the supersystem through adjustable actions and relatable thoughts. To return to history, where suffering cannot be lessened, and disregard the unfolding dimensions of the mutable present, is to deny our own gifts. We are all but one step from our fatal complicities, but the record of capable initiative is the better marker of our purpose. The strands of the supersystem must be gathered together as many as can be reached at once, and the reconfiguration must be deliberate, intense, and productive. In the Obama age, the supersystem received a new paint job and a tune-up, but the underlying structure was reinforced. Gone was the descent into Paleolithic madness of Cheney/Bush, its full-throttle gunnings for all the riches and inequality in the discoverable world living on in the full-staffed heated garages and Palm Beach golf courses for the superrich, along with virtually every inroad on the social compact. The Obama alternative despotic rule appealed on many, important, and superficial fronts. Stem cells were back in labs, torture banished to the fully functional rendition dungeons and not the official letterhead, a percent point or two of tax increases might be meted out as social charity by and to the Obama class, and yet the corporate predator apparatus had succeeded in its new diversity initiative to gather more colonies.

RecBack 46 - DESPAIR

In a generation before TV, Europeans turned off their radios, cut off the record players, put down the Enlightenment books, and began shooting civilians, women, babies, and surrendered soldiers. They gassed, starved, tortured, raped, pillaged, and then bombed, all in service of nation, exceptionalism, stoked anger, fear, and unchecked commanding power, allegedly in a seat of *civilization*. And then was born a *Leave It to Beaver* world, where senselessness of terrible crime and war vies with popular entertainment to describe the human condition. Recent historical truth can never be ignored, it will rise back from the spilled blood and buried bones to condemn our social ineptitude to permit poverty and enmity to join hands with male fear to produce the news of the day's deaths. All over the world and throughout time, the killing propensity and anger inclination of a species erupts like rust on an abandoned bicycle rim. Should we proffer optimism and moral uplift as if the record of our political systems did not populate the ground with innocent and tragic death? Over and over again, from continent to continent, in era after epoch, one life just a trigger or detonator away from senseless cancellation? Who are we claim that we cannot view the world through nihilism, fatalism, or their lesser offshoots?

RecBack 47 - THE GREAT RECESSION AND THE PEOPLE

When do see our arrangements of social truths as too far gone for recovery, too hardened for remastering, too protected for dissolution? At a time of global financial crisis, the ill-read pages and back alleys rang with the promises of economic revolution, nationalization, regulation, reform. Corporate capitalism, vanished in a Bear Stearns minute? Alan Greenspan, hoist by his own petard? Financialization, now an abhorrent curse? The secrets of the temple at long last open to public scorn? Great lies were revealed, to be sure, as fantastic levels of wealth were extinguished in a fortnight, to be replaced by, not by a new economic system, but greater spread of the same system. In the American mythos, if there are problems caused by the greedy rich and their fantastical armed and extortionate corporations, *it's the goddam government's fault.* The legerdemain, the thievery, the callousness, the power, were the replacement, not productive re-organizational ferment. There would be bankruptcies and dislocation to come, from Iceland to Dubai, and the US unemployment rolls would ensnare entire demographics, but capitalist economic management had not shuttered itself, and never would. Losses could hit the elite strata, and reconfiguration could swipe across a few of the most egregious boardrooms, but there would be no popular economic sovereignty, no commissions, nothing but the lightest and most doomed "reforms" that a rabid Congress would set about instantly dismantling. Across the world, people voted their democratic understanding by ceding interest to the elites, not talking about the subject, looking elsewhere for stimulation, giving up on forward economic discussion, a pitiful and abject condition of wise disinterest.

RecBack 48 – GLOBAL?

The national provenance of the Supersystem is American, but supra-national capital all around the world, from Old Venice to Russian oligarchs to Arabian petro-fortunes, occupies leading directorships. These families and mafias and hidden wealth societies direct the doings of power, but to map all the interlocking spheres of influence and exercise of control would be a tedious burden: who needs to see so much fatuous arrogance playing with the good wasting lives of the billions of their serfs? Take a swing from Bilderberg to Bohemia Grove, dip into Dealey Plaza, and Somalia, and Amway, and Wal-Mart, Iraq, and Langley; but this sojourn would only be via the American arm, and where would the co-conspiracies of the elites of all the other major countries fit into your next tour? No developed country can exempt itself from the orbit of the Supersystem, because of the attraction of lesser power towards greater power. In the post-war west, traditions of unionism, of social security for old-age pensioners, of free education, of egalitarian political inclinations, trembled quickly and fell to corporate-driven nationalism, religious fatalism, and imposed debt. Whatever national tradition of righteous democratic integrity was trumpeted as the latest hope for global social change, the fight was to the boardroom'd, to advertising, to supertanker transport, to computer-operated bombing, to profits, collapsing national borders in the supply of created demands. If there are minor regional variations to the supersystem, creating thousands of murders in Mexico yet creating thousands of useless law students in the neighboring US, there are lines all directing back to the central governing forces that enforce such terrible local distinctions.

RecBack 49 -   **VIOLENCE**

No opponent of the Supersystem can resort to calling for an alternative based on "non-violence." Violence comes in many forms, such as through death from a Boeing bomb, or from a punch in the face, or from a torture in a rendition jail cell, or from poverty-induced sickness – all acts with obvious physical effects upon the victim. Violence, as term, is not far away from the pain engendered by a system that condemns a vast majority of the people to unemployment, money anxiety, or unhealthy work. Does an alcoholic do "violence" to his or her spouse though the terrible interpersonal costs of alcohol-induced mania? A refusal to alter onerous actions or communications – in the "violence" or "non-violence" category? Humans are bound by their shared history and ineluctable instincts to violence, the oppression of others through manifold social or individual means, and kill insects, bacterium, animals, with monumental indifference. The current supersystem offloads official violence, incorporates it into bland bureaucratese, delegates it at every opportunity, yet continues to hardwire it into psyches and institutions through its perpetuation of demonstrable injustice. On earth, humans have never been at "peace" - have seen half of its 100 billion ever born die by their teenage years, visit wholesale destruction just through the act of occupying physical space, never to be overcome by good intentions and attempts at self-effacement. Whatever dies can be stepped around.

RecBack 50 -   **THE EASY CULPRITS**

The culprits are always anywhere but with the supersystem. A collective "we" is Public Enemy number two, after the "they" that represents all the wickedness and evil the Other can muster. This Other is fully apart from the "we," but both are evasions of social reality. "They" can so easily be "us," but the only "we" that are capable of governing is the individual self that stands apart from all others, including the inclusive "we" or the "exclusive "us." I am tied to my social reality, to the parameters of my society that have me driving cars instead of tending yaks, and though I am fully capable of renouncing my accrued privileges and customs from within my energy sources, ethical inheritance, and range of employment opportunities, those would be minor deviations that would not deter the known world from its appointed rounds. I could have shamed millions into rejecting the perquisites of violent appropriation that their political forces have produced, but this Ghandian guru-style celebrity has not been my métier, and yours neither. "We" are complicit and guilty only of being worker ants in a colony run on principles of leadership and elite obligations to the furtherance of power, so the charges must dissipate. As individuals, we must stand on our actions, the ones over which we exercise control and observation, and for that which we can be rightly condemned. For those moral ledgers, we have family, loved ones, and friends, and the tumult of social intercourse, but we will create no legacies, nor live on in any form after death.

RecBack 51 -   THE TRAPS

No minority of forward-seeing rationalists has ever commanded the altar of political power to refashion misperforming traditional means of governing social equity. As humans now face corporate-engendered "crises" threatening ecological and economic holocaust, no signs indicate a momentous revolution in legal prior restraint. Talk and anger are in abundance, but misdirected rage is better at strengthening inequality and aiding duplicitous elites than prompting wholesale re-evaluation of existing power structures. *There are no profits in regulation.* Control and supervision of subordinates and subordinate entities is a violent, contested, onerous, debilitating, irksome undertaking, especially of fellow adults. When culturally enforced in the pursuit of profits, regulation and punishment can be performed with a simple goal for a complex procedure, but when denied legitimacy by inherent corruption or immeasurable ineffectuality, the scales are pathetically over-weighted. Inspectors are fresh off the campus, given absurd levels of casework, provided the show when arranged to theatrically be guided through the corporate premises, given the outline of the permissible level of investigation, if any. Others sectors are "regulated" only as a bureaucratic fiction or after-thought, given the open road to fantastical robbery, as in the derivatives, food, and advertising industries. Protection of vulnerable species is not nature's strong suit – the weak are forever providing the food for the strong, and so the supersystem's economics are now crushing the lives and prospects of the lesser situated. No one can undo all the set traps, nor is there the volunteer force to prise all the traps apart once triggered.

RecBack 52 -   ADVERTISING

The supersystem is not mythic – its gargantuan command is built of policies and laws and bulwarks that are innumerable yet part of the daily conduct of economic life. However, there is such an inversion of right and wrong, where the rich criminals are up in the stratosphere of insane wealth and the vast majority are lost to a non-gainful-employment, that the language of social commentary becomes mired in trite, inconsequential, bloodless obvious tossing. No matter what the outcome of any single "problem" or "case" of social injustice, the preponderance of reality accrues to those most in line with the absurd, fascist, anti-rational ethos of the supersystem. Corporations have followed the path of marketing to its logical intrusions into spare inch of the cultural arena – clickable ads on every computer screen margin; ads on highways; ads in the air and in the den; ads in pre-school and ads in the geriatric homes; ads for services, ads for goods, ads for armed forces, ads with distinctive non-people, different languages, slick command, blatant obtrusiveness. Surrounded by this swirling pollution, we have paid for this unelected domination, since corporate advertising is tax deductible. Without designing an inch of this advertising system, facing bare limits on content and placement, the mass audience pays this onslaught through its tacit permission of corporations to engage in well-protected accounting skulduggery to off-set these billable campaigns on the very victims it ensnares in such wide, tensile nets. Where do we think have any capacity to unravel these persistent propaganda delivery systems, ones that do not hurt so much in any direct assault, but reject the very foundation of sanity when lived in as a whole and life-long social layer?

RecBack 53 -   THE SINGLE UNIFIED CRISIS

There is no "Triple Crisis," but rather a " Single Unified Crisis" across all the major institutions of the established world. Ecosystems, energy resources, and the global economic order are of course in grave peril, but there are equally viable threats to the performance of the rest of humanity's daily activities. Politics may be all but finished as an arena for social improvement, establishing an "Anti-Politics," but this is a temporary death in but one form of possible politics (global corporate capitalist command), to be eventually replaced by another form possibly more advantageous to the dispossessed, but more likely to see greater brutality to those arranged in the lower rungs. With liberalism now a desiccated fossil, killed by the twins scourges of neoliberalism and neoconservatism, there is a clearer field. No longer can we rely on the hope of education to change hearts as well as minds – the failure of American education has put a lie to that "Teach the World" ego-stroking. No longer is the Democratic Party to be looked for to be "anti-war" or to be for economic justice. No longer is art or technology or Third-World martyrdom or liberalized sexual or drug-taking or any of the identity schisms to be seen as the ultimate path towards social change. No longer are speeches or books or agit-pop or self-carving to be seen as the Answer. Instead, we have the virtue of seeing neither forest nor trees, but, instead, the pan-optical view.

RecBack 54 -   AMERICAN HISTORY IN 4 ACTS

The curtain has yet to go down on America's Fourth Act. In Act 1, the new nation, victorious in its rebellion against its parents, kills entire tribes of indigenous peoples and enslaves Africans in its youthful campaign of violence. In Act 2, the contradictions between two methods of acquiring property are adjusted with one kind gaining official imprimatur. In Act 3, a worldwide empire of military and corporate infiltration with dominant eugenic inclinations is consummated . In Act 4, the empire is beset by widespread internal and external hemorrhaging. However great this outbreak of largely self-induced disease within the American host, the other members of the global family seem also badly afflicted, whether by contagion or by other virulent viruses. In this 4th act, the audience is likely to become restive and in need of other entertainment – hospital dramas are notorious box-office killers. Is the death of the paterfamilias imminent? With the quality of life-prolonging transplants abetted by the money to be made by corporate-minded interventionist doctors the entire hospital ward could "live" on for dispiriting years, even decades, with no inheritance in sight.

RecBack 55 -   POLITICS OF TODAY

In formulating the theory of the supersystem, very little attention has been devoted to the actions of the "Founding Fathers." Why belabor an over-written epoch shrouded in blathering encomium? Madison, Jefferson, and the other bewigged Tories have their legions of admirers, but the supersystem became ascendant because of the Constitution's omissions and property biases, not despite it. The seeds of today's destructive social policies can be traced back to those tumultuous formative sessions, with the triumph of the rhetoric of "democracy" over its regulatory supports, but the precise delineation of that two-century process demands a higher grade of pay. The present conformations of moronic American political strains are absurd, to be judged by history as asinine across the board, not worth a comment. The Cronkitian intonations of the complete fraud Obama, the hysterical contradictions of the denier Ron Paul, the professional lies of the immoral majoritarians, the loathsome supplications of the political "scientists" - one snapshot is as hideous as any other from 1980 to 2012.

RecBack 56 –   SCANS
The horizon must be scanned – the new dawn will come from that way, and involve the same known entities, in configurations never precisely the same, but only variants thereof. There are bound to be new happenstances, improvements as well as dramatic losses, but we will forever orient for intimations of the realities about to come rolling through. Where is the constituency to provide material support for the fight for the necessary radical redesign of the global economic order? The perpetuation and expansion of the current system of corrupt elite engorgement is moving apace, pausing to shed some excess accumulation while gathering even greater capacity to govern the through the next crisis. The players may change as coalitions crumble before the onslaught of determined corporate re-invigoration, but families stand for generations on fortunes purloined from the endlessly abused and murdered public treasury. The corporations are on the run nowhere, have no organized opposition that is not corporate itself, are in universities as never before sponsoring research, departments, professors, the curriculum, and shopping trips for freshmen.   An anti-corporate party would be the only breath of fresh air this supersystem will have felt in nearly 100 years, but that pipe dream would have to matched by similar hostile movements in the courts, entertainment, professional sports, music, transportation, information technology, health care, and on down the tedious line of areas that will have never seen the light of that magnificent prospect.

RecBack 57 -   CRIMINALS
Within the structure of the supersystem, there are many fail-safe procedures ready to occupy a significant load when one area experiences major failure. The global economic system has been buffeted by major shocks, revealing extensive structural corruption and outright global criminal fraud, but the cover-ups have sufficed to keep the elite criminals running fictitious schemes of "investment" and currency speculation. In systems of extensive duplicity, more duplicity will most often have the system appear to be sound. What's another level of fake accounting when the whole structure is riddled with counter-balancing lies? Professional criminals always imagine an end-point in their lifetimes to their concatenation of deception and violence, in accordance with an over-developed belief in their individual prowess, but the realities of the game are that the con can become too big to end. Too many hands are getting profit off the scam, so the original untruth acquires a shape close to truth as it hardens. The systems that have been built by the fictions of the supersystem are still under great heat, and they may yet lose significant tensile

strength, but they perform important functions that are not going to be obviated by the greater forces of reform, rationality, or the inevitability of change.

RecBack 58 -   **BASIC TRUTHS**

An elephant does not turn into a mouse. An elephant cannot be told or made to turn into a mouse. Complex life structures do not reinvent themselves a simple organisms. The supersystem is not going to bring down itself. There have been great beauty and unimaginable riches that have been constructed by the supersystem. The global system of manufacture and interstate trucking and big-box inventory marketing is humankind's greatest feat – a brilliant, supermassive, incredible accretion of technology in the service of profit and simple pleasure. The global distribution of popular music through nearly complete availability of songs in formats from nano- to expansive remix has been a triumph of corporate research and development. Even as the death knell has been sounded for humanity on the planet, as the warnings of 4-degree Celsius rise issue as the warnings of furiously impending demise, the highways and boardrooms and courtrooms resound with the next delivery, the next financial prize, the actions of a confident idiot.

RecBack 59 -   **THE MADE MEN**

During the 80s, 90s, and 00s, plenty of college -uneducated graduates entered, willingly, lucrative fields of the moment, from computers and corporate management (80s) to Wall Street and corporate management (90s) to investment banking and corporate management (00s). The template was the same for all: firms hired the most craven, unambitious, lickspittle miscreants from the middle to better colleges, put through training programs aping fraternity/sorority drug-taking and sexual buccaneering, then let them loose in a jungle of hierarchical back-stabbing and excessive profit-taking under the heel of psychotic older eminence greasies. Not one ounce of social betterment was accomplished through these bildungsroman sites, not in the sleekest of corporate offices nor in the frenetic gambling dens, but the amount of dollars that were billed and collected and won through these decadent fraud factories was only in the trillions, and defined the contours of the globe's supersystem. Exposes testify to the common methods of brainwashing and reward in these leading institutions, but it took a certain kind of willed ignorance to enter into these depraved halls of commerce. A few egregious behemoths met their demise in the 2008, and there were shocks to all of the bastions of criminal enterprise, but the during that time the ranks were being replenished from the seedier redoubts of the credentialing mills of the US, the seats of power crafted the cover-ups and closed off the entries and papered over the killing fields and kept the mythos intact. They have only begun that phase of criminal theater.

RecBack 60 -   **WORLD WARS**

A complete history of the genesis of the Supersystem will need to focus one bright spotlight on the conduct and operation of World War II, the only one that was fought with grand territorial multiple engagements. In the mistakenly titled "Good War," corporations and governments colluded to bring the forward edge of the supersystem into eternal relief: mass automated killing of civilians, bombed by uranium and incendiary weapons from the sky in the service of ideals of national defense. Racist national myths abetted political notions of "democracy" to destroy a nation's people incapable of control over marauding political elites. Imputations of direct guilt are given to completely removed civilians as well as relatively powerless civilians and low-level soldiers, who are slaughtered en masse to establish some tangible outcome of victory. Burnt, shot, disemboweled, stabbed, poisoned, starved, exploded, gassed, or melted, the dead of that war, along the dead of this and the next war, testify to our errant social institutions, our enduring limitations of perspective, our fixations on nation and race rather than systems of unrestrained power. Our species cannot survive our profligacy of state violence, but those who are not on the receiving end will live as if that practice is unreal.

RecBack 61 -   HOW FAR WE HAVE NOT COME

After the annihilation of Japan through the apocalyptic technology of atomic bombs and conventional bombs, the United States, in the person of mad general Douglas MacArthur, set up a new political system for the vanquished foe. Termed a Five-Point Plan, the US designed five pillars of this new society: Emancipation of women, unionization of labor, break-ups of corporations, democratization of the economy, freedom of speech and thought – this from the governing structure that created the worst mass incineration of defenseless non-combatants. Today, after 65 years of global "progress" in the "American Century," the imperial victor could not pass that kind of document to run its own affairs. Only one point is even possible as a discussion: Women have become emancipated, and gays and blacks and other minorities, but there is no equality, of any sort, nor any great achievement outside of women entering the stresses and deformations of the work force, and a few lesser identity allowances. Corporations have killed unions, taking care of two of the areas, and the bankrupt, fraudulent economy has corrupted thought and speech. 65 years later, it is the American citizenry who is under the heel of the victor, given the dialectical opposite terms from those that permitted the rebirth of Japan from imperial fascism. These developments are not hidden, and have become self-evident truths, not much in need of documentation or revelation. The shadow elites are not in any physical or prosecutorial danger, although as criminals they retain outsized fear of being taken out somehow. The obvious can be belabored, even if it is studiously avoided by tenured gasbags and bilge-spewing think-tanks.

RecBack 62 -   THEN TO NOW

To locate the present supersystem in history, being careful to note the horrors of applicable recent catastrophes, such as in the class-bound rot of Victorian England or the post-Weimar fascism of Nazi Germany, may soften the contemporary sense of being entrapped in a over-complicated and sealed-up maze, since the hell of the common man during those epochs is far greater than a bout of modern ennui. If an additional reason for committing to scholarly history is to vivify the present with dramatic precedents, what then of history when the present appears a defunct terminus, leading only downward in spirals of obligation stripping? Without social capital, any proposal for a "new" society is a sad drunk. Meta- considerations of "Parecon" and "Inclusive Democracy (ID)" can float through many a pdf portal, but the boorish self-aggrandizement of politics has attracted only the most closeted or morally hideous of the damaged class. There is seriousness and rationality behind the "degrowth" ideological movement, yet the current intellectual scene permits lone males a vicious and unheeded biological antipathy that obviates the exchange of ideas. Lunatics take out the garbage and drive within the speed limits, mentally chasing figments and tangible reality alike. Within the supersystem, even this alternating between the fully bizarre and the actual becomes a valid life, since there are so few moments that constitute actual engagement between humans. This is not the default position, but there are so many ways of either denying the morass exists or succumbing to it, that irrationality and psychic legerdemain becomes mired in consciousness.

RecBack 63 -   THE REGUATORS

The enforcement arms of the supersystem have become incredibly lax. No one fears "The Regulators," not in any field, not in any pursuit, except for code enforcement officers. Most regulatory agencies, as agents of state or federal governments, have been intentionally starved of funding, financial wherewithal, staffing, reach, coverage, blood and sinew. Regulators are unnecessary expenses to a profit-driven supersystem, only useful in the fiction they provide of actual oversight, so they become profit-manic, nearly wholly-beholden captives of the corporate supersystem (Moody's, the EPA under Bush II, the Supreme Court, the IRS, Congress, the American print press, the Department of the Interior, higher academic auditing consortia, bar ethics panels, prosecutors, the Obama administration, liberal NGO's, ombudsmen, any of the porous filters employing the once-motivated), Brave whistle-blowers and stalwart opponents of corporate criminality are harassed, shunned, driven to the side, overtopped in rigged floods, marginalized from the minute they are given the orientation tour.

RecBack 64 –   THE TEMPTATIONS

The "Revolving Door" at the top of American institutional shows how ludicrous regulation and oversight have become in the age of the supersystem. There are no real antagonists in the conduct of social affairs – agents dance back and forth from government to corporation, amassing polite fortunes and invaluable shields along the way. Hardened opposition, even if were possible in the softening microwave oven of corporate capitalism, melts when the eyes are on the future riches on the side of the temporary opposition. Who has resisted the blandishments of the corporate representative, that singer of the siren song to come over, just this once, just you, just for your unique genius, for a little thing called a check from us, with more and greater on the way? The hand goes on the back, the ground is solid, the money becomes genuine, and the slide into corruption and destructiveness is now a lifelong condition.   Outliers live in moral cocoons, safe from contamination from the blandishments of the fossil fuel multiverse, but these stalwarts anti-corporatists still inhabit the same doomed biosphere ruled by the insistent majority.

RecBack 65-   WIND

The operation of the supersystem is not a nebulous, unknowable, esoteric matter – it is the wind that blows the pirate sails of corporate criminal catamarans. Where power is exercised to deny human possibility or human innocence, the supersystem is the animate force at the hand of the tyrant, from the lowest to the most consequential. This conduct of authority, to willfully stagger and crush humane opposition and true merit, is the accumulated product of historical fictions and lies, the cause of the lack of an abortion to a poor girl, the gulag inviting dissidents to their deaths, the rotten parenting of Christian abusers, the economic riches of business gangsters, the relentless cavalcade of horror visited upon victim, human and animal and natural alike. Not only are the actions motivated by bestial visions of supremacy, the aftermath and the internment are also under the control and direction of the moronic victor class, whose bank accounts have fattened and grown into incredible mansions and family inheritances. None of this ill-gotten, ill-maintained, ill-distributed spoil of war has parentage other than the supersystem, the validation of mythic command over moral or rational outcome. Today and tomorrow, the rewards go to the top, not because of the elite's superior deviousness or command, but because these masters, in their specious supplications to traditional power, have the supersystem as their unseen sponsor, unseen lieutenant, unseen commander. Try to sail through those westerlies – you will not get far.

RecBack 66 -   ECONOMICS

In the macroeconomics of the supersystem, the forces of aggregation promoted monopoly capital in all sectors. Percentages of market share controlled by the largest firms increased dramatically across industries, as smaller fish became targets for growth-minded larger sharks, who warded off competition by intensive campaigns for territory, favorable legal corruption, relentless advertising pollution. Upstart enterprises positioned themselves to be bought by the large TNCs, or fell victim to closed market intimidation. The formula for this narrowing to ever-larger entities of control was not precise, permitting new technologies to invade and then be co-opted by host firms. Purchaser "choice" could be reduced to an obvious candidate and one or two lesser outside ones, with intense jockeying among these behemoths resulting in only marginal effects. Skippy and Jif and Peter Pan established fiefdoms, with only minor encroachments disturbing the cabinet stuffings of the habituated buyer-worker. Supply chains, and research and development, and marketing, were computerized and micro-analyzed to serve the profit gangsterism of the word's Big Boys, all over fake foodstuffs like machine-mold vacuum spreads. Mincemeat dissertations can be made out of the non-fascinating permutations of our economic age, but the density of production makes any one perspective just one more small-print chemical preservative.

RecBack 67 -   HISTORY

The United States has had a primordial "will to empire" for generation after generation, wave after wave of European invader/immigrant to overcome all barriers human or natural. Under convenient guises of religion and politics and righteous murder, the continent has seen epic conquest by the ancestors of today's role-players. The supersystem grows directly out of these long-enshrined, long-shaped cultural processes of sanctioned domination, now shrouded eugenic illusions of superiority, and fearful violent animadversions against victims. What was once direct killing and virulent treachery is now a deeper, sinuous, complicated bureaucratized version that rules over every sphere of life with momentous tragic condemnations. There can be no sanitized history of the centuries-long genocide of the indigenous peoples, nor of the centuries-long holocaust of slavery and neo-slavery against perceived "Africans," but contemporary Americans are only dimly aware of how to live atop such a shameful and on-going mountain of enmity and pioneer fortitude – with parades and professions of sympathy, with the eyes on the protection of the children and the unearned trust in the verities. History must be washed clean, the unadorned future bequeathed to the living, but of course the legacies of advantage and befuddlement and violence respond only to the strong antiseptics of wealth – all else is stain and superstition.

RecBack 68 -   SLOW COLLAPSE

Rational economics is not active in the dead heart of American politics, which beats only with artificial mechanical means. The culture has become a center of disintegration, as only the gravest anti-liberal arguments have won politicians and political effect. The amounts of income that trans-national corporations have arrogated to themselves are beyond quantification – CEO pay alone, where the numbers for "equity holdings" for Oracle Lawrence Ellison are beyond the spreadsheets for mid-size African countries, is staggering in its depiction of the waste stream of profits accruing to moral failures. The supersystem is not going to be redirected, nor is a paradigm going to "shift." Elaborate constructions are both product and element, both the accumulation of incredible streams of myth and social practice and enforced obligation, and active forces themselves in generating new and greater forms of accumulation. Every day this world of continuously collapsing social reality is met with billions of human striving for a better outcome for themselves, who are sorted by existing social forces into conventional, applicable, and reinforced channels to continue the piling of the sand.

RecBack 69 -   LETTERS TO EDITORS

Heartfelt missives to the president, signed letters to the authorities, phone messages to a politician's recording machine, books written to set the record straight, speeches of conscience, on-line petitions, and testimony directed towards the convincing the powers-that-be to change, all fail to account for the constraining influences that bind the elite.   As with any empire, the people of the current US empire can fairly be asked, "How could you live as if your welfare was so above proper standards of human responsibility?" If the easiest answer is that *advantage will be taken*, to varying degrees, but inevitably, the next stage of explanation is that humans are focused on the immediate ties, the ones that connect the active self to inherited family, inherited co-workers, to the jostling electrons presented right in front, up close and personal. If the repeated accusation is that the American citizenry have become passive, politically inert, stupefied and faddish, then that is result of the confluence of factors that determine social reality, not of some sort of innate ignorant beastliness. Having adjudged, correctly, the political arena to be a manipulated trap, Americans were either at the mercy of its baited predations or fully unrepresented.   Polls served to warn the elite political class of minefields, but policy was in service of the corporate class, and could be resolutely and safely opposed to the majority of upright citizens who might be against particular horror.

RecBack 70 -   JOBS AS GHOSTS

Even at its late stage, capitalism can send temporary workers into melted-down Japanese nuclear power plants, using class intimidation in all of its criminality to send people to their doom. Because there is only the figment of a countervailing power to regulate work so it does not led to the death of workers or the death of the invaded ecosystem, many are at risk of doomed labor or doomed residence, and since these are us only in different circumstances, we as a species fail. None of the hoary social critics of yesteryear can prepare us for the over-complexity of our times – no quotes from the ubiquitous de Tocqueville, no invocation by Adam Smith, no cloistered overviews of medieval precursors. Change may be inevitable, there may yet be birth and renewal of a new global economic order as with our lives, but the number of instant transformations of social reality is rare in the natural world of other species. In the US jobs are a diminishing resource, stripped of many protections and worthwhile wages, a quaint by-gone conceit belonging to the defunct American past of unions, thriving factories, cheap housing. The supersystem holds employers responsible for chasing profits, so jobs can be outsourced, workers replaced by machines, cities overcome by blight, all in logical fealty to the governing order. The US government is not going to go into the expensive business of providing long-term work that pays a stable wage, nor is any state. There is no jobs-producing entity in the US aboard, nor one to come. Whatever jobs that can be claimed by US business will be either non-union, sub-service level, temporary, or tied to radical extractive industries or the horrific war machine. The New Deal is not coming back, the green job chimera is fainter by the year, the masses are getting more trained by the year to accept hand-out Barcalounger unemployment with one house member hanging on to remunerated labor.

Chapter THREE
NO FOOTNOTES and OTHER
LIMITATIONS TO THE
THEORY OF THE SUPERSYSTEM

LIM 1 –   **MISSING**

The theory of the supersystem will be missing its foundations. Where is the grounding in Marx? What happened to even a nodding acquaintance with Adam Smith? Where is the Econ 101 grasp of market fundamentals? Why no disquisitions on Freud? No Shakespearean soliloquies, no quotes from Martin Luther King, entire swaths of Western culture missing? How can the ultimate theory of all social reality be self-enclosed, thinly sautéed, hermetic and featuring a paucity of researched heft? The answer lies in both education received and choice renewed. Youth and young adulthood are a frantic time of accommodation and resistance to existing particulars, and during the American 1970s, a reasonably sane and active young man would have had limited forced exposure to the classical gods. I received a much richer education through the popular culture of my time than through the traditional drudgery of monastic scholarship devoted to antiquity, but the sauce is then without its thickening agent. Who says how this life must be lived in the mind? What part reflection to what parts reaction, brooding, analysis, production, loathing, stupefaction, enjoyment?

Although this is theory, a mapping of the entirety of social reality, it has neither copious footnotes nor ponderous abstraction ad infinitum. The work of other theorists and documentarians has certainly shaped the contours of the supersystem theory, but no one work has offered the blinding insight into any one corner that necessitates a borrowing of a lyric in quotes. In an academic treatise, the terms of jargon pile into every sentence, an overloading that causes the seizure of the brain stem. For this work, boredom and ennui are plausible companions, since the supersystem as the world-swaddling magnificent force denies the primacy of art and good humor. Should you be skeptical of the weight of the social criticism of the author, you have a right to consider the thesis unproven, the facts self-evident, the tone blasé, the consequences unremarkable. No book is a social movement, no writer a god, no story a talisman. However, the critical evidence for the presence of the supersystem is as long as a circumnavigation.

LIM 2 -   **MORAL OBLIGATION**

To have only *exacerbated* the unconscionable enforced degradation of the world's people is a failing greater than any salve from the world's religion, or any obtuse position paper from the conservative think tanks, or any poetic flights from our Yale McArthur dramaturges. Economic inequality mocks all that we are, all that we use to escape, all of our cherished dismissals. Whatever we have done, wherever we have gone, we have defenestrated the very nature of ourselves by amplifying, spreading open, legally supporting the distance between masses of actual, innocent human beings and the basics of human life, while others have basked in profligate, obscene over-wealth. This was not unavoidable, was not visited upon us by some "unseen hand," did not come through unannounced: this was plain as day, right out on Front Street, and it was our doing, either through our outright criminal usurpation or through our inability to be influential against the rampaging global rich. Every child's hunger, every hard-working sufferer's early death, every terrible death sentence from position of birth and location, was from our refusal. Say whatever you want about the tediousness of First-World breast-beating, the tears dripping into Chardonnay, the bleatings of empathy a form of grace before the obscene repast, the worthlessness of liberal condescension, the emptiness of suburban solidarity, but the outside world is always our backdrop. Who are we to ever not pay obeisance to the paradox of plenty amidst suffering?

LIM 3 - NOT ENOUGH DATA – OR TOO MUCH?

Social reality can not be assessed through narrow deep investigations of discrete institutions, like inside baseball reports from the misbegotten courts, jails, schools, families, hospitals, service counters, or other mass common practices of post-war America. Of course these hallowed grounds need their exposes, their undercover sociology, but the far greater reality of the networks of cable and steel supports *between* these pursuits demands primary focus. How can any would-be leftist not see the futility that accompanies criticism that was in full society-wide effect and daily headline power during the 60's, but was crushed by the cabals of mythos and instinct during the next four decades? The need to vouchsafe work status, the desire for self-enrichment, the inclination away from self-denial, the conservative pull of parenting, the seductions of consumerism , and various other natural forces destroyed the social progress movements that flared, leaving psychotic scions in power, the military colossal, prayer cells entrenched in government in business, the environment destroyed by large multinational concerns, youth medicated or committed enfant terribles of the vicious right, and higher education in irrelevance. Of course, this daily menu recitation of today's ills has been footnoted and re-footnoted in books that form a mighty moat around the castle – what could be *new* about any one statistic, any one decrial?   Does the world need one more *statement* of how bad things have gotten? The problem for this inquiry is that there remains no scientific way to establish the quantitative x's and y's of the operation of the supersystem.   How does the supersystem keep its myths updated and functional? How do billions of humans become governed by inexplicit commands that promote subjugation, hatred, warfare, unhappiness, and disinterest? Of course the opposites do find their expression within and through this same supersystem, but only in the interstices, not in the main, and at such miserable cost to the enterprise of human living. How do fear and ambition coexist in the human psyche? Since we lack a good source of communication with our own actions, since we fool ourselves and cheat ourselves with practiced cognitive deceptions, we are foolish to imagine that we have the authority to proceed onto the great mystery of communal social reality, though we must.

LIM 4- LIMIITATION OF KNOWLEDGE

A flowchart could track all the ways our intellectual scene doubles back upon itself, as the supersystem distorts epistemology into an oscillating unknowing. A handy guidebook of cultural literacy, covering the known gamut from computers to stem-cell research to positive psychology to the latest mating habits of the gnarled tsetse to avionics to metabolizing sherry additives, would certainly help matters, but there is no knowledge that is sufficient, no knowledge that is insufficient, because we cannot place the workings of our knowledge into a valuable social production. The theory of the supersystem (tSS) can also founder upon the shoals of the supposed newness of events. This illusion is particularly heightened in the economy, where statistical fluctuations can exacerbate the churn of money, people, and business "news."

LIM 5 -   POVERTY OF ECONOMICS

Much of the problem with the world of economics has to do with the limited choices that the academy has let filter through. A further problem is lack of commendable models. None of us need to redo our decades of non-study of this or that theory, Marxian or Friedmanite, but we could improve the task by noticing that we have no language of economics. With the dearth of individual involvement in economic planning, what else can we do but return to banalities? Who has on their resume a track record of reordering the economic priorities throughout the supersystem? The casual fool has as much an appreciation for the workings of our global economy as the world's leading economist. A brighter day was promised to an unknowing young man, but the reality was built on lies and terror, and no degree of human happiness will cancel that waste of so much human endeavor. These pessimisms and acute truths are well-worn, as endemic to the vulnerable person as breathing, yet they are the foundation to build upon. A farmer plants again, an old lady rises up out of her bed to confront her aches, the quotidian builds through another responsible day to crush the ambitions of yearners far and wide.

LIM 6 -   VASTNESS

The paperage wasted on who called forth what unheeded denunciations of the American imperium is to be rued ahead of its occurrence, since the terrible wasteland of actual causes and events should be our playland, should have been. To unravel the precise nature of the *inter-relationships* among the institutional actors of the supersystem takes a dozen think tanks, or a seized, mentally unbalanced, monastic solo author, and I am neither one nor part of the other. To write a scholarly dissection of the courts, the churches, the schools and colleges, the tax system, the global financial players, the family, the bedroom, the science of a decayed planet, warfare and psychic dissolution, the consumption of entertainment and the, yes, entertainment of consumption, takes, one each one or in groups or in totality, a much-more attuned young fresh fellow.

LIM 7-   THE POSITIVE BIAS

We are primed for action, us thinking humans, inclined towards a positive view of our propensities. How can our life be so circumscribed by unyielding social reality? In a brain capable of self-reflection, how could the image conveyed back not be rounded? What we like, should be liked. What we do, should be done. Self-justification is universal, and underlies a great portion of the momentum of the supersystem, as elites and the various sub-strata act in accordance to situational imperatives. A critic of the regnant social order then is importuned to offer *solutions*, to be *optimistic*, to *find answers*, to *act*, to "be the change," to *lead*. However, power is never ceded to the critic along with the insults, and the damage is then ascribed to the critic, not the perpetrators.

LIM 8-   FATUITY

The world of affairs cannot afford mere documentation, with the books on the last decades of the American Empire providing many an endowed chair with non-perishable publishing. How many ideas, books, speeches, and travels can re-enact the dead past of history, with no redress for the living victims of the present? More letters to the editor, econometric abstracts, on-line punditry, revisionist invocations of Churchill and the air bombings of civilians – or an actual place at the table of Power? Sure, this can be dismissed as a pipe dream, unworthy of serious regard, to unconditionally call for an enfranchised, deep, and resolute immediate global bulwark, but there is no alternative to press for its implementation. Rather than establish an ideology, or march in step with personalities, the future of humanity is tied to the reduction of harmful power. Commerce will have its places, and religion its minor outposts, but never more the inability to connect unseen effects from known causes.

LIM 9-   ORALITY

The tSS is American because of its hegemonic globalism, but applicable to all societies that have established institutions and little way of approaching their consubstantiality. If there trouble in your world – what can be done about it that is not going to be blocked by entrenched forces? The invention of the printing press led to individual minds seeing a chance at ecclesiastical greatness, observing in the responsive movable type a universe for their own manipulation. Oral communication had rewarded the bullshitter, the oracular fraud, but now human expressiveness could command the heights of eternal record. Official speech intertwined with the literate monograph, emboldening the omnipotent author to sweep over complex spaces and times, always seeming to end with a grand exhortation of the looming harmony of the future with the author's view. My work is infinitely poorer for not being open to immediate censure and redirection, but there is also a hell of uncritical comity around the campfire that helps us get no further along to the redrawing of our social compacts.

LIM 10 -   THE NEXT GREAT HUMAN

I have no illusions that through one or two pet issues the world of the supersystem will be overturned. Although religion has been a core instrument in war, subjugation, and oppression, it has also given generations a social bond that now belongs to their television set alone. Atheism is fine as a start, and absolutely necessary, but while it obviates one major irrationalism, that of belief in supernatural control, it does nothing much about the other irrationalisms that permeate our primordial brains. Do I have the appropriate levels of inter-social fears – the right admixture of cortex-based psycho-chemicals, when it comes to apprehending other humans in my daily encounters? I may have enormous reservoirs of unlikely apprehensions, like a fear of snakes, an overactive sensitivity to violence-based taunting, and too great a propensity for self-questioning. Or it may be the precise right outlay for coping with my inherited dramas, making me, alone of the all the humans, both exquisitely fine-tuned for my environment and uniquely capable of withering discernment of its immutable particulars. Or I may be out of synch, somewhat too much this and too little that, with no hope of therapy or drugs to alter my financial/emotional disequilibriums. The glare of the celebrity writer spotlight has become a somatic drug, blasting addictive commercialism into the veins of the little collegiate beasts, making intellectual enterprises lesson.

LIM 11 -   CURRENT REALITY

The supersystem is not presently in any danger of losing its multifold footholds. The criminal masters are not under any imminent threat of indictment, and have new generations of willing minions to staff their organizations. You can find ways to stay the forces of entropy tonight, but there will not be an upswelling of disagreement that finds valuable narrowing towards a societal purpose. Expressions of societal anger by the vaguely discontented slither into new formulations of intrapersonal strife, psychic disturbance, and tattoos on the newly obese. Artists across the decades have built their small castles, adhering to their self-designation as singular talents, nursing dead oceans of resentment towards critical reception, over-valuing the great hand of a divinity guiding their improvisational maunderings. I was the center of the artistic world once, as enamored of my genius as any thousand Mozarts, and there have been good let-downs, when the indifferent, uncomprehending world of right-minded folks has jacked my fantasies of supra-intensity down to the ground.

LIM 12-   EFFORT

How can we quantify the Wealth & Hellness that have been extracted from each and every squalid corner of this earth in pursuit and reach of profit? You can read well-researched books that will fling around the wasted billions, the corrupted bigotries of massive corporate scale, naming a few of the connected names, documenting with curious reserve the criminal machinations of the outward hellions of the imperium, but the earth does not respect knowledge, it only bends according to *action*. We can connect the major actors in the supersystem, replete with professional footnotes testifying to our responsible reading, but the known world would be no further along towards halcyon states of being that will never be ours. We can jibber-jabber until the room clears of all but the autistic vanguard of lonely men, but if the current health of the social world is recrudescent, then wave it through and go see about something else.

LIM 13 -   WRITING

Emily Dickinson exclusively wore white for the last decades of her life. Charles Dickens wrote insatiably over a fear of return to his primordial poverty, and then died of a brain hemorrhage. Mark Twain fought against his true affinity for nihilism (life has no meaning) and determinism (everything is controlled by large forces) by writing and lecturing, though his bankruptcies from failed investments in printing presses and the like also were factors. The Little Dipper is upside down next to the Big Dipper. Rene Descartes was a devout Catholic. Aristotle was a terrible scientist. Humans have stupidly chased dragons, stumbling all throughout creation because they have not had strong critics inserting doubt into their quixotic obsessions, with the effects of ridiculous intellectual pursuits persisting in raging form to his day, and will no doubt continue. What with the hormones unleashed by the 60's and the good times available by the 70's, there was no need or time for a classical education. Although artists and writers are yet capable of producing feats of concentrated art, the question of personal balance hangs over celebrity and genius. Why become monk-like and abstemious or suicide-courting monomaniacal when so many other minor divertissements beckon? The modern historian, like the modern poet or the modern record producer, must sacrifice the modern life to live in the squalor of books to the ceiling, divorces by the pound, children raised by the wild. The joys of abandoning self-imposed imperatives towards ephemeral conquest, the greater truth of writer's block, the sweetness of unfocused brooding, the comfort of lack of responsibility, are denied to the titans of popular culture grandeur. Sure, there must be art product to satisfy the politically-denied aspirations of billions of alert yearners, but sausage-making is not a pretty business, and particularly not for the sausage makers. With the advent of cathedrals of personal performance technology, art is produced by every typist, consumed mostly by them alone, a self-containment and self-reference that makes everyone a winner, baby.

LIM 14 -   WRITERS

A solo writer is capable of great pyrotechnic virtuosity, encasing him- or herself in panopticon virtual reality headgear to visit all the dimensions of other people's reality to summon it intact on white and bound pages. A great trick, in fact better than a three-card monte performance, but only if you are a lost tourist A mark of madness is to continue speaking aloud when no one is responding, and for the solitary artist, there is only the reverberations of the medium when creating. The unitary artist as repository of the world's ineffable knowledge is the major trope of our time, and not worth the remaindered price of Norman Mailer's backlist.

LIM 15-   CONFIRMATIONS

The confirmations for the tSS come all the time, through the transom in newspaper articles, on-line, in magazines, in books. Placing all these pieces of evidence in an order is a Herculean task, and there is no glory in selfless monasticism. This was not an epoch for the shaking of the head, nor could outrage be directed towards a useful protest. What was new or *news* about the sinister, limitless takeover of social institutions by superior interlocked forces of profit and corruption? No amount of informed reading, no grasp of a meta-conceptual framework, no theoretical command of Engels and Friedman coupled with graduate-level neuroscience knowledge, could prepare the critical ground for the tSS. Hopelessness, however, is not a good sell at the State Fair. Other histories could testify, with great professionalism, to some of the Hidden Facts, but if the great point was pointlessness, how could the masses come aboard? Humans have lived and died in arrangements of stupefying violence and incalculable social defilement across dozens of generations and throughout all cultures and continents, burning lonesome anger into heirs who fall into new graves of avoidable construction. What good comes from bemoaning the human misfortune, when unearned privilege can be enjoyed for the price of a withdrawn conscience?

LIM 16 -   REFORMERS

The supersystem relies on a generic acquiescence of the managerial or progressive set, expressed in buzzwords and disregarding superiority. Anger against the practices of the supersystem will not get beyond a tolerating non-hearing, as the complainant gets choked by the tentacles of his or her own rage. If you play the system well enough, even from the supposed critical left, you are accorded a place or a standing, but your words will vanish into the climate-controlled air, as the masters absorb your flailing piety and continue to talk seriously only to those who matter. In the grand tradition of self-ennobling elites, today's putative "reformers" deign to emphasize both "optimism" and "realism" in supporting the command of those at the top.

LIM 17 -   TIRED WORD ARUGULA

There are no characters that stand for a generation's loss of innocence, or a revision to the victor's mis-history that will avenge the blood of innocents. A political economy that looks for divine control from dead theorists is dead itself. Each human generation must invent itself, must speak for itself, must fashion its own social architecture – but who has the time, let alone the resources to get that work done? Instead, we are drawn back ever-again into the muck of tradition, with its religious mire and corruption miasma. In the age of the Internet, with its advertising-saturated formlessness, cross-country textual shouts have substituted for intra-family fights and bowling alley soirees, all clicking for the merry benefit of punk engineer capitalists and live-sex incapable males. Jazz word arugula, however, may have been the rage at early third millennial MFAs, but the global appetite has lost its flavor-appreciation from the dictionary basslines, the hip angles of electric prose, and the bohemian capitalism it serviced.

LIM 18 -   THE LAB

From Marxism, through deconstructionism, past the worries of therapeutic psychology, over the carcasses of political debate, and sprinting around the dying fauna of scientific exactitude, the theory of the Supersystem (tSS) is missing technical words to cement the deal. There is no dearth of doctoral students currently advancing the frontiers of knowledge in any of the disciplines that could be tied to the workings of the supersystem, but there is no road to travel on with this esoteric certitude. Pronouncements herein are made on grave and grandiose subjects as if issuing from some super-lab, a DARPA of the auto-didactic set, competing with intensely micro-focused savants who use every technical means to establish ivory tower command of the ages, but there has no peer review for the tSS. Leave the scientific exactitude to the robots – no human of the Infoworld should disregard the greater imperatives of chilled inchoacy and doubt.

LIM 19 –   RECEPTION

The instant reception for a Theory of the Supersystem will be rejection of its nihilism, or a dismissive finding of *so what? What is so new about that?* However, in its overt focus on large-scale collusion between our panoply of institutional forces, the tSS will bring to our domesticated hunter-gatherer band of strivers its only hope for survival. The point of the tSS is to enjoy the predicaments of modern life, with cynical laughs replacing dutiful greenwashing and guru-venerating backwash. Political philosophy has been dominated by thinkers without a modicum of operational power directing the world with a rubbery baton as if they were the maestros of geopolitical action. The real actors, those of the Bilderberg, Trilateral, Davos, Telluride, Paris, London, CFR, CIA, White House study groups, Bohemian Grove, .1 percent quasi-formalized networks, do not command through instruction from unaffiliated intellectuals. These are structures of dispersed alliances, kept intact through natural systems of predation and ownership.

LIM 20 -   ASTEROIDS

Voluntary asceticism is a minor human pursuit, and will seem foolish if the rest of the "developing" world plugs into the grid and asks for a job and Big Mac. A planetary human population of 9 billion is not going to all sing and dance at the corner pub after a good day of pushing paper in the cubicle. The statistics are known, the Cassandras are accepting accolades in the underground, there are asteroids of trouble all coming in our vicinity, overpopulation accentuating economic inequality exacerbating climate change breaking down family continuity decimating job availability slashed by mechanical technologies, with each asteroid just the half of it, a belt of massive social asteroids each capable of enormous devastation. Such a scenario will not reward expressions of individual resolve, nor be surmounted by strings of private initiative. All social reinforcements must be accounted for, a mapping of global sociology that will place human social power in service of human and natural survival – and look for that on CBS at 9:00.

LIM 21 -   ANTI-tSS

For any work, there exists a force field of anti-thesis. For the tSS, there are many force fields of opposition, including the obvious ones of conservative religious japery, but also including complete drug indifference, scholarly dismissal of unsourced rumination, the rejectionism of the amateur misanthrope, slack-jawed mere dislike, protestations of noxious *repetition*. Why beat a horse you've already pronounced "dead," and keep on pounding it with the same motion, could go the dismissal. Liberal reformists are also in nearly direct opposition, as they posit outside or popular or electoral or cultural control of the supersystem. However, anytime in the news a lack of regulation is cited, as in the hedge fund/derivative economic calamity of 2008 , the tSS is present. Alan Greenspan's life story, in following the cult of crackpot libertarianism to the straddling of the globe of capital, exemplifies the precise fit of rancid ideology with elite command. CIA professors, TASER stocks, the IMF, debt peonage, the SPD, Chavez's claim of US detonation of the earthquake in Haiti – the Supersystem absorbs each datum like more liquid concrete poured into the hardening muck. Neoliberalism has been the dominant mode of operation of the supersystem, as the vestiges of the New Deal were ceded to Big Business in a Clintonian heartbeat, but a new era of crisis exploitation has pushed the supersystem into concerted terrorism against social betterment.

LIM 22-   A NEW FRENCH REVOLUTION?

A theory of the Supersystem must be incomplete, even hesitant. In determining any course of action in the face of such overarching power, the daunting reality of doubling-back occludes the outlook of the most determined strategist. Are the conservatives correct in some respects about the imperatives of raw power? If all that can be accomplished is mere *opinion*, are we to expect endless revision? The briefs against the predatory corporate capitalist state can be voluminous, encompassing murder, genocide, ecocide, any manner of serious crime, but there is no court, never a verdict, just feeble documentation or frivolous indictment. Serious accusations deserve serious trials, and if no resolution ever comes to incarcerate the wrongdoer, the accuser must confront the record of futility. Prisons and jails are notoriously ineffective reformatory institutions, corroding managers, guards, wardens, and civilians as they brutalize the prisoner victims. Why then should we demand the malefactors of the supersystem do hard time? Who will staff the radical prisons for the enemies of the people, and will they be nice jailers? Revenge fantasies are sweet for the dispossessed, but who wants the sour taste of actual retribution? Would it gladden your heart to see a preppie cry?

LIM 23 -   DRUGS, WRITING, AND POLITICS

People have been taking *serious* drugs for forty years by now, over a quadrillion withering, universe-leaving trips, on all manners of pharmaceuticals and natural derangers, from khat and betel to alcohol and the higher formulations, with no end in chemical sight, prompting sensational visages and hallucinations that, though errant and wholly inconsequential, have stripped the art of descriptive writing of any leftover Enlightenment potency. And that is not to mention, for the sober-sided still left out in consumerworld, the equally mood-altering techniques of the modern cinema and televisual apparatus, which have squashed what could ever be left of the pictorial genius of the lonely writer. Who could ever climb above the scrim of the HDTV, SurroundSound, psilocybin madness to see the world from the mediated, black-and-white textual confines of a writer'/thinker's linear confines? The sad fact, however, is that the market spoke: art and exegeses bowed before the allure of the almighty buck. Hedge funds and derivatives trumped MacArthur grants, fiction fellowships, and anti-Microsoft code. For all of the radical lamentation over predatory corporate capitalism, even in its undoing, its unmasking, there was not a whisper of opposition and defiance. Who was more likely to gather the cultural clout to exploit the Quitzicoatl crater left by the Bushite deepening of American exceptionalism: rightist fascists or progressive liberals? With the myths of righteous religiosity, vengeful militarism, anti-intellectualism, and social economic ordering at the antisocialists' disposal, the race was nonexistent. Where did the cellphones of the liberal "opposition" come from – cobalt from the robbed Congo, blood petroleum from where? What could be "sustainable" about the clothing, food, housing, and transportation choices of a globally supplied westerner, with no more direct connection to the sources of his consumer comfort than to the fires of Venus?

LIM 24 -   THE CURSE OF THE SECOND ALBUM

Those whom the gods have blessed with talent, they curse with talent. Writers, artists, producers, signers, actors – once they have made their splash, they get into the pool alone henceforth to recapture that performance. The burden of re-attainment becomes a master to propitiate, with the rewards minute compared to the demands of the excited ego. The fawning by acolytes surely has its serotonal uplifts, but what of the macabre prospect of accompanying criticism, and then self-doubt, all small next to the spectacle of pathetic self-assuagement? The fame, the money, the manifestations of superiority – no doubt better than the unheralded nowhere life of sorrows-drowning, but what human is built to withstand success? The texting, typing, calling, playing supra-reality of this epoch means that there art, once established, then becomes product.

LIM 25 –   DEFEAT

The Industrial Revolution gave rise to the Information Age, burying our consumer connections to the noxious fumes, plastic refinement, and cetaceous oil of past and current despoliations. Any contemplation of the supersystem must absorb the statistics of megatonnage, continental supply linkages, instantaneous crisscrosses of electrons and protons, that have engirdled our supine planet. No novel, no film could properly illustrate the construction of processes and institutions that follow in the wake of technological invention. At last we will admit defeat: we can never hope to supersede the collective genius of profit-driven humanity, along with its attendant horrors of wanton and heedless damage. Though the eyes are on the next brand of human social ownership, the mind sees the trap of trust in its beneficence. All that we do and are is at an eternal cost, and yet there never is recompense -so we are to keep shopping, keep clicking on, adjust the picture.

LIM 26 -   FAILURE WITHPUT INTERRUPTIONS

It is deemed acceptable, just, and nearly inviolate for a member of the writer or professor class to go on, ad infinitum, without challenge or interruption from any interlocutor. Similarly, in established western conversation, the speaker is deemed to have the floor, to have the command to make points without justified objection or amplification. Neither of these two related phenomena of this convention makes practical sense: to be taken seriously, the speaker should be open to illuminating intervention at any juncture. Otherwise, what is the point of speech, let alone argument? No human, and no human point, is above challenge. No argument must be heard in its totality. If a pedant, or a scholar, or a family member, finishes a line of reasoning or elucidation, and is let free to move onto the next, then the chance for a deepening discussion is lost. "Respect" would be lost if interruptive comments or vituperative interjections were made before the finish of a completed statement, but so much is lost of the capacity of our social brain in our hidebound reticence in the face of autistic droning. In an alternate evolution, written communication would be short, subject to immediate clarification, and open to revision. Intellectual life has been an existential failure because of its solitary, windbag nature, promoting withdrawn self-focus instead of the great, chastening interplay of clashing views from relative equals.

LIM 27 -   COMPETING METAPHORS

Lewis Mumford constructed the authority of the Invisible Megamachine, there is Adam Smith's Invisible Hand, and a few thousand other contenders for the throne of the dominant metaphor for our postmodern times. For any thinking human, a rich and vibrant intellectual history makes for an ideal petri dish, but the beauteous charms of television, movies, music, and crime fiction conspired with a post-sixties reeling American educational system to leave the canon tattered and non-drivable. What do the greats have to say on the matter of reinforced social power? Who is up to the task of synthesizing the classical inheritance with the Information Revolution? Which thinker can make the dominant ideologies mesh with the global social effects? Transposed against the theory of the Supersystem are the confabulations of the latter-day Transcendentalists. For this New Age, these overlords of the psychic imagination see mystical depths and irrational realms beyond the mundane social problems of the day. From seeing in nature a purity of cosmic morality, to ennobling personal healing as an ancient medical art, these latter-day Emersonians are heralding the transformation in consciousness that will take us to imminent states of bliss. Coming down from the high, the tableaux are to be ignored. Others are mired in unemployment, other families are riven by stress and incompatibility, other wars and disasters are so much faraway business. The Supersystem is a cold, hard, enduring system of systems, not a poetic trifle, nor a drug hallucination, and not a professorial reverie. We should never be cavalier about our predicament, yet we persist in utopian soliloquies.

LIM 28 -   WRITING IN A HEDGE FUND WORLD

Strafing the Internet with paragraph-long bilious distensions is one way to go through this latest phase of the Information Age, but you no doubt have a better usurpation of your time. I could correct one and all in a one-man culture assault, becoming the belaureled gadfly for a connected hyperworld, but the reward-risk ratio is tailing off to near-asymptotic zero. Compare the writing of a vanity book to the 40-year Ponzi criminal enterprise of the average criminal hedge funder, replete with intercontinental feeder funds, magnificent edifices of performing hedge fund managers, and walls of number-producing computers: who wins the prize for creative effort?   The great stupidity of the epoch is believe that liberal rhetoric will equal "change," authored by the good intentions of smart people.   There are worse stupidities, yet the death tolls and forced sufferings of the reigning hucksterism rival fascist genocide.

LIM 29 -   THE LIMITED DIMENSION

Can a new social conception of an individual's limited dimension of social utility be created? Grandiosity is facet of mental illness, a major disconnection between major ambition and minor reality.   Self-appointed gurus are always garnering acolytes, who now have a sophisticated technology network that reinforces cult obeisance, stranding them far from the ports of cynicism, despair, doubt, and disloyalty – proper varieties thereof, not depression-era theatrics, not vainglorious whimpering, not medicated lunacy. The art of deeply-considered disinterest and disfavor awaits its proper unveiling – yet the masses live that ethos, building grudges and unexplicated animosities that curdle their popular culture dishes. Standard outlets reinforce the uncritical mono-obsession with music, movies, sports, gaming, as if there is no virtue in appreciation of the futility of the consumer/ spectator/intellect.

LIM 30 -   PLEASURE OR WRITING

What could any one person encompass as the oracle above all recorded human social and individual life? What big-think from a one-brain could rock the technoworld? A Chomskyean retreat from pleasure down into vetted, gutted, properly footnoted *research* could produce a "monumental" treatise, an empyrean ascent of high and low culture synthesis that would, in the end, also receive pointed criticism. Why this angle? Why that assumption? Why alignment with that dismissible school of thought? Why no record of influence, effect, or oppression? With the entertainment business capitalized to the tune of trillions, every last popular culture is its own megaworld, capable of sustaining adult immersion forever, or in large doses: video games, poker, dog agility training, yoga, sports fandom, parenting, role-playing games, RVing, amateur classical music performance, NASCAR, local politics, remote-controlled model aviation, boating, drug-taking, extreme exercise, computer social networking, cooking and baking, stock-trading, phone-yapping. Who would want to be conversant with all such and sundry?

LIM 31-   TOO MUCH ENTERTAINMENT

In the Information/Entertainment Age (IEA), there was no logical reason for a grown healthy human to specialize in some indoor monastic pursuit. Who could be an expert in any intellectual field when there was so much in the natural, physical, interpersonal, and artistic worlds to sample? How much reading was good for an engaged 21st century mind/body unit? To any reasonable and critical observer, the human social world was impervious to rational assault, beset by insalubrious forces of control and destruction. Who would want to forfeit the enjoyment of a modern life to become hermetically sealed within some discipline?   The shelf life of the contemporary artist is for a few good years of furious devotion to craft, and then decades of worry and decline. No Athenian cults prosper to promote young acolytes; no devotees of any school or headmaster of thought commander of fiction's call. Books, theses, scientific formulae, and gnostic gospels were written throughout human history by autistic savants, ensconced in a garret, monomaniacs rather than poly-entertained modern beings.

LIM 32 – PURPOSE

Precisely because our lives mean so little in the face of the supersystem, our words supplant what should be our actions. Writing, speaking, speechifying, talking, listening, watching, lecturing, advising, displaying, driving, exercising: the verbs of *communication* of a species unable to find productive action. Our early predecessors had to hunt and forage and develop social practices to survive, but in the oblique world of non-performance, there are impassable borders around work and social interaction, forcing the linings of the brain to be over-saturated with the internal self-references of the synapses. Yet the tradition of obsequious following of our alphas keep the modern individual from creating lives that break from the worship of celebrity, authoritarianism, numerical representations of superiority, and the illusory bonds of birth family unity. No one should need an ascetic description of the modern condition, which is as obvious as the pharmacy marquee, and needs no more investigation or photo-realism or sit-com celebration, just a personal location where the digging and dismantling should start.

LIM 33 - THE SWEEP

Far better the comforts of any work with certainty: conservatism, anarchism, Marxism, liberal reformism, a history of sand, a bathroom potpourri, a compendium of sitcom dogs, paintings of dots, skateboard videos, games with scoring, celebrity tracking, back-to-the-earth how-to's. A baby's cry, a radiant sunset, a lover's phone call, money in the bank, drugs on the way, all preferable to a work of emphatic disagreement. Communication technologies suggest that there will never be a dearth of minutiae that people feel compelled to impress upon others as "remark-able," and it may be a long sail of of specious entertainments until the time the Alzheimer's sets in, give or take a few thousand family mini-crises of money/purpose. Minor philosophical afflictions like how to account for all the unearned accruals beneath our individual destinies, or who died to put us in charge, to what office do we go to settle our accounts to provide reparations to all those who have been diminished so that we might prosper, are to sit lightly upon the near entirety of the populace, foci narrow to home, hearth, grudges, payments, and debts. Who needs more obligation than that?

LIM 34 - NEEDING SOLUTIONS

Importuning miraculous "solutions" to magically hop from the pages of a single author's text to the great and grand global scope of the supersystem has been the stuff and parcel of enfranchised political thought. No matter how awful the litany of statistics that initiate the supplicant to the given subject, from Palestine to the world's oceans to the US prisons and classrooms to the bio-medical "revolution" that awaits our carpeted waiting rooms, eventually to surmount these desperate realities are the *recommendations*, the vague and celestial packaged proposals for instant, future, and encompassing "reform" - from this one mind, that sits at the furthest remove from the actual workings of destructive and commanding social power. Setting aside the problems as described, what is to be done, across the board? Sorry about the horrible deaths and perverse suffering – what can make sweet cries of contentment ring as brilliant day upon that selfsame benighted territory? Only there are no single human rulers of the supersystem, no central locus of authority, but a dispersed   and resistant elite flying onto global tarmac, commanding vast bureaucracies of devoted managers.

LIM 35 -   OPTIMISM

"Rational optimism" can cast the theory of the Supersystem as saturnine hogwash. Look at the indices: so much progress, in so short a time. Cell phones in previously unconnected villagers; longer life spans, intra-country war fading as default option. Explosive population growth, with more people fed, housed, schooled, employed than ever in human history. No skies have fallen, no apocalypse has been reached, cities have been rebuilt, the shows have gone on, mega-malls are bringing snow in the summer to Brooklyn. Look at the latest gadgets, the instant connectivity, the allure of new fields of technical expertise, the progression of the body of human knowledge, "sustainable" mini-mansions, free porn, smart green lives of the new youth. We do not need to be suicidally depressed to clearly see the debased social world that will prove the frustration of continents of hope and desire, and the rotten, corrupt, death-dealing systems of production that are the true "sustaining" forces of the social bounty. Good times will arrive, in and around the supersystem, in various packages and ephemeral delights, but the great questions will remain as intellectual backdrop to all human thought, and no amount of forced happy thought will answer for an interconnected system that reinforces the debilitating perquisites of power. No story of our time can be as great and as terrible as the assumptions of so much power by the ownership class, and no "optimism" will block out the infinite, horrific, lunatic waste of so much human promise by our supersystem.

LIM 36 –   PRECURSORS

There could be limited precursors to this work : Charles Reich's "Opposing the System." The book made not even the slightest splash in 1995 as a follow up to his widely-distributed 60's-defining "The Greening of America.." There were more reviews for that year's Pop-Tarts redesign than for that pocket apocalypse warning, which was accurate in its most fundamental respects expect for its prediction of rioting in the US streets.   There are certainly other points in that slender book demanding amplification and correction that have brought the known world from Reich's "The System" to "The Supersystem," though critiques of social reality should blend into each other if they contain generous helpings of accurate ingredients. No great inventor, nor any great musician, nor any great social critic, works apart from the great traditions of his or her forebears. To have foreseen years of social protest and higher consciousness in opposition to the machine of "The System" was, perforce, wrong and nearly a cancel of Reich's thesis, but the monolith can be perceived to be coming into view through other hawk eyes of the past. Intellectual agreement is an oxymoron- there will always be disputes over any part of any body of work. Far more important than etymology is the introduction of vitality challenge.

LIM 37 –   CRITICS

Great and small fortunes will be under expert care as the supersystem ages. The great uprisings of taxation and representation wither as the dominant modes of commerce and transaction wear down the legacies of French populist anger and American immigrant unionism.   The feudal barons of today pay good dollar for service and protection, growing more untouchable as the cataclysms of their global crony capitalism push consequence upon their lessers and reward them ever more handsomely. Critics are derided either for 1). having no solutions or 2) being negative. What "solution" could possibly emanate from a single person against a supersystem billion-adherent strong, quadrillion-dollar funded, casually and causally supported by history, politics and myth? Give any allegedly "rational" human the reins of power, actual societal-wide power, and watch the games of complicity and avoidance begin, the warpings of principle under pressure, but that scenario is never going to be entertained, because only the most insalubrious brigands have the genetic prototype to seek the center of power. More honest, forthright folk have avoided the spotlights out of genuine distaste for fraud-based action.

LIM 38 -   LOST   FOOTNOTES

Where in the theory of the Supersystem is the scholarship that incorporates all that has gone before: the battles, the Yalta conference, feminism, art, archeology, grand armies and silent diplomacy, presidential letters and Greek city-states, the sheer, documented warp and heft of recorded human civilization? Others, similarly human, have hewed to the extant record, and have the theoretical background in the Christian moralists and Anglo pedants that bespeaks serious command. However, since history is but prelude, and the finale is within sight, our directions shall turn to the portentous present, where the ghosts of antiquity cannot compete with the teleology of technology. Kings, queens, and rebels become unimportant when the bonds of the supersystem become too thick and impenetrable. How can history compare with the stasis engendered by powerful elites in strangling control? Popular culture has been a scholarly competition to the musty files housed in the ivory tower pantheon - more Gilligan's Island than Thoreau, more Mike Douglas Show than Shakespeare, more Wild Wild West than Einstein. The footnotes have been lost to the greater pleasures.

LIM 39 –   OVERLOADED   DATA-STREAM

Words are not prisons, but they can be a one rented room, bad paneling, hotpot and a stinkrug kind of a existence. The motion of a human being at rest is an equation that approaches zero, the physical world has been built by motivated exertions of laborers – though according to the specifications of engineers. The paint is peeling on the edifice, the steel rusting, the chains missing links. Set the mice free, yet they'll still look for cats. At a moment when there has never been more "democratization" of print and thought and text, disseminating the words of billions of humans instantaneously across the ether to innumerable others, mostly without filters or elite oppression, in a planetary data-stream of ideas, reactions, observations, asides, comments, suggestions, monographs, letters, explications, more mediated information than the entirety of prior humanity had ever produced for the audience of other humans, there is, tragically, not a single worthwhile placement or outcome for a single scrap of it. After all that research and development, there is not a need for the product. The culture has been bought and sold, the storefront closed up for lack of sales. So much work, too little organization, no attention to the marketplace.

LIM 40 -   SIZE

The size of the supersystem should be intimidating – each of us humans began our destiny as the zygote product of one sperm uniting with one egg through one act of sexual congress, with no more drama or meaning attaching itself to that procreation than that infinitesimal being you began as could have borne then. You were microscopically small, and through the processes of oxygen-enhanced respiration you became your adult size, and then you shall die, with the smallness of your individual atoms returning to their next journey on planet earth. There is nothing about this immensely reproducible cycle that gives any intimation of a being that can apprehend the great mysteries of human social organization, let alone change its historical and global dynamics. The smallness of man must eternally confront the vast and impenetrable verities, armed only with one brain and a solid mess of incoherent formulations.

LIM 41 - THE FIELD

Were genuine revolution to erupt in the chastened streets of America, were the modern climate refugees to join with the sans-culottes to overturn the theocratic corporate fascist state, the theory of the supersystem would be rendered nonsense. Were secular revolts to jump the oceans from the Third World to the potholes of Route 66, these pages would be ludicrous. However, if the day is to be continued to be ruled by the irredeemable confluence of pro-despotic forces, the theory will be getting its line of beverage containers. Other gloom-and-doom social theorists see looming crises but raise flags of convenience that represent the human agency that both causes catastrophe and then can be summoned to stop them. However, there are no data to suggest complex reformation of regulatory control on the global scale that is demanded by facts of social reality. There are no computer models that generate even the slightest development of a requisite apparatus of global social control of elite capitalist drive to resource-destroying growth. National self-interest abets the rich power grab to snow the populaces under avalanches of blame-the-poor, adopt-the-rich-mentality politics and laws. No guillotines will bring a working restraint upon the globe, but a complete reversal of all existing social reality, where what was up becomes down, is our only way out. Left to become right, dreams to become waking, old to become new, love and happiness to replace anxiety and sadness.

LIM 42 - CONCERNS

If politics is the art of the possible, and nothing is possible, then does art become the politics of the impossible? You can entertain that thought, if you like, with any chosen indulgence or fermented beverage, but you cannot see any future that is not beholden to the past. You cannot overcome. If thought becomes boring because of its lack of effect, can feeling take its place, solo? The thematic consistency and relentlessly similar abbreviated length of these paragraphs of the tSS will be a branding nightmare – who can stand every pop song a 3 minute verse-chorus-verse straitjacket? In defense, how varied in time are any individual's acts of sweet copulation? Once matter is put into its right form, does it need alternates?

LIM 43 - BRANDING

Social critics are fond of whipping that self-selected brand name for all to genuflect before, convinced that some great intellectual tote board in the sky is tallying who came up with what lit-advertorial catchphrase and how many times it gets dully repeated. The complexity of the modern world gets boiled down in one frantic mind to a particular term, and that grateful and greedy recipient starts flinging around the titular nugget like it needs to be a universal incantation. Plaster "the supersystem" around the street corners of the globe like Shepherd Fairey and the

Iron Sheik; invent a moronic yet adopted thought-dumbness like "the world is flat; find the over-inspiration of "Freakeconomics" or "The Mendacity of Hope" or "Eco-socialism" or "Eaarth" a "A Tale of Two Cities" and ride that pony to the profit finish line, but the hard work is in the details, the counter-arguments, the connections, and then in the real work of implementation of ideas into actual reality. In the unfortunate Google-pollution Age, the self-award of "genius" is easily refuted: someone, some digital somebody somewhere, has gotten to that oh-so-special phrase before. This is similar to the social truth that whatever innovation comes out of what remains of humanity's research and development process, there will be a successor and competitor to that product before it even hits the neon stage. Renewable energy innovation and collective genius collaboration may yet hit the vaunted global economy with the force of one-hit wonders, but far too late, far too small.

LIM 44 - POLITICAL THEORY

In all of the possible configurations of political governance, attention to the good has been lost in the intricacies of economic despoilation. What is going to make people of resolute interest find a life that can be enjoyed? Humans must chase visions of prosperity, but when their realization comes with damage to the the the lives and well-being of others, systems have failed. We continue to operate within structures that are guaranteeing the engineering failure of all human lives. What good is your lucky or stolen opulence when it stands atop frantic and arranged immiseration? Yet the way to good times and great oldies seems to be no more than a joke, an excuse for old-time drinking and new wave catatonia. The entertainment appeal of political theory is somewhere below left-handed darts and just above horizontal repose. The seemingly obligatory history beneath even "revolutionary" exegeses implies that the author spent no time above ground, but was poring over primary historical sources with the avidity of a dungeon dweller seeing the world in a passing cockroach. Points are made only after monumental tedium, every book the exercise of a mind convinced of the divine duty to offer reconstitution. While male America cavils over NFL draft outside linebacker previews and female America interrogates mac 'n cheese recipes of last decade's stars, the dirty work of political thought is left to the addled drillers, the disconnected luftmensch, the consciousness-depressing foco.

LIM 45 - THE BLOCKS

For artists in the time of the supersystem, madness and writer's block competed for first billing. What art could be so important when the human world was in such obvious dissolution? In a time of political purposelessness, art could only achieve a distant second to any statement of angered dissatisfaction. The tortuous tedium of family drama underscored the art of the era, with no greater canvas available for the questing mind. The shows, the books, the stabs at profundity and the medicated fulminations of the inward-turning thinkers and creative heroes could fool many with the aid of technology, but an entertainment of despair could never be a common culture. A clicking people have run out of engagement matter, the rhythms of a doomed nature can offer themselves as a substitute for intellectual incomprehension, but fatuous contemplation is not humanity's pinnacle.

LIM 46 - IN THE BOX

The problem with the delineation of the theory of the supersytem (tSS) is that there is no consequent response, no rejoinder, no reaction. The plot is revealed, the truth is out, the twist is resolved, the matter is laid bare – so the denouement is over. All sides are boxed in. The earth is scorched as the nihilist flag flies. God is finally dead, politics buried, education sent packing as a scam, literature revealed as minor madness, science portrayed as aseptic and power-following engineering, the Internet turned off as being unengaging chatter, green purism and ascetic simplicity given the hedonistic slap -so what is the agenda item up for business, then? There will be no shortage of bullshit and attendant foolishness that emanates from the on-going multi-institutional stagger, but that is a cheap sport, when the human mind is also capable of running a productive physical shop alongside fellow human beings.

LIM 47 - PRECURSORS

As with all art, and all thinking, there are precursors and analogues to the theory of the Supersystem, as well as echoes and and inspirations, though no robbery of other acts. The theory of the Supersystem is in competition for world-historical supremacy: other pretenders have been near the post-war mark, from the Megamachine to lesser contenders such as the Central State, the Matrix, the Washington Consensus, the neo-liberal order, or other marketing brands from around the garrets. . Whichever term emerges to define the working order of social reality, the fit has to be both tight and cover expansive territory. Other big-picture thinkers have tended to let their astonishment at the supersystem's reach excite their paintbrushes, with broad strokes then depicting the masses living in a televisual reality, fully mesmerized, insensate, manipulated down to their electrons by all-encompassing authority. Most readers realize that they hold onto their individual identities and methods of understanding their own actions, but still feel overwhelmed by unnamed forces. These thinkers have performed yeoman service, all in a good cause, but the show was canceled for a lack of ratings and sponsor fatigue after the end-of-cable run, leaving the books scattered over rank used-book swaps, the few sociology students dragged kicking into assigned readings, and small-hit blogging. Surely the fate of global social reality deserves better treatment. Fine and astute critics, usually of the kind of conscience-laden intellect that precludes tenure or high monetary ascendancy, are tending to die early.

Chapter Four
THE PROBLEMS WITH
LEFT SOCIAL CRITICISM

PR- LSC 1 -   DEAD LEFT

The Left had its cultural moment in the '68 sun, but it is now dead. The Left has no weapons, no bombs; the Left has no courts, no acolytes willing to be martyrs. The Left has no political candidates, outside of a few college town mayors, and some terribly compromised self-deigned oldsters. The Left has not a military, no pension fund, has no weapons systems, has no collaboration with Big Agribusiness. The Left has no health care system, is not in charge of any tax system, and runs no police. Yet, the Left, oh the Left, leads the world in recommendations. The Left is forever *advising* supersystemic masters on what they *should* do. What should be done better, what should be done nicely, what ten-point plan should be adopted, what people should be released, what should be overcome, what was done wrong by the wrong leaders, what should be the future –as if the Left was ever going to attend to the decisions with substantive power. The Internet has been a haven for Leftists, as has academia, but in neither place has any *movement* or *effect* arisen, at all. Talk is not just cheap: it does not even rate as communication if the other side does not bend to it. The Left can point to its ersatz minor cultural power, establishing identity politics and consumer popular art forms that serve as therapeutic salves, but that is not power. The left must be declared dead for its ideals and concepts to be rescued. If the rout is declared, visible in the global environment and the repetition of the rhetoric and the intractable global conditions, then the game can be joined anew.

PR-LSC2 -   PROBLEMS

Neoliberal leftism features strident denunciations of the supersystem, issued safely from within the great comforts handed to the boilerplatist by the selfsame supersystem.   O how the world is going to the dogs – but boy do I love my (computer) (tricked-out hybrid) (vacations in the Caribbean) (champignons avec beurre blanc) (exhaustive collection of Phish bootlegs). The paradox of this hypocrisy is not resolved by blithely stating that life is unfair – we who see the falseness of our privileges receive no divine credit for renouncing our extra wealth, nor do dying communities eat irony. The overlay of human civilization seems to be best at making the human individual anxious over each and every happenstance, from bad to good, but better would be some eruption of sense that we are, at best, extremely limited social beings. The left cannot be powerless chastisers to power, forever lobbing spitballs of moral disapproval at "The Man" for acting like the Man.

PR-LSC 3 -   NO REAL SOCIAL CHANGE

All of our intellect is oriented toward "change," yet there has not been one enduring, remarkable, solid change to the supersystem in the years after its debut on the world stage when the first atom bomb was released from its bay. There have been progresses of some sort, almost all on the identity front and personal technology fronts, but not one inroad has led to the supersystem itself. With the advent of television, American society has been looking at a social reality, constructing lives that are far more acts of *noticing, observing, condemning, wanting, sitting*, than acts of collective will. The Right has won the social supremacy through its alliance with naked institutional power, but it also can claim a hold on intellectual *realism*, as opposed the stupidly idealistic, naïve, easily deluded self-exculpation of the marginal liberal left. This is a complete inversion: left social thought must be be realistic at all times, forever attuned to history, sociology, and doubt. Cheap talk and pathetic ceremonialism venerating the dead and forever gone past should be the province of the Chamber of Commerce and the NASCAR Confederacy, not the Young Radical Giants. Social policy that feels good but contributes to the enrichment of the elites and the deforestation of the "Commons" should be abjured, not made part of the Progressive platform. The Supersystem can neither be understood nor fought with pious exhortations or generic nitpicking, but with complete reliance on rational investigations, commanding principles, and full intellectual pride.

PR-LSC 4 –   PANIC

There is, above all, a need to panic. In assessing the terrors outside our caves or jungle canopies, humans were in need of accurate, commanding leaders to disregard. Pure animal fear, of the kind that animates the squirrel and the sheep, is within us when we assess the near future, and find it forbidding, looming, ruined, about to end. You too will not like to hear that we have squandered our social capital, are mulish dilettantes, are shameful in our self-righteousness, have no fan club. The tSS is another call to despair, another open-mike depressive, another call about infirmity to a family member, another request for money from a child, another bill, another damaged piece of fairly new technology, lost car keys, bad fruit. The Supersystem will not permit us to rejoice in false verities, intentional ignorance, or cold indifference, since its forces will forever be upon us, wherever we turn. What is the brain for if not realization of others' duplicity?

PR-LSC 5 -   THE MIGHTY RIVER

The positive social changes in global society after WWII were grand, and so rapid as to make the theory of the enormity of the supersystem suspect. . However, the fall of the Soviet Union, the integration of blacks and women into civil affairs, increasing rights for LBGT, and the availability of contraception and abortion, were not the products of elite stewardship, but came from fundamental needs of individual humans to buy, to own, to find relief from economic oppression. Corporate capital pushed this version of mass happiness, finding natural adherents in formerly restricted areas and peoples, who joined the outside of the current, swelling the mighty river of economic expansion. This has sent the river into places it has never been, but it is diminishing in its power, and has destroyed many areas, and we have never shown any capacity to regulate its power.

PR- LSC 6 -   CR

The colossal Right (CR) is first, foremost, and forever the grand enemy of human aspiration. The religion-buttressed killing and and economic warfare imposed upon the people of the world has been the victory of the command of the cR, who may have virtues outside of their ideological imperatives, but are always to be resisted. However, the cR has been greatly aided in America by the folkish left (fl), a now micrometer-sized social power that infests the losing opposition side, corrupting nearly all of its gatherings. The fl is made of the following corps:

- **Noble Losers:** Free Tibet. Save the environment. Question Authority. Save the Whales. The Green Party. All the bumper-stickers of the recent past, attached to only fabulously losing causes. Never acknowledging their ineffectuality, the Noble Losers mount the podium to issue stirring clarion calls for this or that, none of which ever happens, but what do they care, at least they sleep well at night knowing they are Speaking Truth to Power. They are the self-appointed saviors of the downtrodden, secure in their precious essence of empathy, sure to arise to nice Heaven where they will finally, finally rule.

- **Big Charges, No Back-up** The declamations are serious: murder, genocide, insanity, 9/11 building demolitions, chemtrails, impeachment, ecocide, species extinction, southern ignorance. The indictments are voluminous, detailed, delivered with the most fervent of assured conviction – yet in the next moment, the BC,-NBU go for a smoke, grab a beer, check the cell, pet the dog, look up the investments, accept the encomiums. How can a prosecutor of the gravest charges known to humans compile a completely indictment-free career? America is conducting an illegal war – so let's go vote for some Democrats? George W. Bush is a murderer – did I remember to put my account number on the tax returns? You're a fascist – do you think our kids will like a play-date?

- **Conservatives Using Discredited Institutions** Even with a basic understanding of social ills, the folkish left clings to conservative institutions with the fervor of their CR brethren. American exceptionalism is common to both, whether in shop-keeper Jeffersonianism or in Austrian-school corporatism. Forever voting for losing candidates, always supplying the American higher education establishment will their own victim progeny, abhorring all the liberations of the true left in sex and music and literature, listening to nonsense from all sides, the folkish left demands "solutions" for the insoluble. They are the putative rebels, the saviors infiltrating the dominant institutions with liberal innocence, reforming these oppressive systems – only in their self-conceptions, while legitimating these defunct monstrosities, providing cover for their more rightist overlords, succumbing to innumerable imperatives to contort their liberal intentions towards deleterious outcomes.

- **Actions Belying Slogans** Self-styled "humanists," waving banners of peace and harmony and toleration, they react as curs to direct criticisms of their anti-humane personal conduct or complicities. Inheriting money washed with the blood of genocide far and wide , they draw a circle of purity around their steps. Never averse to dispensing moral guidance and command to others, the folkish left tries to ignore the justified reproach of others. Inside these dishonorable folkish left are bilious interpersonal cruds, spilling ad hominem animadversions upon any question of their product. Who are they to order the affairs of others? With such a impurity of conduct, such hollow hubris and vain smokescreens of intellectual pretensions, how they can serve as anything but as poster children for the faults of the Cause?

- **Tin-Pot Potentates** Every stance, every opinion, every view of the folkish left is deemed to have world-altering capability. The poor and suffering of the earth are awaiting, not succor, not food nor medicine, but the well-considered conclusion of the far-away viewpointist. All that reading, all that anguished reflection upon the mighty events of time and antiquity, find their flowering in the announced inclination of the fler. They are against this, for that, a follower of such-and-such but not his contemporary, most likely for another few thousand things, which will demand a lifetime's sinecure to undertake. This is all to be debated, endlessly, mostly within the solitary mind but occasionally in tedious consensus-building workshops, as the fires of the wretched burn with feeding wind.

- **Class-Down Warriors** The only class antagonists during the rise of the Supersystem were fully not of the targeted classes, but were in fact well-ensconced corporate-money aided upper class beneficiaries. Whenever the rich were derided, correctly, the second half of the sentence would include some allusion to the crumbs left to "the rest of us," a fallacy given the carpets and 401 (k)s and tenures and privilege options available to the social critic. With investments in Wall Street or progeny tuition and remodeling costs to calculate, the bold denunciator of all things corporate was left far from his declared intellectual mooring. If somehow a trust-fund rejector, the ascetic revolutionary was seen as beyond foolish for his or her refusal to grab that porferred golden ring, if ever so gently. What class war can be fought by the other side's double agents?

Declamatory leftism demands recitations of all, and at all times, of the maladies and suffering and bad signs and poetic despair and collapsing realities of the times. The throne could be gilded below the leftist, and the tears of existential solidarity barely dry, underneath these tales of woe from 401(k),brand-name sunglasses refuseniks. The few critics of the supersystem are drawn from the guilt overclass of mis-educated burghers, while the flag of the bosses is waved by Jesus-loving proletariat, now in serious economic terror. Shopping and owning are oft-rewarding pastimes, not the endless loops of dissatisfaction that anti-corporatists abjure, so the clarion calls of "protest" go round and round the ivory tower circle, not the dens of unemployed America. here have been great riches of technological plunder that the American imperium has arrogated to itself, and that prospect of "more" will drive generations to come. A good many of the leftover leftists still orating today have had dismaying associations, have been "talking left and living right," and have left the good cause open to the charges of impurity, overzealousness, injudiciousness, half-baked conspiracism, and hosts of other variations of hypocrisy. The amount of transnational corporate mining extracture that goes into the average "green" American's daily upright posture is a small mountain of self-deceit.

PR-LSC 7- TEDIOUS CATALOG

The present status of the American version of the Supersystem is not particularly noteworthy. There are innumerable ways in which the supersystem fails us, is bogged down in what will seem pathetic and laughable now only a couple of years later. Because there are so few political openings in the supersystem, culture has assumed a stranglehold over lives. All that time spent watching and playing and downloading and driving occasionally reading across the universe has produced a habituated being, but a dead social sphere. The workings of corporate capitalism in the globalization age are but dimly mapped, and no one has developed the vocabulary to even begin the measurements of its active state. What metrics could suffice to quantify the physical supports that power enjoys across the social and political institutions? What language even approximates the subtle, pervasive dimensions of ineluctable governing multidimensional capital? The assumptions of priority that invaded the brains of the worldwide elite during the Information Age are beyond appreciation – do you want to catalog the erroneous myths of superiority, philosophical advantage, unstated inheritances, overwhelming rectitude, that the investors into the expansion of worldwide capital enjoyed? Make a quick inventory – what is the current balance of the global corporate elite, from its military to its Happy Meals to its business class flights to its deregulated utilities to its endowed MBA professorships to its ad clicks to its clothing manufacturers – undso weiter   - compared to the assets of honest social democrats? 17.6 trillion, available at an instant across the globe, to a negative equity?

PR- LSC 8 -   OUR   RECENT   PAST

Imagine that all of your life and work was for naught – no worse, that all of your life and work was for *bad*. . Throw away all of the newsprint, strike the theses and the departments – it's been a slow strangle of all decency, hope, and honor in the abattoir of politics. The purchase of global resources to furnish the toylands of the American rich and the debt-ridden large dens of the uneducated American middle class was accomplished through the Phoenix program, enterprise zones, W-I-N, "lust in my heart," Contract with America, CBS Evening News, the War Room, financed and governed as if by stealth with the colossal acquiescence of hundreds of millions disparate actors. If you were ever one in the victorious crowds, jumping up and down at the winning vote totals, your man or woman now the Leader, the Reformer, the Fuhrer of the Republic, can you say what went so right for the American supersystem because of this one satrap? Or was this just one more functionary in a frivolous whole, a pathetic charade of self-aggrandizement in an unworkable whole? The lone wolf is a wanderer, not part of the pack, so there is no need to lionize (mixing the species metaphor) the crusading "progressive," the marginalized ineffective supplier of outlier credibility to the inner core.

PR- LSC 9 -   LEADERS TO FOLLOWERS

Our leaders are known lunatics and genocidal dissemblers, and our global political institutions are as dangerous as tissue against them. We know that human beings possess great weapons of self-annihilation in and about our governments and controlling corporations, from the obvious nuclear bombs to the researched bioweapons, and including our promotion of the spread of virus and bacterial slaughter from the poor or citizens of outlawed states towards us, wherever we are. Despite the constant advancements of science, and also the growth of the environmental "movement," both the political reality and the environment have gotten worse. Corporations have dominated the legal oversight of their secure theft of natural resources Destruction issues from my person, trails like noxious vapors, but I have done far better than my alternate corporate personality, and have seen far more of the bounty of the natural world than Suburban Man. The dramas of our lives lie much beyond our words, rendering poetry hypocrisy and hypocrisy something entirely beyond the plains of cognition. There is development and genocide beneath every inch of American soil or asphalt, the purchase and employment of nature and people in the service of profit and conquest. Fair enough for a run-through-the-mill through "radical environmentalism," but where do we go to get our sense of living back in the land of "property rights" and the Interstate? The fissures are too great to support politics, conversation, or homesteading in a country riven by economic inequality and despoilation. The quarter-measures by the left: its measly marginal street "protests"; its merely "speaking" truth to "power" rather than grabbing the power away; its egotistical gurus and vain devotees; its "solidarity" and sympathy and guilt and good thoughts without action; its endless "dialogue" with itself over the inanities of "process" and arcane ideological spite; its antediluvian adherence to the two dimensions of writing and speaking; its asceticism and discarding of its once vital young traditions of sex, laughter, and music; its enforced rubrics of race and class and gender; its organizational incompetence and capital avoidance; its acceptance of its assigned perpetual "weak" and "loser" status within the supersystem – that is a "movement"?

Conspiracy-mongering can be a fruitless game of speculation without a portfolio to prosecute allegations, but I do admit that I have been conditioned to be naïve and credulous, not the worst of traits. Our government/business elites have been proven to have been murderous, complicit in great and varied genocide and pillage, but who has won convictions against them? The verdicts of history do not go to the promise of eventual power, but the actual exercise thereof. JFK/911/vaccine endemic establishment paranoia may be justified, but the supersystem is not going to be slain by the expose of one or two sinister mega-productions. Instead, there has to be a massive hollowing of its accumulated privileges, wealth, and ownership. And that is going to happen how?

PR-LSC 10 - NO IMMINENT COLLAPSE

In this economic branch of the supersystem, the connections to other branches are too great for words. Given the numerical amounts of privilege, and paved driveways, do you think finance capitalism is going to let its power walk out? Whatever vocabulary you might use or encounter to describe the global economic disorder, there will be psychic resistance, yours and others, to the puerility of your words in the face of such a colossal monster. Economists may find inner validation in aligned with various sectarian arguments, using a mathematical calculus to chase some esoteric side movement inside the beast, or revisiting long-dead revanchist abortive revolutions. Here, the supersystem is all but impervious to action from below, controlled now in its economy by solidly entrenched and guarded observant myrmidons. These few oligarchic central bankers and their next level of sinister moguls are subject to a few times and tides, and their progeny may prove relatively dissolute, but only a fool would look at the flow of capital and domination and see collapse.

PR-LSC 11 - SPEED HISTORY

Ascetic liberals (ALs), such as the kind that received tenure, got degrees and went out into the corporate business diaspora, or gave interminable speeches to well-heeled sitters were fond of airy disdain for the economic order, but thought a few minor acts of charity would absolve a tidal wave of rotten privilege that accrued into their back pockets . The growing cynicism about the American political system should be matched, though, by a similar distrust of the pace and scope of economic reform. American individualistic exceptionalism (AIE) pushes workers to consider their immediate banking and pricing adjustments as the primary economic measurement of the entire economy. With unions dead and bills crushing the middle class, economics has ceased to be discussed, only bemoaned or celebrated in fearful privacy. The practice, the structure, the common understanding of economic reality has been traduced by the post-war victory culture Life took place in water for billions of years, then our ancestors escaped to land 365 million years ago. Do you think that we, as humans, so lately in the great blue, know much of how to organize the equitable distribution of wealth and natural resources? We have great skeletons for moving and evading, attacking and wandering, but our minor cranial reserves do little for the grand tasks of constructing a happy civil society – and are in the midst of a Great Meanness. Choose whatever statistic glazes your eyes – 50 million without health insurance; the millions of poor and unavenged dead in Vietnam; the accelerating profits of Goldman-Sachs. The economic branch of the supersystem is run by similarly evolved fish, no more repositories of "evil" or "sin" than any lobster. In the supersystem, we play our roles in our inhabited territories, driven by chromosomal madness and bouts of acute perceptual clarity. The leaders of this recent manifestation of the supersystem are "normal" people who are twisted into grotesque monsters of capitalistic manipulation by the contours of the economic game. Some were born to this elite status, others elevated themselves to these positions by force of will. They have applied their basic native intelligence to the common forms of business and academia that were before them, and yet they are no greater than the complaisant, dutiful boys or girls they once were, back in the days of television, dancing, sports, classes, and alcohol. The elite were not used to being questioned then, about their ill-formed philosophies least, and in pursuit of higher office they have left whatever could have become of their integrity and self-analysis. I do not doubt that these judges, lawyers, professor/consultants, CEOs, foundation officers, investment bankers, writers, creative honchos, musicians, hoteliers, and sundry other million-five plus apparatchiks are in some ways a more advanced me, but they possess no special magic, and are in many ways a thoroughly incapable, denuded people. What did they think was being accomplished as they fattened their bulging bank accounts? As the supersystem smashes its way through the neoliberal crack-up, a few of them will be looking for answers, support, intervention, assurance, but they had the best of a popular cultural upbringing in an enormously rich world, and they deserve no great sympathy. There will not be reckoning for the masters of the universe, most all of whom will grow old and senile surrounded by their ill-gotten, protected bounty.

PR-LSC 12 -   AMERICAN BARBECUES

I can relax and partake of all the glorious technology that fate has sent my way, but this is not, and never will be, a world of consequential rightness. In order to get products to our table, at this moment in an empire's time, it should be understood that violence permeates every facet of the goods distribution process and market history, and that others' dismal pain is the reason we can afford our intensely profligate First World joyride. None of this can pass the slightest moral test, but humans must choose whatever happiness they can derive from their circumstances. The chance to have fashioned even fractionally workable system, where the rich were taxed, capital reined in and jobs distributed across the spectrum from private to public, was lost, conclusively shattered, long ago, and no amount of gossamer "progress" gainsays that historical *fact*. Once established, great concentrations of wealth and material advantage will support only a slight oversight that reduces their appetites for expansion There is a structural bias in favor of agglomeration of economic power, as Big Wealth rides its malevolent way into every arena of individual life. We let this system become outrageous and the final definition of human folly, because post-60's thought was omnidirectional and subservient to Renaissance traditionalism. We, as a world headed for continually escalating disaster, must agree that good people, with good minds and salubrious intent, permitted Large Money to play without restriction, and now we have excellent TV, good high-level medicine for rich folks, and children without food, a querulous distracted populace, and enough intimations of looming disaster to dominate backyard barbecues forever. America will cling until its death to its cherished mythos of the evil criminal/virtuous common folk, despite the scoldings from "radical" social critics, tin-pot Jeremiahs, unvarnished beat poets, tattooed therapy gods, professors, grad school wunderkinder, and the lesser minions of the decrying-my-food-while-I-eat leftoriate.

PR–LSC 13 - VEAL CALVES

There is unity to the course of events in our time. Across all the institutions, the developments and corners and interstices and outlying areas, common imperatives were operating, shaping these disparate entities with oceanic might. There was no central design or planning, and the various elements of our world were affected in ways subtle, profound, and across a continuum of effects, but the financialization of all was a pure form of erosion. Corruption follows from power's domination, in innumerable ways of stealth, rhetoric, and crime. The *common* practices across all these dimensions could be plotted in a book, featuring revealing interviews and telling exposes that dovetailed every prominent edge of the American empire, from steroids in sports to lying EPA administrators to white-collar religiosity to decayed inner-city parks to CEO academic managers to nuclear arms to, and you see how this would become tedious in its obvious theatricality. Without an overt platform of fascistic fealty, and with a fraudulent campaign of "education" and "bottom line" and MBA/JD/MD/Ph.D/investor credentialing, this program of increasing numbers to sustain accumulation turned all of the institutions into conspiracies of accommodation, silence, distrust, and duty. The hollowing-out of existing, yet puerile, "checks and balances" and "regulatory agencies" and "fourth estates" and "democratic processes" and "governance" and "auditing" and "legal review" was a purely natural triumph, done with legislative and cultural piracy and subordination. The rhetoric of any putative opposition was appropriated and employed by the perpetrators in the commission of their criminal enterprises, a destruction of language as well as environment. How far away is the French Revolution to you? Does it enter your mind when you enter the grocery store? How about Lenin and the Wobblies – are they alive for you as the news breaks for its Pfizer advertisement for chronic pain self-assignation? No – you are as remote from politics as a veal calf is form the herd. Within the governing idea of profit-seeking without responsibility, every sector became controlled by invested, evading elites enjoying broad latitude and insulating myths of earned privilege.

PR-LSC 14 - NO PIES

Words have proven to be the cheapest of both recent and historical vintage. Another global war for the American empire, with the embers, landmines, and physical legacy of destruction of the southeast Asians colonial wars still active. However, unlike the great radical left of the thoroughly defeated past, I am not preaching for a better world that is unreachable. No "paradigm shifts"; no planetary alteration of consciousness; no do-overs; no penitent marches-in-the-street under the aegis of the plain-clothed authorities; no losing minority shareholder resolutions; no hoping and waiting for another Great Depression; no calling of elected officials' 1-800 numbers; no appropriation of violence; no grass-roots organizing that changes no outcome; no Statements; no World Social Forum of the marginalized; no lectures to the possessed; no academic sinecures; no performance poetry; no theocratic denunciations of the warring wicked.. To contend with global corporate power and all of its ancillary supports, every public deliberation, every convention of institutional actors, needs to be subject to the intervening presence of the force of social evaluation. Because self-generated virtue is tiresome and easily avoided, this force will generate a broad system of regulations and incentives, but precisely because the supersystem has inculcated a mythos of *anti*-regulation and *anti*- communal responsibility, the prospects for this force can only be found in the lsot mists of Port Huron, Haymarket Square, Wounded Knee. No one should be asking for incrementalism, nor are we crapping fatuous hope. The scale of corporate criminality is so vast, so endemic to the operation of global commerce, that we cannot ask for United Nations this or governmental aid that or little voluntary efforts to grab a moment's drippings off the slaughterhouse floor to press into a jar of disposable salve. This is not bongwater utopianism – the human social world must find a gargantuan authority to bring the truths of secular humanism into full-scale operation.

PR- LSC 15 -   TORTURE

Yes, stop torture! Of course, the progressives are not the correctional officers, the jailers, the police, the military, who torture for systemic sociological reasons that are endemic to human violent folly. You may not torture, but others will do it in your stead, for your benefit, in your system, under your averted eyes, because of the ineluctable horrifics of crime and punishment. "Not in our name," but to our benefit. Not in our name, but not needing our name – where does that place us then in our moral objections? In "friendly fascism," intellectuals are not surveilled or yet shot, and have not been purged, denounced, or cast aside by my traditionalist families. The drama has been kept to a minimum while power aggregates.

PR LSC 16 -   CONTEMPT

Social criticism cannot be practiced as a denigration of the witless lower class morons who have had the audacity to live as their social circumstances permit. Call out *the people* for the various ways they fall short of the Cantabridgian ideal – but there are an equal thousand ways in which the derider is him– or herself the epitome of sense-defying habituation. All culture is affectation, a gathering of particular acorns of differing sizes, dependent on place, season, supply, infatuation. If there is a single life that is both exquisite and supremely ordered, consistent in its details and breadth, subject both to passion and reflective organization, the passage of time will not register the magnificence of a life completely well-lived, rendering it pointless. There never was golden age, nor a charmed circle, nor an upper crust, nor social achievement that allows for withering contempt, of the kind that sustains us in our private rage.

PR- LSC 17 -   NO OTHER WORLD POSSIBLE

The Great Bailout Swindle of September 2008 was the confirmation of the theory of the supersystem's (tSS's) structural rot of endemic criminal elite power. The sums of money were astronomical, the lack of responsibility by the moneyed class incomprehensible, the evident necessity for reform never before as clear. The despoilers and ravagers were all over cable news and radio, blathering lies and cover-ups with the true command of military propagandists. Radicals and liberals and middle-class anti-intellectuals were united, for this once in American history, in their calls for "reforms" and "regulation," but there was no place for them to land, no way for them to raise a sail. "Another World is Possible" only if you leave the realm of reality. In this world, another world is not possible . You will never live in another world – it'll be roughly the same, absent a few details, plus a few more. Our social world is built on extremely complicated powers of human obligation and habit. If some wish to see revolution and rupture, a vivid contest of opposing theologies and principles that have taken mankind on a whiplash tour of rapid progressive change, others see the enduring verities of want, unfocused need, and churlish resentment that ever explode inside the human cranium. Superficial shaping occurs naturally as humans wobble towards new technologies, but traditional institutions persist for millennia without much rational foundation because of the immense and immovable dimension of the supersystem. Forget living in "another world" – you're not going to wake up President of the United Marijuana States, the hurting are not going to be healed tonight, money isn't going to rain out of the sky, the ones you love aren't going to cease their petty irritations, the Revolution is not going to preempt local programming. Hello, Occupiers!

PR- LSC 18 - DIFFERENCES

The virtuous, ascetic left (VAL) arrogates to itself all *caring* about the damage wrought by humans unto the world. Others may cluck sympathetically with their poetic raptures about the horrors of modern society, but only they, the VAL are in tune with the sick and sorry of the known and unknown worlds. The VAL write fine books, lead worthy conferences, are espied doing the good deeds that shame the rest, are sensitive, and can sling denuded political phrases like the best mid-range philosophes of antiquity. The true and natural world, however, does not respond to individuals, words, ruminations, potential change, or hope. All human beings think and act within the confines of their working supersystem, and the true and natural world moves in constant flux with this collective madness. Each of us humans, as short-lived protozoa, has only the most tangential, most minute, most ephemeral of effect upon the entirety of the ecosystem of Planet Earth. We can contribute mightily to destruction on our pitiful own, of course, and our regret and apologia are wholly insufficient to counter our disturbances of the natural order, yet we do and create and as a whole, as one unbroken chain of humanity, living completely disparate lives based on our particular inheritances and minor choices.

PR-LSC 19 - NO FORCE FOR LEFT TURN

A "Left," or even a "left," implies a force with enough power and command to warrant an inclination worthy of a turn signal. As if the trillions of defense wealth can be unspent. As if the trillions of corporate and financial wealth can be recovered and its mansions reverse engineered to pastures. There is not a court, not a department, not a foundation, not a police precinct, not a conference, not a supervisor or manager who is left in outcome as well as analysis. Good thoughts from good people abound, promoting sterile or discredited buzzwords like "tolerance" and "democracy," as the grooves of enforced inequality become ever deeper. Then we face the eternal vexation: what do we do now? Okay, what do we do? Is what I have done enough? Is there more, is there better, where to and for what purpose? This, the garden-variety of remorseless interrogation of a vaporous and insensate human world that leads down, way down, to Budweiser-and-Barcalounger oblivion. With food on the table, roof over a head, and gainful employment in a wealthy country, that would seem to clinch the question with a self-evident answer of unearned plenitude. However, and this is but a small point, humans are built for movement, and do not react well to diminished vistas and stationary loss. Here the supersystem promises entrapment, not the kind of technological envelopment that is consumerism's greatest feat.

PR-LSC 20 – INTERNECINE

In the reformation of the supersystem, who would be the vanguard? The American left was studded with schismatic antagonisms over allegations of doctrinal impurity or overbearing pomposity. Though functionally without power, the left attacked themselves with the battle cries of the losers determined to vanquish its former allies turned enemies. No one alive is above this charge of misplaced antipathy, in this case weighted far too heavily against would-be compatriots of the liberal left who fail to see where the pegs go to hold down the big tent. Mewling and squalling against one and all, including former versions of every self, is possible only when the consequences are few, since there are no real-world effects to opinions, not imprisonment or loss of a house.

PR-LSC 21 - PREPOSTEROUS

Pie-in-the-sky leftism lives on, in the absence of any political or legal status, from Die Linke to sustainable development to green capitalism. Without any operant power to smooth over the stylistic differences, the kind of financialized bounty that allows old-money Republicans to count their millions with beserker crypto-Christians under their low-weight tent, the "left" devolves into squabbles of leftier-than-thou-ism. On the good far left, absolutely correct fulminations about the catastrophes of the "megamachine" occasion absolutely preposterous envisionment of sudden flowering of that could be holy true and paradisiacal. Even anarchists are marked by this stupefying summoning of all that does not exist and never will exist as some global utopia, right here, right now, denying all that has not come and all that heads our way. Corporate structures have ensnared every single member of the western civilization membership drive. The libertarian goat left falls victim to having its milk curdle, inevitably, into a rancid rightist abjuration, skewering "liberals" even more vociferously than the supersystem-owning panjandrum. Justice for all; everyone has a say; universal high-quality health care; and Gummibears and love beads raining from the sky. Where is the sociology of functioning power in this folkish world? Where is the calculus of social reality? This Coca-Cola advertisement of singing harmony all across the world could not get the Vietnam War stopped until millions were dead, had nothing against Clintonian neo-liberalism, was safe in corporate back-pockets when the Bushes occupied the throne, and now has had its pretensions to a softer diversity panacea crushed by the brutal Obama con. Since there is no "change" coming from the machine, we need to take our losses and move on.

PR-LSC 22 – SUSTAINABILITY

In the kitbag of the contemporary social reformer, the word "sustainability" has become the buzzword of all, conservative to radical. Nothing is world is purely "sustainable," of course – unless death is a form of it. Conversely, if you keep your foot on someone's neck, you are "sustaining" that action, but is very likely not pleasurable for that person. For an American of to imply that his or her life can be made "sustainable," after all that has gone on below, history must be wiped of all its blood, spilled and yet to be spilled from the unfortunate occupants of resource-rich environs. The word "sustainable" should be canceled and replaced with "equitable " - not that there is ever going to be that forlorn impossibility of "equality", but at least there is some consideration in that word of injustice and real accounting, not greenwashing and a-sociology.

PR-LSC 23 -   LIBERAL   CONFUSION

Those with a liberal humanist bent are urged by their masters to "make a difference," to be "part of the solution," to work for "social change." By that standard, every liberal humanist worker in the US of the last 40 years has been an abysmal, incompetent failure, since the indices of social equity have stagnated or dropped. What do radicals have to show for themselves but the truth of their once-strong objections? Since far too much of life consists in fending off the weight of reproach, there should be greater allowance for the right of the individual to refuse to accept the doings of elite power as his or her own. Vainglorious self-ennoblement of the lowly individual is as maleficent as the depressive's inability to perform basic human functions. Do we expect the world to conform to our wishes? And conversely, do we expect our self-drawn impositions of existential misery to be a positive expiation of the world's undeserved sufferings? Should mammals be "blamed" for performing according to social norms when they are profoundly social beings? Liberals did not make the world of oil wars buttressing after-school specials; malarial deaths and inter-racial dances to Aerosmith and KC and the Sunshine band; A- papers on Marx and Hegel and Goldman-Sachs interviews; pop trivia and the Moral Majority; $1.99 cut-outs and B-52s; napalm and sex - but they became warped by that world's dimensions, enjoining them from anything but superficial niceness, directing them in countless unjust and murderous campaigns as they took turns winning elections and occupying managerial slots.

PR-LSC 24 -   THE YIPS AND THE KIDS

The would-be US social critic almost inevitably falls victim to 1. *The Yip*s and 2. *The Kids*. In the case of the Yips, younger professionals freeze when their criticisms hit the public air, and what in private may have been impassioned condemnation, or strident fact-calling, or resolute denunciation of injustice, becomes retracted pabulum. A young hearts beat fast when its owner's career looms in the imaginary cross-hairs - Who are they to cut their own throat, to invite the wrath of their masters with endless attitudinal rejectionism? At their core these are dutifully educated nice boys or nice girls, not capable of wearing outrage like a shunned coat. Why not backtrack, give outright concession to the putative opposition, let the calm waves of beatitude smooth over angry stones – such an easier walk along the beach. Though the truth can never be left entirely, the suffering of others recedes, and the Yips guarantee that there will be no assaults after the talk, no summons to the supervisor's office, no lifelong censure. As for the Kids, this is now an even possibly late-in-life parenthood that takes radicals from the spittling rage of youth to the twin poles of A). more liberal, it's-a-great-world-after-all folksiness, or B) dyspeptic attack/defend conservatism. Now that Junior or Cieran's world is Daddy or Mommy's responsibility, from the last cupcake to the smooth educational sailing into a high-paying sinecure the scions have as their right, old political analysis is replaced by focused association with traditions. Alone, the young radical can take on all manner of overseer; with-child, then it becomes a wider world where even bankers can become sugar daddies down the road, who knows?

PR-LSC 25 -   ART'S AFTER-LIFE

Artists and writers must persist even when the competition is on a roll and besting the unpublished self, the published scrap-heap denizen, the backwater prophet, or the unregenerate psychic layabout. In his 1988 slim classic *What's Left: Radical Politics and the Radical Psyche*, Michael Neumann dissects his people, the Marxists and 60's left, deftly flaying the enduring social theory and causing great qualification to the word "radical." Power-pop bands of consummate musicianship sell in the low hundreds. Documentary film makers produce marginal epics that see the back of the line only. Did the intellectual excitement of the creative delirium fade for these progenitors? Has the relentless cascade of the Information Age left them dismissive of their youthful eruptions of hyper-associative exegeses? All authors want the most for their paragraphs, the very best, and for all their sentences to live in a delirium of appreciation, bringing the shining light of the self-understood cosmos to dark and sad abodes. However, the after-life of art, whether a "masterpiece" or completely failed, is an alternate universe, airless and without much point, unrealizable beforehand and bound to be monstrous in the incessant din of the artist's mind.

PR-LSC 26 -   THE BULLSHITARIIANS

As long as we have breath we rage against those we consider our lessers, invigorate ourselves with delusions of superior intelligence or superior aggressiveness, to   neglect the brushes of the very beast that threatens our existence. Nature has placed us as the victims of our own capacity for excess power, to be devoured by the creature that our own creative instincts fed. Who wants to traffic in such horrid irony? Instead, we have the odious political landscape of malevolent conservative fascists merging with the obtuse corporate liberals, drawing in the professional Bullshititarians, who are characterized by 1). autistic intellectual unresponsiveness 2) complete lack of societal consequence, and 3) chronic inability to confront self-futility. They, the front row Bullshititarians, include   the lectern-mumblers of the eliminated US left, side-instructing the remnants of the scourge-ascetics, the greenwashers, the sacredists, the Cammers (complementary and alternative medicine), the bookish family commanders, and the remaining shunted-aside intellects of the good folkish reform.

PR-LSC 27 -   DAYS OF FUTILE RAGE

Since the days of rage in the 60s, anti-supersystem protest has been widespread, yet spread thin, and   based on epic weakness. How to challenge an entirety? How to make statements that do not result in death or long imprisonment yet display force? Across the decades, gatherings across the globe have expressed views against the supersystem not as a whole, but in discrete and often single areas, followed by a nice beverage. Nuclear power brought out the fury of the German middle class, but not the toxic waste they shipped out by world record amounts. War and globalization have seen their battles from civilians, but the results are one-sided in favor of the authorities that guard and govern the spoils. The possessors of truth and honor and moral righteousness make the police act with restraint as they flex-

tied by the hundred-thousands, but the supersystem has yet to be diverted from its conquering demarche.

PR-LSC 28 - LEFTIER THAN THOU

In the game of leftier than thou, which was all that was available to thinkers, each *position* was advanced without reference to its effects, since there were to be none. No putative leftist could offer a defense of his or her associations, since there was no way to live and breathe that was not conditional upon the largesse of the supersystem.. Anti-empire critics were tenured professors at corporate academic universities. Civil rights pioneers were tax-favored bureaucrats of racial corporate evangelism. Tree-sitters, money-eschewing community activists, international solidarity penitents, blogging seethers, foundation functionaries, conspiracy cargo cultists, were enveloped in every space by the supersystem. The count was not in consciousness raised, or in identity politics established to continue the non-meritocracy in a new direction, nor in single issues, but on the ground, in the dirt, on the hillsides, in the graves. How could there be a number on the board for the great DLC hoax of Bill Clinton? Down 2? What would the loss be represented by his ideological heir of corporate deceptivism , B. Obama? There was no social need to be satisfied by any left program, since all the layers of society could trade in anger for the corporate right's directed passions. The left didn't even have lemonade stand in the post-war economy, not a dime coming in. Liberals were no leftists, and there was no category of radical achievement beyond that.

PR-LSC 29 - THE TRAJECTORY

"Speakers" for the poor, the disenfranchised, the marginalized, the oppressed, the violated, the polluted, the forgotten, or the unknown may hit the big time and become administrators of the system. They acquire an office, a budget, start to hire, become directors, move up in the hierarchy, attempt to place their principles into the maw of the supsersystem, and the deceptions start as soon as the diplom ais on the wall. In way over their heads, these "reformers" are easy game for the bureaucracy of elite power. Down go the gates once opened for "the people," as exits for the conscience become sealed, though the rhetoric of righteousness must continue. These politicians, or academicians, or movement "leaders," recapitulate the corrosion of good intentions that meets the cold steel of existing power . Yes, they now have hard-earned "wisdom" about how the real world works, but no one listens to these stories of contextual resilience, so they tell lies that gladden their acolytes with thoroughly discarded versions of courage. Whoever has staked out a public image as liberal at any level, from parent to Bill Clinton to Van Jones to this year's model, rapdily becomes this deceptive performer. This syndrome of incipient bending will afflict anyone within the purview of the corrupt supersystem, which has many subtle yet profound ways to push away the large focus.

PR-LSC 30 - THE DEATH OF UNION HALLS

The great corporate takeover has been noticed many times in print, and even some who have testified to its totalitarian scope. Yet there has been scant appreciation of its resistance to amelioration. Tenured critics have tended toward blunt appraisal and then delirious praisesong of countervailing forces and gathering insurrectionary *developments*, yet the Supersystem has ground into the tarmac "corporate social responsibility," "parecon," "Nowtopia," "permaculture," "institutional shareholder activism," "socialism," "stewardship," and a thousand others deserving of tedious listing for the fascinating deaths they have all received. The sound of "democracy" in America is lost to the decrepit 1930s union halls of the immigrant Midwest, now empty, birdshit-floored unheated wrecks. Once there was debate that led to action amongst workers, many of whom were destined for early, employment-derived choking and wasting deaths, others genetically able to transmute hard labor into a paid-for house, presents for the grand-kids, a sense of contribution to the upward trajectory of humanity. Now work is a sequence of Taylorist engineered structures that are running on the fumes of tanks from bygone eras. Doing the same thing over and over should be reserved for antiquity's beasts of burden, but the modern functionary either has the yoke firmly in place or wishes he or she could only find a yoke that could bring the comfort of the master's obligation for feed and care.

PR-LSC 31 -   THE DECLINE OF THE CRITIC

Critics of an established order become known for their own foibles and theoretical holes, as the envious strain of human emotion crowds into audience appreciation for skill. Marx is quoted splendidly to this centuries-later day, but the dictatorship of the proletariat has not worked out too well as market share. Minor political or cultural power has deformed many a lion of the expansive treatise, of the male variety. A pre-fame litany of out-crowd brilliance can be undone in a late-stage informer, war-apologist, sexual trespasser, or bilious prevaricator descent. Often the lines are not fully toed, and the once-mighty revolutionary becomes just another authoritarian drudge, a conservative libertarian, or, even worse, a Speech-giver.

PR-LSC 32 -   CLIMATE CHANGE AND NEWS

Severe global climate change is coming soon and hard, no matter what we do in the dimming interim. You may be at a loss as to *what to do*, and guilt trips and retreats into apocalyptarian anxiety and guru instructions towards your martyrdom may proliferate, but you need a better sense of the system than anger at its typical players. The minutiae of who is up to what in the supersystem's current global ballgame can preoccupy engaged satraps (whither Russia? Who of the Chinese remnimbi? Who holds today's cards in the Gaza Strip? What will become of Wall Street? Who calls the Silicon Valley shots?), but without a dedicated line for such esoteric knowledge, the swirl of electrons is unreachable. Each news item from the non-corporate mainstream source can be coded and assigned numerical value: A. Bad News Signifying Looming Catastrophe (BNSLC) Score B. Record of The New Idiots Ascending to Prominence (NIAP) Score C. Fatuous Out of Power Suggestions to Redirect Marauding Power (FOPSRMP) Score and D. Clubhouse Pep Talks (CPT) Score.

PR-LSC 33 –   PROSPECTS

How was any of this going to get better? Through *meetings*? How much of the American Dream has been wasted sitting around, either of the suited or student or family type? For all of its vaunted humanism, the left progressive sub-stratum democracy-in-action featured petty feuds, barely concealed contempt-hurling, specious grievance-airing, mendacious pettifoggery, and gifted ideologues. The corporate daemon, by contrast, could produce a dynamism of active greed pursuit along with its interminable sit-arounds, moving mountains while the opposition moved fetid air. Following the next dollar bill was an easy trance to put under the populace, have them talking about the fractious details of accumulation rather than the real political questions: Why pursue war? What makes people poor? What kind of work will make a life worthwhile? What are families for? Can I grow old without becoming broken? What is the value of knowledge? Who gives a damn what you think? "Intellectuals," or "rebels," or "malcontents" in this supersystem became susceptible to the easy hell of drugs, or quiet late-night nursed rage foundation, or unacknowledged desperation – no more than a margin of inchoate dyspepsia in the entertainment penumbra.

PR-LSC 34 -   KEEPING SCORE

Is each development or new item a win for the aggrandized forces of the supersystem or the opposed   forces of moral justice? Do not count *potential* indications, minor suggestive leanings, silver linings, marginal yet sorry bills, and the baited like. What is the score, as you see it, not only for today, but for the recent past, which will have so much to do with our near future? Did the cries and tears of others obtrude into your life, or did you sail on your leased ships of ambition and techno uplift? As the observed losses mount, you should consider that 1. You cannot isolate one problem from all the others. 2. You cannot offer criticism that is not based on a comprehensive philosophy. You may scorn this or that, offer judgment on any cultural artifact, proffer an opinion, issue a fatwa, upend convention, build an ark, or simply stand dumb in uncomprehending place, but   all thoughts revolve around basic suppositions. How do you want this social world of collective human enterprise to work, give or take a few levels of complexity? Who will reap the benefit of each and every profit, to what degree, and to what set of overlaid regulation? What of our ambitions- how far should they extend to our concerns? Without a title to social phenomena, we speculate about its ownership, reducing complex provenance and inchoate events to absurdly reductive *influences*, and thereby never find connections to the beating, acting, moving loci of power. We cannot ever see wide enough, nor affix real stamp of governorship. With no real targets and no territories uncolonized in part, the rhetoric of a "democratic uprising" is fatuous and immovable, able to self-captivate the professional few.

PR-LSC 35 -   ASCETICS VS. THE RABBLE

The New Ascetics have preached a virtuous return to the innocence of a prelapsarian age of comity, amity, and fawning deference. The New Ascetics sold many books, occupied many professorships, gave quite a few autistic speeches, and headed the liberal ship to be dashed on the shoals of cultural irrelevance. That trying-to-be-hip-professor; that aged poet maudit; the artiste manqué with the spiritual bent; the New Age mother; the computer programmers from Opus Dei; green "lifestyle" magazines; schoolteachers, professors, CEOs and loan officers; a continent of anti-cultural self-ennoblers. For them, the rapture of a self-assigned morality compensates for the wickedness of the easily-manipulated hoi polloi and its evil overlords. Nature, or an entity called "god," or Literature, "Democracy," or the pursuit of numerical financial "growth," or some other singular righteous transcendence, becomes the monotheism of the New Ascetics. They bathe the past in glory, valorizing their alive triumphs: Montgomery, the Mobe, Summerhill, Stonewall, book readings by tenured savants, "effecting social change," - a pro forma litany of lost causes that is minute compared to the cultural command of the illiterate opposites.

PR-LSC 36 -   THE LOSSES

The Left won nothing from 1968 onwards. Not a candidate, not a cause, not a movement, not a victory. And yet the Left was writing and talking and speaking and writing as if every day was crystal clear purity and green fields of clover over the rainbow, if only, and when only... From Israel to Katrina to the Bushes to Reagan to global arms sales to the BP Gulf to cars to plastic to corporate media to neoliberal IMF to Bilderberg/Tiralteral to unemployment - who won the political wars? Not the "Better World" Left, with its notion of incipient justice and anti-miltiarism "Support the Troops" and family values parenting and command-the-lectern pontificating and workplace climbing – that was far from a Left, and not even close to "the" Left. Hearts might have been in the right place, some cynicism might have crept into the bank account, but righteous moral uplift always won out – and gave us Clinton and Obama, corporate CEOs talking "sustainability" and Wall Street Democrats "progressive" in their child-rearing and sexual permissions, just not in their corporate criminality. So to the land of obesity, cognitive impairment, and virtual violence the world went, trailing bank account numbers and the naked results of dishonesty.

PR-LSC 37 –   ANTI-THESIS

The anti-thesis to the tSS states that the revolution is happening, right here, right now, in the local, personal, de-commodified spaces that have grown in urban and rural locales throughout the known world. This is over-estimation – human lives can indeed stand against the overwhelming tide, but the tide is, was, and shall be the force. Are we to see incipient collapse in the regular crises, or is there a damaged but intact superstructure with a long lease? This over-large issue may be one of orientation, a neural tendency which divides the pessimists from the habitual fantasists of left inevitability, but few humans enjoy the psychic taste of realistic despair.   Where do we go to rescue the damage that should not have been allowed to occur? Who can repair time?

PR-LSC 38 -   PERSPECTIVE

For minor alterations of the existing supersystem, see every other American spouting an opinion to a co-worker to close cell-phone friend. On the subject of "politicians," make sure to point out their greed, a stunning revelation of corruption that never seems to trouble the speaker on Tax Day. What are they thinking – how could they be so dumb – can you imagine the nerve – a daily recitation of the same theme, how the others with power are not you, the sainted, unappreciated figure of untrammeled moral purity, a self-absolvist unwilling to apply that same rigorous theocratic condemnation to the rampant cheating and doltish disconnection from human sympathy in their own lives. Never can they see themselves as subject to the same distortions of pressure if they had applied themselves more vigorously in the political realm.

PR-LSC 39 -   CTS

Conspiracy-theory Speculation (CTS) has been the bane of the left. Out of power, the left sees nefarious ber-plots from those in power, ones that reach heights and complexities that are viewed only dimly, from below, but with great confidence. In great logical fashion, those in power do collude and conspire and *cover-up* and bomb and imprison and fix and corruptly govern, but those without prosecutor power apprehend these vast to minutely personal rings of deceit from far outside. History has not been kind to official pronouncements of democratic virtue, but in the day-today present, those not on the calling lists of the punjabs and majordomos are mineral speculators. We may have no reason to *trust* the actions, intents, or apologies of the corporate/financial/governmental elite, but those on the receiving end of their operations cannot assume to see through to the encrypted cables and unstated commands of these thousands of labyrinthine cooperators. History will cover over nearly all the extensive felonies of murder, robbery, fraud, and terrorism from the great political/corproate governing conspiracies of the late bureaucratic era, each evaded crime papering over the last generation's commissions. Without a statutory authority to investigate boardroom crimes, the lower orders are left to shake their fists as they choke in coal dust and plastic-induced palsy.

PR-LSC 40 -   CEDING GROUND

The supersystem's totalitarian ownership extended high into realms of police and incarceration, obviating the direction of leftist resistance to elite control through violent protest and attack. Quite rightly seeing the draconian punishment and relentless infiltration visited upon even splinter groups, anti-corporatists and anti-militarists ceded the ground of violence and torture and decimation to state forces. From Iraq to the 50 state gulags to the regions of resource extraction, the American empire used its technological and economic means to remove the means of sustenance for true unfortunates, and there was not a firecracker that could be lit in response that would not activate a sensor, mechanical or human, in the police underworld. Other means of escape towards some, even minor, forms of protest grew in the farthest left hinterlands: skepticism, double lives, interpersonal intransigence, frantic reading, anonymous blogging, corrosive doubt, loneliness, aimless cognitive dissonance, outright confusion. With each thwart of leftist "hope," that ceaseless valorization of every fillip of remote popular uprise as constituting the dawn of "revolution," the true believers faded into integration with the powers-that-were.

PR-LSC 41 -   PROTEST

Protest within the supersystem is as threatening in its forlorn placard-holding might as the status of smaller placard-holding begging by the homeless. To the commuting, purpose-driven hoi polloi, those are not with the program are lunatics, willing to don sackcloth and ashes for disruption of the agreed-upon mythos. Direct-action might stop some traffic, bring the grinning rent-a-cops who get to pad some overtime to try out those new and shiny and expensive technology toys. Street theater that might prove that Bohemia has yet still a post-60's market share preempt more sober, non-drug programming. The rag-tag opposition is "permitted" to assemble on a designated lawn within corporate control to listen to amplified autologic speakers, the easier to be surveilled and cataloged. Each tried-and-true micrometer Left form could create some wave of "dramatic" resistance, or it could serve as further confirmation of how pitiful "resistance" has become when the levers, the doors, the guards, the courts, the papers, the parks and the communications infrastructure is owned and monitored and activated and strengthened by the command of the elite. On-line and through crowd-sourcing and by various social network means, an alternative of "protest" can spring anew, to sweep the land with great affiliations of pro-social technological innovation – or the other side can hijack these same means to provide a superior form for elite co-optation and infiltration.. The future does not portend much in the way of rebellion - not in the land of networked cameras and "terrorist" eco-defenders doing 25 and elected born-again prosecutor vipers. The Occupy movement has come along to galvanize the lost and new lost tribes, but without an entry into the political system, the process and non-violence and non-demand has led to

PR-LSC 42 -   CARING

The elemental matter of "caring" is predominant in the upper reaches of the supersystem. Being alive within it necessitates a concern with self-advancement and the acquisition of money, but such a crass preoccupation demands a comforting fallback position of of "caring": parents care about children, siblings care about each other, the rich care about the poor, the healthy care about the sick, the profligate care about the wretched, the thrill-seeking care about the bored, the sane care about the depressed or insane, the bombardiers care about their victims, the First World cares about the Third World in history and the present. This "caring," however, comes in great varieties of thickness, and is confined to a general quarter-measure of caring "about" rather than caring "for." How can a privileged individual display a requisite level of "caring" for those on the left-behind station of life? Write an annual check to CARE, adopt a foreign child, vote Democratic, teach, volunteer at protected events, do some pro bono, buy green, raise Jesus children, listen with passable acting skills over the receiver to decomposing others? The woman getting your your Mickey D's dollar fries may have two kids that need to be fed at the food pantry tonight, and this may trouble you some, but, hey, what are you gonna do? Live everybody's pain for them? Jesus, if I could help, I would, but everybody's got problems, what the hell are you gonna do? Basic connections between social policy and human suffering are too large to absorb, so folks become selective in their concerns, if they care to exercise that non-financial emotion. The horrific discontinuities and marauding acquisitions of the supersystem are protected by this progressive balm of "best intentions" belying bad outcomes. The large rung below these staffers of the elite colossus are the beneficiaries of the murderous and toxic institutional practices, the middle class who do not trouble themselves about their direct involvements, since they can validly claim next to none. Those who claimed to "care about" deserve no special dispensation compared to those who "cared less about," since the grand effect of all the tributaries of causes is a fraudulent wreck of a society. An understanding of the fundamental inequity of the supersystem should be a pillar of a moral intellect, but there is no schematic for how how to look at your own life in relation to the misfortune of those below you. You'll never sort it out, nor can you get it out of your mind.

PR-LSC 43 -   THE RESISTOR

If raised inside the supersystem, subject to its massed imperatives yet cognizant of its operational vacuity, a buffeted resistor can become, at most, an observer. This mode of being entails participating in most all of the contemporary customs and rituals, but with judgment held in reserve, a compelling internal disquietude, and about a five-second delay in social situations. Quite usually perplexed as to *what is supposed to be going on*, this upright quizzical ape is fated to be without the focused direct energy of the supersystem's more loyal adherents. There can be a great deal of mostly inherited social and economic support below this out-of-phase seeker, but there will never be a suspension of that skeptic's disbelief that social reality is undergoing renovation. Under control because of the supersystem's command of threat/reward, the neither enrollee, nor registered objector will be less than a rebel, more than a guard. Life will disappear beneath his or her feet, native intelligence meeting self-understanding to guide the performance of the available social roles of profound uselessness. Good intentions will fade into unproductive decompensations, but this is a social system at work, in all of its magnificent command of every corner of reality.

PR-LSC 44 -   PROTESTS AGAINST PROTESTS

Against the supersystem, the micrometer left (ml) has written books, essays, pamphlets, essays, blogs, posts, and analysis. Often devastating in their critiques, sometimes lucid in their theory, and once or twice compelling in their sociology, invariably at the end there is the call to left arms: utopia is but a step of reform and commitment away! To the barricades, comrades – victory of the People is nigh if We but get right on it, fortwith! The plaintive call for this or that reformation of one or more of the major arms of the supersystem goes unheeded, destined for the textual scrap-bin, instantly shredded by a corporate-legal-political connection, or a furtive friendship agreement between planning board lawyer and corporate assistant vice president, or any unrelated machination of the amorphous big-cheese entity. The awful varieties of human cruelty have ruled the course of humanity, determining the sky as well as the night, mutating "I Have a Dream" into a 2010 "I Have a Dream that after a $20 Trillion Dollar Bailout of the Stupid Rich, 90% of African-American children will be on food stamps at some point in their childhood." What gift of prophesy our doomed Gandhi had! The protest "movement" has a staggering line of decline from actual effect in the civil rights/Vietnam era to the anti-apartheid protests at my college targeting faraway racism while allowing its homegrown version complete reign, to the anti-war marches that gave such a fine send-off to the Bush bombing invasions. When do noble sentiments never heeded transmute into condemnations of the self for continuing to see possibilities for placard-based reform?

PR-LSC 45 -   CONTEMPORARY FASCISM

The impoverishment of political science discourse leaves social critics employing terms that are outdated, inappropriate, or insufficient to describe new reality. "Fascism" was a specific kind of political rule employed by Mussolini and then adapted and expanded by Hitler, wherein political murder was a daily practice and on a mass scale: trade unionists shot, communists shot, students shot, a campaign of crime and murder and robbery that used these lawless means on a grand scale to acquire political power. The KKK and the CIA were American variants of this kind of poltical killing to effect rightist control, but the supersystem of today does not need domestic murder to achieve its ends. American political opposition is not shot dead in the streets, nor sent to the gulag for its speech. Instead of mass murder and intentional genocide, the overt means of control are through supersystemic devaluation of the concepts and practices of social and economic justice. The neoliberal elite are in too great and too wide of a control – the opposition becomes a tiny band of cranks and loony freaks, though it may have broad popular support. The technocrat in his suit and tie inhabits the definition of serious rectitude as he ratifies policies of utter insanity, while the ranting goober is mocked and left by the wayside for noticing some form of disconnect.

PR-LSC 46 - MORAL GREENS

The liberal social critic issues fatwas against himself. Under the ownership of the supersystem, even "opposition" within social reality is dependent upon the very institutions it derides. Down with corporate rule! says the sign, Up with corporate rule! say the clothes, the job, the 401(k), the sneakers, the music, the movies, the beer: Talking Green, Living Brownish. The electricity, the tanked-in oil, the taxes for the security police, the investments for the endowments, the board of directors for every still-solvent company – where do they come from but from the inner sanctum of the putative enemy? The thoughts may be resolute, the vision of a better world detailed and inviting, but the castigations of the fallen world seem to always land so close to the near ground of the inveigher. "Movements" that award themselves medals for the slightest "good work" while the planet burns and produces huge increases in CO_2 emissions have all the moral integrity of the US military.

PR-LSC 47 - TOMORROW'S REBELLION

Any day now, we are going to take to the streets. The tarmac is going to shake from the thunder of our righteousness. Cosmic injustices are going to be righted from the force of our suddenly communal articulated grievances. Feats of surreptitious organization are going to bedevil the authorities in a rolling cascade of non-violent street direct action. The poor are going to be willing muscle and ready reinforcements, supporting the vanguard coordinating the barricades. No one is going to watch TV or game or chat the whole revolutionary night, as the second coming of the Days of Rage finally materializes. After all this prelude and false starting and ineffectuality, that prayed-for outcome will have descended from the Jesus heavens – the will o' the people, in an unstoppable wave! Then, upon waking, we will see that the streets are swept clean by rent-a-cops, the proceedings monitored and frustrated ahead of time, during the time, and afterward, in excessively-funded legal-police sync. There will be no resurrection. Democratic insurrections are creatures of simpler history and pre-technologic societies, plus a few European blasts from the past – some left-over sound and fury of no comparative strength to the supersystem.

PR-LSC 48 - NICENESS AND REWARD

Against all the insane inanities of religion, against the fervid naivete of the liberal reformers, against inward depression and reactionary suicidalism from ill-equipped doubters, the individual reveler should look after the fortunes of him or her-self while investing adequate effort in understanding the fortunes of the outside world. With all recent trends oriented towards exacerbation of all profound inequalities, sustained by all institutions, the band better start playing some dancing music. Although the supersystem rewards those who "play nice" who were well-situated to begin with, there is not much morality in being inoffensive, "tolerant," not very ambitious, unable to look to long at big pictures, unconfrontational towards those below and the few above in the social hierarchy, easy to led to socially acceptable pursuits, marginally competent at specious but well-rewarded tasks, frightened of scandal and drug excess and penury. The world came to these labeled as "nice," "educated," and "smart," though of course these were outlooks and courses of action permitted by the particular circumstances of global disequality, and the possessors of those qualities could have proved to be the opposite had those latent antitheses been brought out by more parlous or threatened times. Avoidance is a mark of wisdom in the natural world, as prey avoid predators by quivering anticipation, but that does not make the prey heir to magnificent prizes in the way that nice, well-intentioned American life-lottery winners came to epic splendor.

PR-LSC 49 -   THE CONSOLATIONS

The weight of the supersystem lies behind anti-reform, rewarding mountebanks when they mount the feeblest of counter-reformations- and the good liberal secretariat is left, always, wondering why its nuanced, in-depth, voluminously researched initiatives get the cold shoulder. The liberal-left has its outlets, in a few web corners and TV outlets and a few graybeard professors and their more connected younger juniors, but the game is absurdly tilted towards the conspiracy of marinated dullards. . A few tweaks of the knobs of the messaging apparatus, and Middle America is having conniptions about some benign or conducive step by a liberal target. In a rigged game, the designated victim side may continue to participate, but only with spoken contempt and outright hostility, not with naïve faith in the justice of the referee or pathetic fealty to hope and civility. The private compensation of rectitude in the micro-left has no translation into food for the poor, nor homes for the foreclosed, nor health for the poisoned, nor return for the extinct. The social needs of humans outweigh the real consolations of intellectual fortitude, but ideals can only be refracted in the human form, never duplicated, so disappointment lives in utopia.

PR-LSC 50 -   THE PRETENDERS

Claims will be made upon the world scene: here comes the new revolutionary, here is the real street protest that will threaten the edifice of corporate power, here is the indigenous leader to conquer the mighty West. Each post-WWII generation has its pantheon of the Opposition, from Arbenz and Allende and Mossadegh and Guevara to the intellectuals to the Oaxacan take-over to the latest dumpster diver. Hairstyles and books, big rhetoric and undeniable condemnations of Western perfidy, then either complicity, or worse, once set in the unforgiving glare of actual power. What was that plan for "democratic governance" again? Where is all that extractive profit-making going again? Show projects and side reform aside, what happens to the structure of power once you have entered that worldly abode of true influence? Old age is too much of a series of fattened bank accounts to be the only stage where accounts with reality are reconciled. Social reality needs its true accounting as it occurs, not decades later in specious memoirs from academic sinecures.

PR-LSC 51 –   TACTICS

Adopting the tactics of the enemy is not going to reverse the course of the Supersystem. No advertising binge is going to re-frame next year's political dilemmas to capture the viewing attention of the insensate and the lonely. Brainstorming and re-branding and going door to door and penning jeremiads may contain the seeds of true and lasting revolution, but in the present conditions of the field, growth will be accidental, at best. Nothing will ever be as it never was. Local eruptions of plant growth will undoubtedly occur, as some protests and rebellions and takeovers begin the next phase of organized minor resistance to the neoliberal order, but the dead do not rise – unions, mass education, government works programs, progressive taxation are several decades moribund, at best. Only the unforeseen holds promise, and there has been only the usual scene in the last period.

PR-LSC 52 -   BURNERS-ON-HIGH

The anti-systemic rage of the oppositonists can have a fatal admixture of mental illness. Burners-on-high fictionists patrol the subterreans of their consciousness to great acclaim and once family-supporting sinecures, then hang on by rehabbing serially or become Likudnik Republicans. Anarchists intake copious drugs, straight-edgers overdose on Jesus, home Dads play with toys and misbehaving brats to strike repeated blows against the patriarchy while living off the partner's corporate checks. Where are the pure, rational, resigned yet intact left life models? They will be needed in the future: as humanity crashes its overloaded cart of civilization around a carbon-drenched, flooding, parched, 3 degrees C and above lunar landscape littered with bodies of climate refugees and climate-extinct species and rusting snowmobiles, the quest will remain to find some quiet way of understanding human folly. The past greatly influences the future, so without established avenues of rational command of social processes, we cannot talk about de-carbonization and de-growth with anything less than laughter.

PR-LSC 53 -   SCHOOLING

At the "elite" level, where the hundreds of billions of empire's booty landed with the most authority, the mix of inward ambition and noblesse non-oblige led to verdant Ivy swards populated by versions of the clinically not-well. Instead of paranoid schizophrenics batting away imaginary saucer beams at McLean's rec rooms, colleges and universities contained lecturers focusing on the theatrical holiness of the curdled greats. Here's how the world worked, said the nation's most hallowed halls of Enlightenment wisdom, and then served up unassailed, enclosed trite canonical re-heatings in its grand courses. No theory or day or faculty meeting or paper or conference was particularly vicious or consequential, and identity politics and computer networks received their due strengthening through approved endowment distributions, but all of the reigning institutions produce passable plays and happy lunches, minus the bombast and moral overreach. The greens got cut, the teams played their games, the degrees were conferred and the patients returned to society, the twin engines of medicine and law fired in sync, but only in the corporate conspiratorium was the new world constructed. Schooling was a beside-the-point warren for intensely hormonal rabbits, given its command by the assumption of tradition and natural fear.

PR-LSC 54 -   REBELS

If you see the odious supersystem and begin to "monkeywrench" your way through without a prison record, when will that new system begins its appearance? Are you going to go the way of the "alternative" folk, driving and tattooing your own individuality to a crowd-sourced corporate similarity that provides drug buddies, secret corporate rebel clubs, fun twenties, and a trail of petroleum tears? Lost in the tangle of geo-politics, where nations fight for resource supremacy through the machinations of shadow corporate cabals, none of us are going to be able to live in a world that reflects our intensified desires. The lists of socio-political nonsense that our forebears lived under and through dwarf our own more refined dilemmas and information-aided discrepant insanity, but that realization of relative cultural betterment has been every generation's inheritance, and does nothing about the on-going failure to get the program in gear.

PR-LSC 55 -   THE fL and COUNTER_ACTIONS

The folkish liberal has a professional investment in seeing green progressivism as being in the near ascendancy and imminent triumph. Disdaining "despair" and placing halos of light around every gaseous emanation coming from the high priests of hope-bama, , the folkish liberal discounts prior history and current capitalist hegemony to see great awakening, paradigm shifting, consciousness raising, redemption, salvation, a new dawn for a New Age, love and spiritual renewal, creation in a child's laughter and a lamb's frolic, human empowerment in indigenous resistance, the realization of thwarted human potential, a return to Nature and its motherly commands to cooperate and gather at the feet of the masters. This line has been peddled stateside for a half-century without a single territorial acquisition. Professionals in the uplift business cannot countenance the rejection of their self-assigned purity, preferring the comforts of fantasy to the pain of social reality. Without the necessary knowledge of human perseverance in deleterious but immediately compelling social practices of working dumb jobs and having no social voice, refuge for the fL is always found in the promise in intensely minor initiatives. Whatever good was in the protests of yore cannot be located in the abandoned stateside sites of today's counter-actions, as the police and surveillance teams chalk up another successful intervention.

PR-LSC 56 -   DRONES

The gasbag, droneous, without-surcease auto-fired leftish mono-maniac was born by the Beats, flowered during the 60's, got an academic job and a line of bullshit during the 70s, made a killing on the stock market in the 80s, turned ascetic and bitter in the 90s, issued jeremiads and ten-point plans in the 00s, and has not stopped lecturing, hectoring, chiding, and blithely intoning for the 10's. Every microphone-hogger, every rewarded dull pedant, every book-jacket aesthete and armchair revolutionary, every closet manic-depressive had the Secret for how to reform the known political world, if only there would come a duchy or a principality to give the squire the actual club of power. Accurate diagnoses of capitalism's maladies and fortnightly assaults could tumble from the solo mouths of these brilliant bookworms, but never a room for debate, and always spurious uplift and terrible culture-jacking for their own hermetic purposes. Events of the day were mixed with superficial hijackings from the cultural totems of the day to create a bland, off-key remix suited to down-headed audiences and scourge-minded NPR penitents. Rich Hollywood matrons were doing blow into their late 80s, but these parsons and ascetics were staking out for a nostalgic Puritan land of never-was and never will be, where every farmhouse had a philosopher-poet and whittling was the most exciting event of the forenoon.

PR-LSC 57 -   THE NEO- AGS

All around the collegiate proximity, neo-agrarians are heeding the call of ecological Armageddon, and heading for the land with their ideals flying high. Drummed out of the corporate rat race, uninterested in the white picket fence house with the anti-depressants and early divorce lifestyle, disdainful of the cul-de-sac of publish-and-perish, ummoved by the call to be a Peace Corps imperialist, the neo-Ags are getting down and dirty, home-schooling their Jesus babies, composing sonnets and threnodies as they slaughter their organic animals while hosting city slickers for costly "retreats" in their hardwood-floor yurt performance spaces. As early Transitionists, they understand well that the suburban American Dream was a destructive delusion, but they are adopting pre-Enlightenment nonsense like dowsing and beyond-overweening parenting in their quest for psychic fulfillment. Why live like the Amish until it is necessary or common to do so? The fate of the world hangs not on these still-supersystemic neo-Ag muckers, but on the collective adaptations of the near-7 billion humans and their unfortunate anti-regulatory processes. Opting out of the consumer-purchaser delirium is excellent in concept, beyond difficult in execution (where are those shoes from, how much hidden fossil fuel usage is permitted, how much corporate family money is credited to the farm operations), and a form of anticipatory drudgery in evaluation.

PR-LSC 58 -   TERRITORY

"Making the scene" is a fulfillment of our social instincts, when humans come together in social cohorts. This can be in a family, but more today in self-chosen affinity groups, cultural bands of commonly-interested folks who are drawn towards that temporary world of shared private "work." The language to certify this positive attraction is far more pedestrian than the feelings of greater purpose that are elicited, but there the culture has evolved many new meeting grounds to compensate for the old discarded ones of family, religion, and capitalist labor. Many people of today search in vain for these digital or cultural watering holes, and far too many others are forced into intrusive and over-reaching enforced affinity groupings of the ivory tower classroom and the post-Fordist cubicle workplace. Unless the co-determined fate of humanity is advanced, the convolutions and inexpressions of the communicative individual is of no particular larger dimension. Down-in-the-gutter sociology may tell important stories, but the moral is lost when the gutter starts to fill up with evermore bodies injured by the supersystem: the mentally downtrodden, the terminally addicted, the spendthrift and the class war casualties. Rather than gathering strength from small, disregarded acts of anti-authoritarian humanity, the opposition needs to acquire a territory or two where the Big Hand of the supersystem is reduced to a proper peripheral, frightened role, and not a Germany of determined renewable energy revolution contradicted by waste-exporting corporate banking inequality structure.

PR-LSC 59 -   HISTORY"S VERDICT

What story ends happily with "Then she was beaten and shot"? What gratification attends to, "Then he was convicted and sentenced to ten years in prison"? What uplift permeates, "He died working on his next book, broke and living in a small apartment with his cat"? These are the refrains of the modern left, honoring its ill-observed martyrs, seeing purity and valiance in a pre-incarceration speech, forgetting an indefatigable researcher. Why does such an "informed" audience fall, beyond repeatedly, for the elevation of the trivial and the marginalized and the defeated and the beaten and the traduced and the doomed? There is no righteousness when the spoils of victory mean the perpetuation and expansion of globalized suffering. Others have "fought the good fight" and headed to death secure in the justice of their cause, even as the cause was never possible, never to be. The other side plays with its riches into its old age, laughing at the foolishness and obtuseness of its victims. The other side has its investments expand, now into the trillions and all across the continents, while the ascetic side of moral beneficence gets T-shirts on its way to the unemployment line. During the Terror after the French Revolution the opposite result obtained, as the alleged rich nobility were guillotined, but this is no comfort to the employed modern left, who are separated by class standing from mass violence, and are not quite sure where they would be judged to stand on the question of immoral financial gain.

PR-LSC 60 -   THE GOOSE AND THE HOSANNAS

The liberal left called endlessly for "activism" to thwart the expansionist aims of the supersystem's real estate developers, corporate lawyers, venture capitalists, military, police, privatized security directors, foreign energy pirates, investment banking criminals, corrupt judges, and religious mercenaries. The goose was being cooked in the oven, and though the diners complained about the smell and hurt feelings of the goose, they surely sat down and ate. After they ate, they complained about the smell and the hurt feelings of the goose, and resolved to give some crumbs to the next goose they might happen to meet, but there would dinner the next night, and it would be goose. The 60's left lost the war to the corporate hegemon by refusing to investigate power dynamics and hypocritical complicity, investing fantasies of Arcadian withdrawal and Jesus-children raising with unwarranted social consequence. Each outgrowth of this revelry has occasioned graybeard hosannas, each a puerile valorization of the outsized dreams of conquest by imperceptible orderlies.

PR-LSC 61 -   UNEMPLOYED BUT WAITING

Who were the "rebels' against the supersystem of the 80s, the 90s, the 00s? If you were not working for it, you were scratching a living from its detritus, or going back in time in some Galahad quest that attracted no sane followers. Anti-imperialists, greens, liberals, academics, open source computer techies, peoples' lawyers, squatters, back-to-the-landers, Battle of Seattle vets, vegans – who wants to claim a record of success? Who took back the upper hand from the powers-that-be? Who started hiring? The "jobs" that can come from such an absurd arrangement of technical subservience to the superstate can only be servile or sycophantic, or deceptive and marginal. The repeated trooping of unformed college graduates into the giant morass of the corporate supersystem has become a sad march into oblivion, attracting the venal and the stupefied into subordinate prostitution, only now the paper-circulating jobs have dried up. For those not able yet to climb into the cubicle life of corporate food and corporate drink and corporate clothes and corporate transportation and corporate fuel and corporate energy and quasi-corporate work and corporate entertainment and corporate health care and corporate insurance and corporate-mediated social relationships and a corporate mentality be replaced? A few anti-corporate moments and some chosen anti-corporate expressions do not even mildly trespass upon the entire realms of space owned by and devoted to the expansion of the corporate supersystem. An ocean of digitized favor flows toward this false light: people, their money, their political systems, the law, the military and its "adventures." A trickle flows in the opposite direction, a universalized hatred of the supersystemic command, the human response to an anti-human construction, but even a dying animal clings to a doomed fight.

PR-LSC 62 -   BIZARRE REALITY

Conspiracism starts from a fine and good place: authoritarian structures are certainly capable of, and have generously throughout history indeed committed, nefarious plot-mongering. Treading on lies, duplicity, official propaganda, intimidation of opposition, murder, and extreme marginalization, enfranchised manipulators have been at the Reichstag, assassinating foreign reformers, holding Inquisitions, torturing dissidents, creating secret bands of cultist murderers, framing anarchists. There is a much larger dustbin of erroneous conspiracy theories, promulgated and accepted by the credulous and incapacitated. Most of these false allegations of elite criminality stem from theoretical possibilities branching off from actual events, then taken to untrue heights, but without the social power to substantiate the charges fo murder and genocide, conspiracies inhabit the the airless world of speculation, often diverting the precious remnants of social capital on the weird and the unprovable. In the Am-Left of today, the real possibility of conspiracies underlying recent historical assassinations generates truthers of all stripes. Correct suspicion of the immoral status of capitalist medicine begets the embrace of the traditional practice of worthless folk-cult medicine, from homeopathy to herbal placebos to the spine-tingling of chiropractic reimbursements. Accurate understanding of the killing propensities of corporate manufacturing leads to the easy adoption of chemtrails. Awareness of US political fascism leads to 9-11 truthers, Tea Party paranoia, and tin-foil hat websites depicting a reptilian elite. Further examples are tedious – government AIDS connectivity, pedophile hysteria, anti-Communist and drug war paranoia, religious insanity, UFO hauntings – but there are always genuine bases of social problems that underlie the grievous extensions into irrationalism and delusion. With inclusion into the open realms of social power and intellectual command, these theories collapse, but with a fractious ineptitude regnant in the political arena, the hinterlands will be rife with percolating nonsense until the sands sweep over all.

PR-LSC 63 -   DISSIDENCE

To answer the correct charge of boredom ensuing from being trapped within the supersystem, critics engage in radical anarchic "play," from Situationists on stilts to steampunk soirees. What about those more tied to a bourgeois style of alleged fun? What is the "transgressive" appeal of annoying clowns and spontaneous idiocy? Workers and the under-employed and the unemployed are not always brimming over with prosocial enthusiasm, and can be excused if the traditional expressions of anti-authoritarianism strikes them as far too much mind-blasted weirdness. The known world is not going to be overturned by overly familiar "deviance," the worn channels of tough-guyism that animated temporarily antagonistic "rebels" since VE Day. Determined folk-savants have foresworn the 9-5 for generations, finding a better version of themselves with contemporary outsider stylings, but lifestyle choice is not going to print money nor stop the killing of species. High culture and forest wanderings may make the individual rebel feel apart from the concrete jungle, but the global economy is forever in the path.

PR-LSC 64 –   OPPOSITION

Opposition to the supersystem is not short on facts, nor theses, nor evidence, nor stalwart antipathy, but it founders on the central irony that the fiercest critics of the supersystem also have derived lifelong benefits and superior standing from it. Marxists, liberals, anti-neocons, eco-saboteurs, Battleists for Seattle, no-nukers, Democrats, union leaders, agitprop musicians, tenured radicals, ascetic simplifiers, all cannot claim to have de-corporatized. Second homes in Wellfleet, metastasizing corporate investments, family inheritances derived from marauding robber barons, suits and dresses stained with sweatshop blood, high-percentile tax avoidance returns, children raised in technological affluence – the Am-Left is shot through with these disproportionate, compounding gains from the supersystem. No fight can be won when the spoils from the enemies' warring against the opposition go directly to the coffers and habiliments and magazines of the alleged opposition. Fights are won out of desperation, not removed inclination.

Chapter FIVE
NIHILISM as DEFAULT TRUTH

You will need a variant of nihilism to contend with the Supersystem. Philosophy has fallen in disrepute, religion has become absurd in the more advanced regions of the world, but we cannot sustain an alternate faith in "science" and the progressivism it appropriates. Atheism has become a momentary minor sub-region of bestseller world, but atheism, as a rejection of supernaturalism, must do better than the obtuse secular humanism that presupposes a wonderful, Up-With-People bathos to human society and technology. Science, in the form of a technological focus on the objective testing of natural hypotheses, has created incredible electrical feats and structures, but it has been equally misused to destroy the very natural gifts it depends on. For the purposes of the propagation of the supersystem, science has been generally left to the scientists, who are are quite poor moralists, with the result that non-scientists such as myself cannot tell the difference between a quark and a photon, and have vast reservoirs of scientific ignorance as debilitating as the astrological fixations of our herd forebears. My credentials as a *thinker* should not permit a further recitation of my ill-educated gaps in scholarly command, but we are neither building a rocket-ship or diagnosing your genetic markers. Scientific insufficiency is part of the tSS argument. We will never approximate a working knowledge of our natural world, but even this knowledge is immaterial, because we lack demonstrable effect on our own social institutions. Without entry to the operation of our supersystem, we are forever dumb, outsiders clicking on endless distractions.

"Nihilism" has been the favorite target of late-stage academia. How can any one idea/worldview/all-encompassing belief system (AEBS) be so important that has no one, not a soul, for it? Why all the worry if there is a not a single declared adherent of this AEBS, outside of the clinically insane? Nihilism takes the air out of pedantry, stating forcefully that our social institutions, since the demise of the frightened solidarity of the hunter-gathering bands, have become ethically and functionally defunct. Nihlism celebrates the verities:

- We are not getting out of this alive
- Knowledge is not power
- The truth shall not set you free
- Whatever bad is in place – check back if it ever disappears
- What goes around does not come around
- The worst of us tend to make the most money
- No one really gives a damn what you think
- We cannot think our way to happiness
- We are but one incomplete arrangement of protoplasmic atoms

This list can go on in dull pessimism, countering all the happy think that does not do justice to the glorious experience of cognitive wonderment, and you should feel free to offer pith and rejoinder to all the clichés that permeate our western stratosphere, but that exercise, too, needs its comeuppance, because the universe cares not the slightest for our despair or frustration, but rather waits for our intellectual commitment to active exploration of all that comes our way. A cheer, also, for solipsism – why not think as if your conditional existence is the most important thing to hit this benighted blue orb? Who is not committed to his or her Weltanschauung?

This book is its own negation. Obviously, in the face of the Supersystem, there are better things to do than write books, which are a low-tech leftover. We are all going to be playing in the daisies and swimming in marmalade pools one of these days, if about 10,000 unrelated forces switch their polarities, yet without that direct concatenation, we are going to see our world go down, one CNN headline after another, from shooting to bombing to sex sting to cover-up to "hate" speech to new drug to Christian apologetics, at the end of our work evasion days.

NI-DEFTR 1 - HISTORICAL TRUTH

The supersystem is simply human social power, writ large. Social improvement can only come an epochal redistribution of power towards beneficial regulation, a requirement which clears the shelves of just about every earnest political science, philosophy, sociology, and history tome. In the annals of popular resistance, what has ever produced a concentrated upwelling of anti-statist oppression? Ah, say the ancient guard, surely we can glory in the Bastille, in the civil rights movements, in the Lincoln Brigade, in Seattle, in the Enlightenment, in Chiapas, in freedom and righteousness that are the legacy of the finest progressives "movements" that swept the fascistii to their doom. However, not one of these flag emblems conspired to deny the victorious march of this supersystem. Where in history was the anticipation that all of that blood-won struggle would result in class-dominated economic inequality, terrible want amidst elite prosperity, and monolithic corporate militarism? Only the pessimists and the nihilists were right in their debilitating and sometime suicidal depression: this human world was in a slow track, fated to be governed by incompetent, arrogant dullards seeking individual reward in systems shot through with corruption, propaganda, and killing. Of course there were improvements, cancellations of terrors, obvious benefits that accrued as the generations moved through irrational systems of slavery, abuse of women, workplace degradation, sexual paranoia – to produce a supersystem of continuing misperformance. We have not achieved a utopia on earth, nor have we created real institutional forces to counteract destructive inheritances, so we are stuck far behind our destination, with no means of transportation to get there. Unconvinced? Seeing this as sour dyspepsia? Then deny the connections the unite the frustrations that you and your fellow humans will encounter in your daily stumbles. Are you ready to continue to ascribe evil depravity to all the authorities and manservants and minions that have bedeviled your awake hours? Clearly, you have also failed others, as they have failed you, and it cannot be the light of Jesus' last breath and Mohammed's innocent favor were visited upon you only – obviously, there are *motivations and compelling influences* that constitute our social reality. You just need a guide to clarify the overt conspiracies of action and inaction that co-animate the gouging doctor, the terrorist judge, the psychopathic general, the proud slumlord, the unrepentant tax haven vice president, the sinister psychiatrist, the paper-pushing criminal.

NI-DEFTR 2 - THE TRIPLE BIND

In this approach to the mountain of the supersystem, we are not doing any real climbing. These questions are about *outlook*, not action or existence. The standard social science indicators can be trotted out to measure the worth of our present social reality, and if you want to say that matters have gotten substantially better than the cave days of raw meat and hunger, then you have a point. Yet we live in the shadow of the much better world we could have become. And we are haunted by the barriers to the much better world we could be. Put those two realities together, and you have an untenable present, a present that cannot be defended, but one that we must live with, in gratefulness and cosmic happiness, with sunshine crullers for every sweet child and bumptious dancing nightly on the veranda. You will have your precious cultural and inter-personal sustenance, as I do, and I gainsay none of it. However, others are denied what we have, not through the faults of their character, but through the strictures of their provided circumstances – and now humanity faces what Tim Garrett of the University of Utah, among others, has delineated as the _Double Bind:_ if we do not decarbonize, we face devastation through ecological collapse that will cause massive economic devastation including inflation, but if we rapidly decarbonize, it will be only though the collapse of civilization, a similar horrible result in either case. We may say we can do nothing about the suffering of the mass of others, but that is simply not true – our social realities have enormous, global dimensions, and we control them all through the fractious workings of the supersystem – or, in the _Third Bind,_ as if two weren't enough as looming calamity, we also cannot control them because of the massivity of vested interests.

NI-DEFTR3 -   BONDS

Pessimism meets the conditions for our understanding of history, reality, the odds, the outlook. This gargantuan human social enterprise is doomed, listing badly, and odious in its unjust outcomes. We are caught in the supersystem, acting upon our honed instincts. The F-word of "family" is exalted in the place of a community of common purpose, with adult children having long outgrown the now fictitious bonds of "family" forced by the expansiveness of the concept to maintain long-distance fealty. There is not a single moment that is not a confluence. There is not a single action that can be taken back, not a single memory that does not get superseded by the demands of living. We all have a responsibility to govern our own actions, but where are we ever called on the carpet? Where are our local halls of shame? Where does morality lie? Through conversation with those unfortunate enough to be near us, we get some basic ideas, we are given some degree of both positive and negative feedback. These judgments become internalized, often in the form of grudges, some as effective barriers against our own volition, but the human social enterprise goes abandoned, as the bright lights of the telescreen and the warm ambers in the bottle invite the recline before sleep.

NI-DEFTR4 –   RESULTS

What is the _point_ of all this writing and discussing, this obeisance to monologue, when our actions, both collective and individual, have such innocent effects? Unlike in earlier times, when the individual was valorized as the apotheosis, unlike the Peace and Love 60's, the Cocaine 70's, the Greed 80's, the Clintonian 90's, there has been a terminus achieved in the 00's and 10's with the Bush junta and Obama con. Take all of your earnest efforts, add in all of the books and the research, mix in all the hedge fund trillions and the money market investments, and you are still left with imbeciles in charge everywhere, from the most egregious of mutant rapscallion boors in Bush-time to a constantly updating world-wide gang of prevaricating pedants. There is not an education in the world, not a platform in the universe, not a position of intellectual command for any human, that can be equal to the sense of vigorous despair at seeing such a debilitated supersystem. Since we know that time is short - that all human systems break down under the weight of ego + greed + violence + endemic enmity + disinterest in strife by the well-intentioned – we can only raise to a toast to the wonderful exasperations of environmental futility, lockstep social disintegration, and minor repairs.

NI-DEFTR5 -   DOUBT

There are bookish savants who supervise a vast region of cyberspace, who have their files neat and cross-referenced, who know the minutest details about their chosen focus, who can be oracular and profound only because of their deep and long study – but where is their sense of doubt about themselves? Where is their cynicism? How can we be lectured to by those who have not stared into the abyss of nothingness, who know only the merest intimation of oblivion?. The worlds of nature, of athletic strain, of domestic labor, of people-watching on the tube, of brooding and anxious contemplation, of onanism and monogamous sexual harassment, are at least as valuable as straight scholarship or remunerated managing. Of course, not many of these pleasures benefit the mass of humanity, are more receptive than active, and so must be balanced by the musty pursuit of supra-intellectual grandiloquence.

NI-DEFTR 6 -   STORIES

The industrial entertainment industry can keep the channels going, the stories now with a war backdrop, there with a green tinge, updating old favorites, recombining classic texts into jaded teleplays, luring new thespians with immortal small-town dreams, upping the tuition for MFA on-line programs, occupying the night-time hours with edgy violence forays, calming the engorged modern psyche. Practitioners and evaluators of the dramaturgical obsession will provide the overlay of commentary for this latest iteration of the post-war urge to stand apart from the quotidian maw of life, but the fiction has shredded into sheer indecision. You will find in the screen what you want, but will it be enough to stay the demons of political hell that have gathered to produce family stories of no more interest than toaster instructions?

NI-DEFTR 7 -   UNRECONSTRUCTED VILLAINS

What should have been the most relevant, most necessary study, sociology, the investigation of the social corruption of global power, was translated into incoherence, dropped, and then left for the back alleys of higher academic irrelevance . The only sociology that makes it into the back racks is the sociology of the underclasses, a natural curiosity that certainly gets the normal collegiate vote, but a predilection that ignores the far greater venality, duplicity, irrationality, and malevolence of the upper classes. Gangs, prostitutes, drug fiends, killers, sexual deviants may have gotten the researchers and the scholarly overviews, but these are no more than local color, good for stories, professorships, and foundation credibility, but not the villains of our world. Where are the examinations of the flattened ethics of the suburban churchgoer, or of the summary misjudgments of the commercial banker, or of the depraved familial hurts of the distorted modern family? Better to have our freaks represent the obverse of the folk goodness in our sociological imagination, than to find our common areas befouled and rotting.

NI-DEFTR 8 -   THE LIMITS OF NIHILISM

No one *needs* an extended lecture about any of this. The pose of no pose, the stance of no stance, the theatrical art-nihilist of "*It all means nothing*" is as useless a by-product of the supersystem as the megachurch devotee. Social reality is of enormous consequence to the prospects for work, home stability, and leisure enjoyment of billions of our fellow humans, now and forever. While we have life, we are endeavoring to placate its own neuroses, see our way forward, shape the cosmos better to our liking. Unfortunately for the project, we as a rooted species have lost command of our institutions, and so descend into domestic madness.

NI- DEFTR 9 -   PESSIMISM AND DIVERSITY

To accentuate pessimism is to go against every human's instinct to protect self-worth. Otherwise percipient people, decrying every manner of injustice, seeing all varieties of devolution, rear back from the conclusion that matters will not get better. There is plenty of depression to go around the globe, a full planet of frustration, self-castigation, worry, but the individual will seems to demand, in public, valuation, no matter how dismal the recitation of exigency that precedes the uplift wrap-up. Die-hards of the folk left point to the antiwar and civil rights gains of the 60s and 70s as the rebuke to any doom-'n-gloom. Look how far we've come - America was in the icy grip of Pat Boone and the Chamber of Commerce of alcoholic whites - and look at us now, transgendered, biracial, tuned in, tatted up, a civil rights explosion that took us from three channels and Lawrence Welk to a forever altered diversity of lifestyles. These epochal advancements came in the specialized area of *identity power*, and resulted in no lasting effect upon the socio-economic power of the supersystem. Visible bigotry and monumental economic disparity remain layered into this portion of this mix. Potential and uplift are not going to rise out of the human sea, summoned by a call to our real and demonstrable better nature. We all have a duty to look on the bright side, to refuse to wallow in debilitating moroseness, to get busy finding the beauty or comfort in life, but this mode of thinking and living cannot come through dishonesty. If things don't look good, if the signs all point one way, we can allow for a sudden shift of wind, but we must act according to the dictates of nature. Assess the conditions, then go find it elsewhere if it can be found, or if moving beats sitting.

NI-DEFTR 10 -   RESIST ALL

All this hue and cry about the supersystem will be worthless if we do not produce a social movement or two worthy of the name. I have faulted the sainted left for its crippling lack of realism (CLR), and I would be happy to build a new left from the ground up, with a existentialist atheism that blocks autism, inhibits self-promotion of would-be leaders, enforces sociological discipline, and foreswears righteousness, along with a few thousand other traits for self-improvement that cannot, will not happen. Why pine for a 60s "movement" that arose in a specific moment, was beaten by the violent forces of virulent counter-reaction, and exists only in the mists of nostalgia? The pockets of true intellectual rebellion against the dominant anti-humanist ethos of the supersystem are without social capital, allowed the space for minor growth because of their financial and cultural lightness and sparseness. Globalization has already happened: the die-offs have already occurred, species after species, large fish after large fish; malarial victims after the prior hundreds of thousands - our recent human record of disease and starvation and enforced poverty has sent record numbers of our fellow humans and animals to this avoidable fates. Why look at our common trail of colossal devastation? Because, for one, that view down the horror of our path-walking ought to give us, the living, the breathing, the sentient, the humility to stop our puerile genuflections to tradition, to hierarchy, to narrow subservience. Instead, we can resist, resist ourselves, resist exhortation, resist resistance.

NI-DEFTR 11 -   THE VERDICT

If, in expert judgment, the game is over, and it cannot be won, the only responsible action is to declare the mathematics unwinnable. Considering the institutional actors operating with destructive vitality in the supersystem, assessing the balancing and countervailing forces, forecasting for the resistance of entrenched interests towards pro-social regulation, crunching the numbers and facing the verdict: it's over, Johnny. Small, incremental, unthreatening up-turns in the numbers that matter would be welcome, but are not expected, and would not signify reversal even if occasioned by crises or temporary liberalism. The Gini coefficient; the rate of resource hoarding and extraction by the G-8; civilian deaths and injuries due to war or civil political strife; premature deaths from pandemics, malnutrition, and insufficient equity in resource access; enforced social despair based on gender, religious discrimination, or tribal antipathy; conditions of working labor – for all these determining numbers of human life, even if there are gains in the coming years, which is doubtful, the perpetuation of immoral, illegal, or deleterious discrepancy means immense, inconsolable suffering.

NI-DEFTR 12 -   POLARITIES

With no shortage of experts for any social position you wish to find, there can be an endless confirmation of your bias. Although the neoliberal American model became a flaming wreckage in the late Bush years, none of the radical relocalizationists could draw a vision of how the mechanisms of social power were going to be seized by the flotillas of right-minded folks. The hinterlands of thought were replete with moral urgings of the most puritanical sweep, to repent drastically from happy motoring and televisual stupor and growth mania and puerile xenophobic politics and littoral littering, but the pies went spinning into the sky, Pollyanna entered the kitchen nook, and Don Quixote dropped by for a latte. A few ascetics seeing the cosmic truth emanating from their craniums was not going to alter the dynamics of a late-stage corporate consumer stranglehold. What would be the mechanics of global social regulation? What might even count as a *start*, when the scale of operation had to begin at such an elevated level?   The institutional implements to transmute theory into social revolution were hopelessly corporatized, from the universities to the think-tanks to the foundations. Populist revolt inspired by martyrs and led by self-designated saviors was theoretically possible, but the theory had not been invented. Who would risk imprisonment, forgo health care, eschew a paycheck, say goodbye to lovers and a family, just for the sake of a dimly perceived outline of an unreachable social utopia?

NI-DEFTR13 -   REALISM

Realism may be a hackneyed appellation for a social theory, yet the supersystem is all too real Not one of us is going to find hope in parables, or in the magnificent workings of a few local martyrs and saints, or in the rescue of one foundling. That kind of hope is always self-referential, focused on small victories that are pathetic against the infinitely grander larger scale of defeat. No theory can encapsulate the many-splendored dimensions of power relations, and there is great temptation to go sit on the curb and watch the traffic. No argument for stasis will stand the test of time, since from any one perspective, all subsequent events are effects from identifiable causes. Accepting this tendency to discount nihilism, the truth of our relentless predicaments are observable in the similarity of the human struggle to work, co-exist, occupy time productively, and calculate meaning since the dawn of civilization. What could redefine that repetition of thwart, alloyed desperation, and inherited treasures? From inside the power structure, self-accusatory tales of deception and willed ignorance can be found, as the elite confesses to non-prosecuted crimes, or finds comeuppance in family and personal travail. Scientists become whores for industry, shifting their research to bend to the flows of available funding capital. A model of production that causes widespread cancers through industrial exposure can rely on the educated consciences of judges who offer, in 2009, a 22-year prison sentence for an ELF protestor who set property fires in GMO research labs and luxury homes. We all know the score: we can harbor all the antig-overnment paranoia a brainstem can generate, but as long as we go to work dutifully, leave the planetary damage infliction to the corporate masters, and press no cases, we might consider ourselves *free*. Waste, death, avoidable suffering, despair, graft, the arrogance of unexamined power: these are the trifles our age cannot solve.

NI-DEFTR 14 -   OURSELVES AND OTHERS

The record of social institutions in the liberal Enlightenment west is one of enormous systemic resistance to transformative justice. How then did we raise ourselves from the muck of the cave to the dawn of the New Age of unbridled leisure?   The precise psychological mechanisms that smooth the cognitive adjustments for the supersystem's multiple generations are going to be lost to time and over-complexity, but we must confront the victories of sustained injustice and sanctioned terror if we are to approach the legacy of humankind. Who can do this and remain functional? Who lives with the burdens of humanity's rottenness dogging each mundane and minor little step? In our roles as individuals, we let others do the supervising, the managing, the interpreting, the investing, the judging, the dirty work of empire and accumulation: our function is to stay in the flow of whatever large forces surround us. Now the entire credentialed sector becomes part of the national security complex, attached to the advertising industry's dissemination of pollution and noise, interfacing with the industrial discharge of toxic effluent, all sectors impinging on the edges of the others. If things are looking so bad, why care? If nothing works, why pay attention? If things look hopeless, why look? If there is no telling what can be done, why talk about what chances we never had?   The sweep of recorded human history dictates that quietude and intellectual honesty lose, if they ever appear, and the bonds of integrity that an alleged democracy must derive from its structures are easily surmountable by greed, rapine commerce, powerful corruption, and inertial misperformance. Yet to be ignored is both our fate and our honor - the only call a bird can make is the one nature has intended.

NI- DEFTR 15 -   HONOR

The supersystem gives enormous precedence to elite power, foisting the burdens of work and struggle to the lower orders. Honorifics in this faulty enterprise make no sense. A "Reverend" is decidedly *not* to be regarded as worthy of being "revered," given awe, deference, and devotion for what? "Professors" derive their paychecks from a thoroughly corrupted system, in which they sat their spreading butts in seats in front of old-generation intoners, followed their precepts and musings and bloviations until they, themselves, got the ersatz sheepskins that entitle them to "profess" – what? And to whom – the progeny of Donald Rumsfeld and Sarah Palin and CPAC cretins, college graduates all? "Father" McSlappy and Rabbi Lech and Imam Anti-science – they have "earned" their titular supremacy? Or are these and all honorifics conditional, suspect, and then bogus? How many honorees in the supersystem have refused their medals, their designations, their accruals, their MacArthurs, their Twitter access, their spot on the dais? Hit the delete key, and feel the elevated rush of the clearer path, the discarded affectation.

NI-DEFTR 16 - GOOD INTENTIONS BULLDOZED

The think-tanks have been in overdrive since the great fortunes needed outlets for their global embezzlements, but the papers and manuscripts and conference minutes and ten-point plans have had the unfortunate occurrence of being fully ignored, except for the PNAC monstrosity with its well-connected authors. The mountainous sludge of other, well-intentioned vettings of the modern social world have been immediate refuse, never finding the light of a powermaster's eye. The Tobin tax, carbon trading, single-payer health care, harm reduction, 350.org, Club of Rome, the Oslo Accords, and new thousands every year have disintegrated, to be buried by history's bulldozer. In the realm of social power, nothing is so disposable as good intentions. Earnestness, ambitiousness, and competence-directed work have animated the forward wing of the American empire, leaving the marauding to the lesser, easily manipulated anxious males. The American B.A. is a certification of *niceness*, as if being reasonable, accommodating, mildly polite and forgettable is the ticket to the acme of human accomplishment. There are worse ways to go through life, but you will not make the supersystem flow like honey just through naïve intentions and unobtrusive toleration. Do well, feel bad for others, self-criticize, brave public scorn, bring problems to the fore, articulate skepticism, or plant flowers – not one of these minor initiatives cancels the immovable concentration of oppression. Where will be the purchase on this gargantuan edifice of the supersystem? What be the catalyst for this catching of a hold on the sheer, slick rock? Down the country lanes, past the happy restaurants, into the vibrant art district of a major city, the promise of a modern world of variegated fun and social good times once existed, can exist, but only for fleeting few or time. Every socialist "leader" became a statist, every advance of civilization destroyed the supplying area. If you condemn a system, you also deny its pleasures and perquisites, the ones that only a few can reach, at least fully, but the others below are always looking above for instruction and below for disfavor.

NI-DEFTR 17 - OBLIVION

The supersystem does not permit easy entry. Those with the personality and the family history can drift early on, and then become unaligned, rootless, lost in the sauce. Others are in tune with the dominant requirements, and can plow through the social mores and educational games to a house, career, and parentage with only the lightest of self-questioning. Oblivion awaits those who feel its pull. Drug habits, loneliness, and nursed anger can occupy the suburban easy chair as well as the skid row, and with the privatization of all that can perceived, the dollar sign is attached to even the feelings of happiness. How can a theory of social power account for all of the intensity of disaffection that ruled the land of plenty? How can a social theorist not place his or her idiosyncratic life experience into the equations that activate his or her sensors? Where can you see that you will not get there? If the way has been long and undistinguished, which way does the journey turn?

NI-DEFTR 18 - SPEECHIFYING

On the left, especially the young left, a primarily campus artifact, there is intense declaiming. Righteous passion grabs hold of the critic's resisting métier, and the mike gets a wind workout. The tragedy of our time is that such perfervid opposition gets nowhere in the face of the supersystem. What, precisely, was there to *do*? Where was there a social outlet for empathetic pessimism? The marches on Washington were now in the pre-epilogue history pages, the liberals had been siphoned off in an Obama-Clinton minute, and yet the roads bounced with manufactured determination. The popular culture fabulia were ever-ready and blinking, canceling social engagement in favor of the minor and the personal – each mind a big screen destiny and social whirlwind.

NI-DEFTR 19 - LIVING WITH NIHILISM

A narrowing of life to the quotidian does not plow over the fields of larger social purpose. Growing a rose does not cancel the foreclosure debt of a medical-bill-induced bankruptcy. Strumming a dulcimer to the pausing chipmunks will not bring secure jobs to the destitute. We can not avert our gaze from the governed arena of the supersystem, though we can recognize the chaos, the vicious irrational judgments, the sinister triumphs of entrenched elites and their poisoned lackeys. The horrors of the world are visited upon people just like us, placed in irredeemable social circumstances, yet the political culture denies this heavy burden upon the fortunate, and places more and reward for them. Look to Mexico, to Afghanistan, to America's inner cities, to Africa, to the suppliers of all your goods and trinkets, and you will see that this has become the dominant tendency, unstoppable.
area of predation.

NI-DEFTR 20 - HEROES

If all talk and forecast and deep knowledge and cogitation is a conditional scream at the void, then your reaction to equivocation will be a petulant yawn, demanding *to be told something I don't know*. What will the future bring, what will we know then that we should have known now, what is way out of this mess, what is the proper balance between dread and enjoyment, who is to be trusted with your intellectual loyalty, who is above all reproach, who risks much but not all, who is grounded yet brilliant, who can operate all the levers of thought and action and enjoyment and evince a coolness that is the summation of all the personal lifestyle rebellions of the 60s on over – that is who you look for in an "Author," what you demand of your pieces of technology, what you believe is your due from all that you behold. If you are told that no person could possibly that be that action figure of wisdom and physical guile, and that there is no better world to come, you should be prepared to accept your own powers to contend with social reality.

NI-DEFTR 21 - CONSPIRACIES

On a continuum that ranges from crop circles, lizard-men, Jesus and Mohammed in the sky, the Phoenix Program, the Inquisition, the Salem Witch Trials, talking frogs, portentous rabbits, omens on the dinner plate, lucky numbers, CIA false flag operations, Yakub the mad scientist, hidden family abuse, subliminal advertising, Protocols, sub-humans, life after death, to every other speculated deep truth and misinformed half-baked urban suppositon, we tend to cluster around some, deny the rationality of the many, and find plausible many alternative scenarios. For the purposes of the theory of the Supersystem, those in power are allowed their backrooms and their secret handshakes, their murders and their corrupt visions. Who fully understands that which cannot be seen? We need evidence, we need to follow the logic and the recorded propensities, but the lone observer will never get the justice that the lower orders demand from the upper stratum, so we will catch glimpses of the necessarily colluding elites, but will only be able to see the next generation arranging the next level of deceit. The mighty can fall, but not because of their past deeds, but only, if ever, because of their present overreach and inadequacy.

NI-DEFTR 22 -   WANTING SUBSTANCE

Usually, our intellects are *onto something*, though imperfectly, without full apperception, informed by our well-chosen readings, educated by the resistance of others to our will, churning with remote chaos, marked by neural pathways we share with no one. For some, the communicated words of others are often enraging, indicative of incompleteness, arrogance, self-absorption, risible funk, familial intransigence, or obtuse philosophical venality. Although well-practiced in the arts of intrapersonal avoidance, I know that the articulation of chastened doubt, more properly known as nihilism, can clear the room. Our antennae are oriented towards human *performance*, not to the observance of the troubled human beset in quietude.

NI-DEFTR 23 -   THE DANGER OF REALITY

Humanity will never create social systems that place humanistic leaders in actual positions of power – too indecisive, too capable of listening, too riven by doubt, too incapable of dissemination. Those looking at the supersystem from below are in charge of nothing, the opposite of *authoritative*, the halo of sanctity secure around our president-of-nothing heads. The powerlessness of the individual and the mappings of invisible power are the great unexplored themes of art and the great areas of unexplored sociological reality, and unavailable to the modern psyche. We know that time is short - that all human systems break down under the weight of ego + greed + violence + endemic enmity + disinterest in strife by the well-intentioned – so where is the remote? *What else do you want us to know that we feel all the time, can do nothing about, and can see nothing from you that will help us against the beast you claim to have named?*

NI-DEFTR 24 -   REFORM AND NIHILISM

Nihilism can be the valid skepticism about human social reform that notices the insane repetition of evasive, doomed, massed tropes. When observing the continued vitality of war, economic devastation, religious bigotry, triumphalism, judicial obtuseness, corporate malfeasance, health care for the rich, bad politics, reruns of bad sitcoms, what discount is applied to the retail price of reality? There are good pockets of fun, privileged oases of great times and good oldies, but across the whole of time and space, given the endurance of idiocy, and factoring in death's ultimate sting, who places what bet on social betterment? How many psychodramas of national reform have led to this epoch of social incoherence ? Didn't the rivers of blood in the Mekong Delta flow into the paper history of our futile mass death actions and fascinations? Why are we continuing to be such purveyors of the Fake Tough Guy Mystique? There are many fights we cannot win, will lose if the fight happens to come our way. Our strengths do not include an imperviousness to trouble, nor a transcendence of our refracted fears. Our pain is yet to come against us, but it waits, safe and surreal. How many more iterations of political and cultural disappointment will be needed to disincline us toward the illusion of reform?

NI-DEFTR 25 -   BETTER NIHILISM

Shall this argument of supersystemic disconcert be dismissed due to its obtuse pessimism? Are there the proverbial "hopeful signs" burgeoning in the spinning globe? Until death comes or destruction becomes monumental, those presented with a structured and gainful life are obligated to dance, sing, eat, have passionate sex, and foreswear prayer. What kind of fool engages in endless questioning leading to doleful pensiveness? The strength of the supersystem cuts pastoralism, literary obsessiveness, quaint melancholia, the withdrawal into retrograde family instruction, and hobbies. Who cares where we find solace below the industrial gray and the global technological bit display? Our times have been records of chances lost, needless building commenced, mass communication barriers obliterated, chatter and gradual ensnarement of the living in their boundless systems of accommodation and latent desiring. Whatever you can cherish within the purview of the supersystem, it will be accompanied by its inexorable regressions to, and then below, the mean. Not a bad way to go, most likely, but nowhere near its infinitely more comfortable better dead twin.

NI-DEFTR 26 -   PHYSICS OF SOCIAL REALITY

We have demonstrated as humans the ability to produce alternate social realities for entire classes of fairly similar folk, so we can produce better or lesser social realities through managed institutional forces. We are not predetermined by mechanistic fate, but we are shaped and shined and eroded by our social conditions. Take away productive jobs from a populace, strip them of a source of realizable pride in their earthly efforts, and the masters will end up with acutely evident social decay, which will be used as evidence of innate worthlessness justifying further repression of the social conditions of these victims. Once on a circular path, centrifugal force impels the traveler onwards around the bend, never off.

NI-DEFTR 27 -   INSIDE THE TUNNEL

The supersystem has produced nothing in the way of an *outlet* for the interests of other-regarding people. Instead, the good and the brave are imbued with guilt over actions they were never consulted about, imagine grave consequences of global degradation to their minute and tethered lives. In an atomized social world, the only actions in which there is an actual physical *we* are those in which there is an active criminal elite conspiracy. The decision to invade Iraq was not made by the American people. The brutal and absurd tax system was not designed by you. There are, of course, aiders and abettors, cheering crowds and complicit quislings to all manner of global horrors, but we cannot get to the actors themselves due to the protections erected by the established and constructed bulwarks for them in the supersystem. The royal "We" becomes the commoner's yoke. Yet there is no future in detailing the the ways we Lost It All. If the tunnel leads only further into more darkness with no opening at the other side, and we are incapable of working back to the beginning of the tunnel, then the   Great Liberal Experiment of Education,

Rhetoric, War , Culture and Incarceration can be pronounced a wretched monstrosity, yet all we have, and all we can work with in our places inside, lit by artificial means, digging for no real purpose outside of our need to be active.

NI-DEFTR 28 -   THIS WORLD

Towards the source we incline – where is that animating control for the social reality within which we are entrapped? Since a god or gods is so obviously long dead, we ask for a political system of systems, determining overt policy through debate, elections, and competing policy papers. Yet the more talk about "change," the more social reality doubles back upon itself for tiresome mocking of sweet desire. Americans by a growing majority understand fully that voting is a superfluous act when large corporate entities determine the scope and theater of the political game. Honest brokers give up on the possibility of adult romance, going to sleep alone after another night of televisual non-sexual entertainment. Authors give up on book projects, give up on being an author, as musicians abandon the band and athletes retire. The supersystem specializes in providing dreamers the adult knowledge that they will not "overcome." There are fully realized aspirations, of course, beautiful products of relentless preparation and risk that place their architects in great and exalted superiority, but these are exceptions, quite minor in number, that testify to the totemic nature of human frustration and loss. The best of times is no match for the times that the best is gotten of us – yet that is just pure fact, to be fought by the glories of this, the best and most salutary world we shall ever know.

NI-DEFTR 29 -   GOODS AND SERVICES

Everyday living within the supersystem is dependent for its contours on large and semi-guaranteed forces. If born to a generous station, most factors are in place for a quiet ride through the vicissitudes. Without having wagered much, legions of college-educated boomers have shouldered their way through recession, war, and famine (continents away) to become first in line for the suburban spoils of a well-born suitor. Not much had to change, nor did the basic choices of this life offer much contest or flavor. Doing the bare minimum of what was asked, answering placidly a series of broad questions posed by an arrangement of social forces, saw the man or woman to a large home with a monster garage and children off to their well-funded sports events. Whatever more life could or had to be due to the grinding of the gears of the supersystem, was a reality that others, not them, had to face. This augury was of no moral consequence to the universe, which rights no wrongs except through massive failure. Some had it very, very good, and yet so many of them could never perform the most basic of human niceties, that of *appreciation for the hard work of others*. This should have not been too hard to attempt, though most likely overwhelming - the horrific inequities, the blatant crimes of ecological devastation, , the abysmal exploitation of wage slaves, that factor into any item or good distributed to the well-off of the post-war era, makes any moral accounting impossible. The scope of the corruption that metastasized during the rise of the supersystem can never be documented. Money power flowed into every crevice, creating a second universe that featured the worldwide banking syndicates and their pathetic non-regulators, like BCCI and its connected American politicians Jimmy Carter and John Kerry., to the Rockefellers and the Duponts, Coca-Cola and every stained hand that was touched by the winnings of the elites. The post-war epoch is a record of liberal rhetorical persiflage amidst growing murder and global rampage from the finest corporate suites mankind will ever witness. Do you want to be the presiding judge over that case, and begin to rationally begin to sort out the levels of guilt of the perpetrators, likely from within your own extended family?

NI-DEFTR 30 -   CHANGE

There are social critics Waiting for Godot, seeing not the Continuation, nor its obverse of an imminent Flowering, but yet an eventual reckoning of social affairs in which the bottom shall rise to the top, the elite smit'd by their own accords and inevitable decline. How shall the Near Future look? The purpose of "witnessing" now, in the face of the looming supersystem, is to pave the way for the ascension of the righteous by as yet indistinct means. However, the "change" may as likely be in the opposite direction, the one where injustice commands the arc. There is no over-riding likelihood of social reformation along the lines of good times for more people, songs in the parks, love and tenderness for quality human beings. Where are the signs that these conditions shall be the pillars of human society, rather than the elusive and mocking unreachable condemnations of our present circumstances? What is the promise of better tomorrows for almost all that sends so many to the distant thrills of optimism, even as the litanies of incredible and mounting despair precede? Fuddy-duddy critics, the ascetic repastors drawn from the high-classical mode who have made their bones by condemning the brutishness represented by TV and pornography, are always hair-shirting the great unvarnished by invoking some mythical great libertarian past in good ol' Jeffersonian small-town racist-sexist alcoholic America, but that banner is not going to fly in Dollar-Store America, where TV and pornography are about the only good things going, outside of a few enduring socially cohesive cultural practices. If things are going to get better, let's see the plans, the blueprints, the recipes – run the numbers for us, show us the prospectus.

NI-DEFTR 31 -   SPEECHES

Together, we cannot change the world. Life, in the supersystem, consists of dealing with the feeling of being left behind. The blue orb keeps spinning, but there is no social momentum. Somewhere, out in that cold and distant night, there are other people making technology jump, but you, the recipient individual, the face looking at the superimposed sheet of glass, are not that governing architect. You can listen to TED speeches from steroidal snake oil salesmen following professional gee-whizzers from the Radio Shack academy, but the political system lists without a functioning motor, obese conservative pundits appoint themselves "philosophers" on CNN, and countries die from external contractions. Can there be a cheer in the seated crowd of elite invitees for that? Are the Bioneers and the Imagineers and the DARPAnots toiling deep into that green corporate supersystem night to bring about a megaworld of stunning beauty for the entire globe of waiting children? Will humanity finally stop the rat race, pack up the accumulated nonsense from generations of anxious strivers, and redesign the maze to favor some for all, not too much for any? Take a look around, past the screens and the pages – sense any real action?

NI-DEFTR 32 -   THE ELITE

The elite cannot be excused with the alibi of the supersystem, as if the machine and the matrix worked inexorably, without human divination or agency. The people at the upper level of the supersystem know precisely what they do, whom and what they serve, and what effects come from their common actions. War, economic inequality, and environmental devastation are not mysterious deus ex machina, unseen and unknowable. Bombers know what their bombs do; corporate lawyers know what will happen in the communities they exploit, businessmen and -women know, to the deepest recesses of their psyche, the imperatives of the bottom line and the continuance of a position. . There may be protestations of ignorance and self-justifications of ultimate morality, but the elite and the rich and the connected layers immediately beneath them have active minds, quite able to see the foolishness of human social action. They simply choose to push aside those evident truths with all the force of circumstance and diversion, spending their ill-gotten loot on walls against reality. They become functional morons, encapsulated in protective sheaths that are of no use in the recesses of their minds, where they know, and wish forever to conceal, that they are as dirty and pestilent and illegitimate and blameworthy as the phantasms of the "immoral" lower orders they publicly abjure. Yet, in this world, they will be the suits behind the desks, rubber-stamping the vicious orders of the cruel state.

NI-DEFTR 33 -   THE BACKDROP

The present supersystem is built of "mechanisms," operational processes within our large social institutions. How does the same news keep reoccurring? Why are discredited "initiatives" given constant re-birth as problems multiply? Within these mechanisms, large-scale foundational imperatives and inclinations override reform. Casinos crop us as economic "solutions." The Federal Reserve allocates "quantitative easing" to cover its existing crimes. Confessed war criminals sit on talk show couches. Quack alternative medicine is bought to contravene corporate conventional medicine. Faith healers prey upon the poor. Judges sentence political protestors to life sentences. The US military investigates its own crimes on its own battlefields. Google sends its profits into offshore tax schemes to steal tens of billions from the US Treasury. Events have antecedents, events emanate from existing laws and by-laws and confirmed structures. Observers take snapshots of crime scenes, and publish them for voyeurs. Social reality cannot be "halted," be evaded with a flick of dismissal, nor consigned to the backrooms of the corrupt and the indecent – with the presence of information technology, social reality is as much a part of nature as the sky or the air. As "weary" and "know-it-all" as happy nihilism appears, the operations of the supersystem will be the backdrop to human life, and will be as dismaying and enraging as any infestation or chronic pain, and endlessly confounding. No one should see utopia emerging from any scenario, but will it be too much to ask for?

NI-DEFTR 34 -   CLIMATE CHANGE

The world's governments will meet into perpetuity to discuss a global framework to curb carbon emissions, in cities that will acquire the ghostly assignations of World War I battlefields – Ypres, Passchendaele, Verdun. Now, Kyoto, Cancun, the one in between - papers and talks and coalitions and walk-outs and speeches as doleful and fatuous as the shots and charges and defenses by those doomed youthful soldiers and their delusional generals. No colonial power has ever agreed to terms before its wars of conquests became waning, so what will bring the victorious corporate economies of the developed world to lower their guns? Until the daylight skies darken or the oceans roar with fire, the carbon emissions of the working and building structure of human society will be uncapped. Endeavor to construct whatever working blueprint of governmental restraint of trade you wish, but even if such a document of cap and fee could be produced, the violations hatched in corporate corridors would start in frenzy before the "send" button could be hit.

NI-DEFTR 35 -   FALSE LEADERS

The ills of the supersystem are easy enough to identify – anger all over the place, even from its stalwart rightist shock troops. However, the opposition to its practices is mired in its hallmark paranoia or hallmark sectarian clashes. No "movement" can thrive on exhuming a century-and-half dead theorist whose tattered flag has been flown by repressive regimes. At some point, the painful variations on the theme indicate that the theme itself needs to be scrapped. Although corporate capitalism is not worthy of any further study or defense, neither shall we collectively inter the Grundrisse to see what we should do next. A diagnosis of the ills of capitalist power is not difficult to do from any armchair, but then comes the difficulty of diagramming a power distribution system to combat it – about a light-year from "replacing it," but who is counting? Who guards against the abuse of power by the various competing factions? How does the replacement system stop those who accrue greater economic power from acquiring greater political control? How do the inevitable differentials shake out? Did we all miss our chances to become leaders, movers, or shakers, so that now we can idly speculate about the fallen world until the final supply of bile courses its way through our dying body? There are some American "liberals" in positions of some managerial power, gurus of the classroom or the hip technology start-up or the hard-bitten Third World non-profit or well-read carpenters with tenured spouses or baristas with the art studios, but the exercise of power in their hands is never as beneficent as their hearts would intend, and involves a fair amount of public self-love and enforced tedium.

NI-DEFTR 36 -   THE BLINK OF A LIFE

The rotgut fulminations of tanned golfing religious criminals curiously redound to the benefit of the micro-left, their blood-sworn enemies. The horrific wars of Iraq and Afghanistan, witless exercises in craven national territorial violence, did not hinder the flow of oil and gas to the energy appetite of the west, liberal and conservative alike. The flow of murder and species extinction and enforced poverty upon the rest of the world to irrigate the fields of televisual leisure for the west ought to have troubled more than a few kind minds, but there was no mechanism to register communal disengagement. Just as criminals are driven to commit terrible acts when in the company of semi-goading others, so do the fair folks of the west keep the malevolent gears of the machine churning through obligations to associative others – the kinds of entrenched lives that will flash by in an alcoholic second.

NI-DEFTR 37 -   HAVING CHILDREN

The enduring power of genetic affiliation explains the continued practice of producing progeny, but from a systemic financial angle, the added burdens unto late age are farcically burdensome. Factoring in day care; the costs of rapidly escalating clothing and footwear; the demands of supplying up-to-date yet semi-controlled technology; the necessity of finding extra bedrooms in functioning school districts; the legal system's concentration upon parents as the source of moneys as well as ultimate responsibility for child misconduct;   the insane increase in unproductive higher education; the costs of summer camps, summer programs, summer daycare; the driving to sports, family events, Sesame Street shows, and Disney World; the constant supply of palatable foodstuffs and trinket-bearing snacks; the health care imbroglios upon any slightly complicated health interventions; the disputations attendant upon any of the fore-mentioned upon spousal affection and attention; and the bill becomes monumental, for each and every child born to parents ensnared within the supersystem's extensive command. There are no forms of discipline that can satisfy the protection of children from the storms of childhood – physical abuse is not on the menu, but "time-out" and conferences and contracts and bribe-rewards and gentle chastisement and adult pleading and grounding do not constitute an arsenal of parental authority, but a pathetic desperation against that time when the first accusation of "bitch" or "asshole" emanates from the emboldened tyke of either gender. Of course there is a new generation of wonder children sensitive to injustice and capable of triumphant sweetness to the parents they cherish and the world they have been so delicately prepared for with sing-alongs and soup-kitchen Thanksgivings volunteering, but they, these top-of-the-line jacobins, are destined for a work-less post-graduation. Good luck to one and all.

NI-DEFTR 38 -   COMMENCEMENT

Successive generations of would-be leftist students have been exhorted to "fight the power," to re-enact the grand theatrical gestures of the long-dead 60s peace protesters. Destroy property, break the law, tie up traffic, get arrested, risk prosecution, talk with self-anointed heroism, live poorly among indigenous grateful charity recipients – don't worry, you are bathed in righteousness, all the 60's rebels ended up fat and rich, curse the Man and get it out of your system before you become him. Going to the jail in the 60s was rite, but now it has gotten serious, expensive, a barrier to future employment, and bad for health, as well a case of being deprived, in rough and stark ways, of the essential condition of liberty. Prison was no joke before, but in the surveillance and computer-record society, it is positively a terror. The destruction of property is not likely to impress the rest of society, and youthful passion has shown the greater capacity to turn into a disavowed past for dentists. Scores of 60s heroes and their fans have delivered homilies and commencement exhortations to successful classroom toadstools urging some form of anti-authoritarian life stance, disregarding the simple enduring fact of power flowing from on high towards those at the bottom. There is no need to rain on any parade, but if you are imagining yourself a one-man band in the grand parade, take a listen to the on-lookers are saying as you go by: "Look at this fool – what a goddam idiot!" Banging your cymbal while pounding the drum, wheezing on the braced harmonica, clacking your knees together and initiating some head noise, doing the endeavor called life all on your lonesome, by yourself, looking out for number one and never being denied, being the best that ever did it and ever will, made Ford tough and the best, a winner and the World's Greatest – that's not what the peanut gallery is saying. You are another holy foolio, lost in your own special world of just you, while others see the need to find some companionship as the supersystem organizes the route. Get out of that ridiculous costume, grab a hold of yourself, come back here with us.

NI- DEFTR 39 -   BETTERMENT

The entertainments kicked out by the supersystem are robust and expansive, continually tested and refined to both excite and reflect the attention of the audience. Whole lives can be lived inside the popular electrons of games, chat, views, gambling, harassing, griping, masturbation, celebrity devotion, hobby partnering, photo-sharing. Cultures of scholarship and religious meditation may be waning for all the most fanatical, but the grand popular election of electrical self-stimulation will only be a successor to these failed obsessions, more time-wasting for a species unable to tend to its territory. Deep thoughts and brave encounters with despair are the birthright of every human, heretofore flourishing in the lower bars and stranger night-time back alleys, where desperate people blow their security out on vices and teary monologues. Since the value of any one person in this supersystem is infinitesimal, these dark moments are as expressive of the human condition as any other, but if a social purpose for humanity returns, there will be much greater reward for smarter living. Blasé above-it-all-ism ruins the baleful screeds of ex-conservatives assaying the denuded intellectual landscape – the supersystem may be a monster, but it has real and terrible effects, infiltrates whole colonies and produces widespread blight and waste, and will be outside the door no matter how hard we refuse to recognize it. Nothing is beyond rational improvement – health care needs a dedicated single payer system, banks needs regulators, elite liberal arts colleges need dissolution, the military industrial machine needs severe disintegration, the safety net needs the beginnings of repair, social truth needs some light, lives can rewarded for righteous toil. So little of that real improvement is augured by the current supersystem, but the right conditions of principle and solidarity can come through the darkness, the glory of social betterment that can produce the next improbable social adaption.

NI-DEFTR 40 -   **OPTIMISM**

Against the pessimism of the theory of the Supersystem is a well-funded cottage industry of Cantabridgian "Rational Optimists," gathered around Tory apologetics campfires by the gated mansions. By the measures of the present against a horrific human past, the lot of humanity is wonderful and getting better, with trade and technological innovation giving the lucky global tribe of today a rosy and tender shine that looks like nothing but sun and flowers ahead. Yes, for some, for that slice of over-privileged applicationists the world has been their oyster – and their pharaohic fortunes have skewed averages towards the positive side, but the over-accumulation for these superstars of advantage is not the proper vantage point to evaluate human social organization. If the proper variable is that of the individual human being, what statistical number can illustrate the unearned suffering by those in the non-elite who have been denied a reasonable share of extracted bounty? What number emphasizes the misfortune of those whose horrid lives have kept the averages from being higher, who were born to near-certain exclusion, lived in the consequences of poverty, and died in avoidable and staggering profusion? In each of the institutions strangled by the supersystem, the theme of "collapse" can be delivered in mainstream books: the collapse of the legal system; of higher education; of health care; of journalism; of public education; of the oceans, of fisheries, of old-growth forests; of foundations and non-profits; of the Peace Corps; of sports and fitness: of agriculture; of energy systems; thousands more to come, needing to replace the theme of "collapse" of a more accurate apocalyptic term from physics. Yet each worthy dissection ends with ten-point plans, with liberal reform proposals, solutions and ways forward to rational social harmony. None have so far rescued any institution nor arrested the speed of collapse, which in all institutional cases has many more miles to go in its grievous implosions. On the other side, where true power lies and performs its daily stupefying functions to prop up the supersystem, the bullshit forms mountains, of incredible texture and command.

NI-DEFTR 41-   THE GAPS

What history or what topic or what cultural artifact or what grand theory of everything will bring you that optimism you are hardwired to expect? What can take your mind off the Troubles? All of us need focus, as well as a focus, a guiding light for this temporal journey across the sands of oblivion. If all ends badly, what good is the prelude, the character development, the wordplay, the exegeses of themes? Even if the scene is buzzing with Information, pouring through every portal as raw data and overviews and memorable experiences and mountainous trivia and dull disharmonious stupidity, the human brain can only process so much before the result is either insanity or cold, hard anger. We want this social reality to work, to keep the hordes relatively contented and the overlords in check, to take care of problems while strengthening human reliability. Yet if the project appears doomed, the drift-away by members will gather rapid momentum and leave only abandoned flotsam. Human life has been beastly during so much of the preceding times- violent, pestilent, brutish, senseless in its operations and lack of rationalism – that to decry the present in its misperformance is to be ungrateful, preoccupied, morose and depressed, unbearable. The gaps between yesterday's social realities and today's are great, of course, and to be saluted with parades and holidays, but the gaps between today's realities and their improvements are equally as wide. Utopia is not ever to be within our reach, but to call our present social institutions functioning or intact is offensive.

NI-DEFTR 42 -   OPERATIONS OF POWER

The dominant ethos of the upper level of the controllers of the supersystem is of fitful expansion, mixed with consolidation and infiltration of powers into all social and individual areas. This constant power grab is not totalitarian nor radical, since it is marked by diffuse and corrupt means that vary widely in levels of intensity and overt misconduct. Governments are large actors beholden to their supervisory cohort: corporations, corporate benefactors, military, military contractors, inherited-wealth patrons or antagonists, banks and investment criminals. The threat of supervision is omnipresent, but regulatory reins are usually far less effective than the exacting whips wielded by the other competing large actors. With a petulant tough-guy mentality animating the little dictators of the assistant vice-president class, the spread of legalized robbery and remote bombing and ruthless business conquest has given us a social reality that manages through language as well as enforced expectation.   Power comes in many forms in social institutions, from militant intimidation to crass hypocrisy, but the results become a mush pile of discarded and thwarted human initiatives.

NI-DEFTR 43 -   TRUTH

Preparations for the apocalypse should accentuate the fun and games we can enjoy along the way. Knowing as we do that death and slow decay are encoded into life's structure, we have to see the limitations to exhortations of constant uplift and transcendent purpose. How much killing are we going to accomplish today, versus how much killing are we going to avoid? What systemic losses are you prepared to accept in the name of furthering your immediate situation? World-weariness, mock despair, depressive monotonal self-focus, blithering anger, vicious inter-personal calumny – where do we as humans think that gets us, where do we think we could be otherwise?   The sorrow is that pity for ourselves is of no value except within our own mental processes, so the better move is to construct massive defenses against imposed entropy – through technology, sex, entertainment, skepticism, habit, and the capacity to engage with the most complex of existential conundrums when given the prompt. The truth is yet to be established, so if the invitation is forthcoming, we can find all the purpose we need.

NI-DEFTR 44 -   HYPOCRISY

The supersystem can run far into the future – decay and collapse may be built into its practices, but those twin forces can last through many phases of global social disintegration. Although the permafrost is melting apace, the over-topping seas may not wipe out the Hamptons until more great fortunes are stolen. In the environmental forecast business, the greatest liability to claims to knowledge are the triteness of the dates: what was true back then is true now, just more so. The jeremiads against the conduct of the industrial arm of the supersystem were written long ago, and the only question about their confirmation is their specificity of actual appearance. Make your calls about the remaining wonders of "creation," see a bright and pristine future appearing through the concerted global elimination of fossil fuels, but that will be a tomorrow that has never existed before, and a past that should never have been. As in every epoch, the cultursphere is that which we know, the standard and judgment of our circumscribed actions, with only variations of hypocrisy attached to all of us: greens who drive and mow lawns; corporate critics with investment portfolios; conservatives with drug habits; professors without intellects; judges without morality; pedophile priests; broken and strained family-heading family therapists; diesel-spewing organic farmers; nice murderers; beautiful alcoholics; manic-depressive geniuses; book-writing nihilists.

NI-DEFTR 45 -   PENALTIES

Humans have thrown off the shackles and blinders of religious irrationalism, in a growing and salutary global movement of atheism. Despite the weight of ecclesiastical power and wealth, far-flung rationalists have cast off this unnecessary limb of pernicious nonsense, in ways that may have only a private independent cognitive process in common. Given the brevity of life and the enormous crises now confounding humanity, no one in this camp needs to study any of the great religious texts or traditions for any reason, least of all to try to convert religious dimwits to skepticism. Why become conversant with the intricacies of fatuous poppycock? We, as a species, cannot begin to justify how those in the global North shall live long and healthy lives with abundant energy stolen from the benighted South, but that is our past and the looming future. Our international institutions, from the United Nations to the World Bank to FIFA, are sad and listing wrecks sailing in circles after their prominent and fanciful beginnings, and will be wholly unreliable in the coming global lurches. Once an entity misperforms in a spectacular and rewarded way, it acquires an ineradicable virus in its core, which animates its subsequent self-aggrandizing ways, so it must be abandoned. Religion, the United Nations millennial programs, the international courts, western political "science" - all fatally compromised, all deserving of dismantlement.

NI-DEFTR46 -   NON-INTELLIGENT DESIGN

No "movement" has ever featured the losing of ground upon conception, the acceleration of more loss during promulgation, and no evident sign of ever arresting the acceleration except through unimaginable calamity, yet the answer to the Supersystem is said to lie in "decommodification," a term that has no physical or historical referent. Where has humanity undone the purchase of death? What gun's bullets, once exploded out of the chamber, return to the chamber? Try to decommodify that which has been commodified, taking out out all of the research and design, the mining and the manufacturing, the transportation, the storage and the delivery, the advertising and financialization of the profits – but there is no product recall on that which has already been commodified, used up, discarded and abandoned to create more complications in its dead stage. What "better world is possible" that incorporates the dull insipidities of the present one? Transitioning to a "sustainable revolution" and new technological forms and adaptability to explosive climate change will certainly preoccupy the sentient followers of the coming long decline, but the intrusions of the lethal powers of the malevolent corporate forms favor disintegration over guidance. With intransigent exploitation marbled into the structure of our social reality, who can see intelligent design looming over incipient crises?

NI-DEFTR47 -   NEGATIONS

No nation is an entity. No government is itself governed by "the people." "We " cannot be "responsible" for that which we did not do. No human being is the sum total of his or her ancestors. No fiction transcends reality. Information of all kinds may have been reduced to bits, but that is a technological process, not a state of being. Humans have no souls, nor a definable "spirit." When the communicative babble of humanity ceases to have a marked impact upon social reality, other human endeavors, though without larger intellectual dimension, seem more apropos. A garden becomes poetry, a motorcycle Proust, stippling on canvas sublime, a child's touch an affirmation from the deity, food ecstasy itself.

NI-DEFTR 48 -   CALL AND RESPONSE

Redistribution of wealth was never going to be an easy task, even if the wealth was stolen in the coldest and most brazen of daylight. Kickback, as in outright theft and retaliation and alienation of rights, from the elites to the misbegotten descendants of the New Deal has been world-definitional, a totalitarian stealth of command of all institutions . The presence of liberal nostrums has aided the brazen class assault of the neo-conservatives, providing the institutional faith in capacity and innate goodness that keeps the courts, the sacristies, the lecture podiums, the shareholder meetings in continuing working mania. This is our known world, where we chase illusions of progress or inevitable positive change as the underlying conditions of myth and operation became over-saturated in mendacious governance advancing the interests of the upper few. Corporations have proven to be spectacular failures in the choice of products, flogging the deleterious products with all the moral command of carnival barkers. This is our civilization, however, the accretion of profit-centered ingenuity into every space of human existence, the car and credit-card world that erected McMansions on every suburban hillside and every broken-down farm. And yet the calls go forward for the cleansing of all, this manumission of mankind from its social reality, the turning of asphalt and concrete into loamy topsoil, the enactment of utopian dreams into the ceaseless horrors of the past – as if we will provide a sweet and sustainable home for all the unknowing and defenseless creatures of the natural disapora, diverting mass extinction of innocent species into salvific and heroic establishment of the eternal rule of rationality. Whatever we can salvage from the looming sequence of catastrophes will be only a fraction of what we could have become.

NI-DEFTR49 -   NOT IN EXISTENCE

To speak of that which does not exist in social reality as being in existence is obscene. To claim that which does not exist will exist without providing specific evidence of antecedents is obscene. If the X that is said to exist, does not exist but its obverse Minus-X exists, then to claim that X will appear belies logic, and is obscenity if repeatedly invoked. The world's warring or competing nations are not going to sign any agreement to curtail practices that establishes massive costs on the powerful.   Not over nuclear weapons, not over commercial trade in lethal weapons, not in destruction of fisheries, not over climate destruction caused by Northern countries' energy demands, not over trans-national corporate extortion, bribery, control fraud, or ecological terror. In no possible logical world are we to see prior restraint of extractive trade. There are no legal frameworks, no political philosophies, no democratic tendencies, no signs of elite reformation, no methods of counter-imperialism, no means of resistance other than dull and contumacious waiting on crises emergence.

NI-DEFTR 50 -   PROPOSALS

Every proposal from the right-thinking side, based on extensive research and deep and lengthy concern, from the reforming of the monetary system into a U.S. Treasury control of the monetary supply, to prosecution of Wall Street gangsters, to public financing of elections, to single-payer, to strict separation of church into completely private, to animal liberation, to labor rights, to non-toxic sex toys, runs into the terrible contemporary control of productive means by its antithesis. Every protest can seem like a last-ditch revolt, exciting the latent desires for triumph by the diehards and the professional optimists, but coalescing into hardened opposition that will go down to another defeat, still determined that to lose with nobility is to gain. Old slogans never die, even as cause after cause resurrecting them suffers ignominy. The onslaught of global warming, caused by the laissez faire corporate energy market system, will appear through a global energy order requiring 55% more energy by 2030 – time for a nice book and poster and lecture on how that's going to go?

NI-DEFTR 51 -   THE LIVES OF DOUBTERS

Pessimists should live long and well, knowing that anxiety-suffused aspiration for dramatic social improvement is small beer. A new kind of "best that we can do" may have to be constructed, where the endless harm that we perpetuate through the attempt to have multiple cakes, even of the smaller variety, along with their somewhat more constrained eating sessions, can be folded into the batter. How are we to sleep otherwise? The science of despair needs its invention, so the better nature of skeptics and malcontents can make its emergence as a viable form of living against the propaganda violence of the re-education camps, the free marketeer pirates, the fake populist Democrats, the real estate quislings and the well-paid gurus of the padded lie. There is nowhere that the truths of ideological antipathy can go, though couples may try to share secrets of resistance.

NI-DEFTR 52 -   BAD REALITY

The supersystem was not built by symbolism, but by cold, hard facts of profit and loss, and yet its opponents think of "imagination" and other symbolic forms as its potent antithesis. This is trivial, when the steel girders of monolithic buildings stand strong in the polluted night of the world's cities, as mentally damaged under-employed cope with various forms of medication to keep their life-affirming machines switched on. Reveries of a post-capitalist future evaporate instantly when confronted with the capitalist present, as fully moronic political approaches receive their latest infusion of social capital from under-exposed self-defeatist natives. No one can escape the implications of current social reality, yet when the details of the supersystemic breakdown are delineated (the on-going sixth great extinction; Wikileaks of governmental deceit; the massively fraudulent Green Scare; record government payments as share of national income), the "radical" or "critic" feels obligated to wrap up with some self-aware promulgation of "hope," as if recited self-assurances will make all the bad signs go away. Hope? Yeah? What specific indices are available to suggest supersystemic redirection towards social betterment? Why see portents of doom and explications of powerful corruption in selected social areas, and then turn away from the stark vision to embrace some fanciful land of vague but enforced comity and enforced justice?

Chapter SIX
LIVING WITHIN the SUPERSYSTEM

Over the course of our Enlightenment out of the muck of ignorance, many thinkers have endeavored to name the dimensions of our social reality, The occupiers of the pantheon, from Plato, Marx, Rousseau, de Tocqueville, Sartre, Shakespeare, Freud, and Goethe, to lesser and sundries, have given us terms, notions, entire philosophies, treatises, whole movements, governments, studies, wars, devotions, cults, and versions of the nature of social reality, but they all have been engulfed and drowned by the mind-deadening ascendancies of the rule of corporate industry, Information, and education. The classical education that would have steeped a callow youngster in the bitter tea of the pantheonistas was moribund by the time the American public high school system absorbed the culture of the 60s, and there was a desiccated version available to others at my ill-chosen college, yet there was nothing that screamed "great insights" to me from the assigned antiquarians. There is not enough time in a human life to become "educated" to whatever fare-the-well the classical pecksniffs set out, yet the world has never ceased to offer instructive "reading." The forebears belong, all belong, to the dear departed past, before the architecture of human social lives became so irreducibly complex by its reach and so maddeningly simplified by the bubble of atomized non-work and anti-politics. Our social reality must be described anew, and as it has become ever more agglomerated and awesome, we have fallen continents behind in our control of it. We lack a working vocabulary for our times, for our social realities, and so we fall ever always back in the quest for a productive knowledge. The loss has been of blood and desire, to the causes of suffering, of omnipresent unhappiness, of stunted or stillborn lives, of humans caught within the terrible maw of the gears of an unaccountable, derelict inter-supportive perpetuation of social institutions.

LWSS 1 -   **INEPTITUDE**

The Supersystem is a superstructure, of course, the architecture of our institutions and traditions that interlock, inter-support, interface, populated by regulated, subservient, observable functionaries, you and I, they and them, the faraway, the unknowable, your masters, your children, your ancestors, your celebrities, your dead and dying. We would like to think our technological change brings us to a New World in each generation, but that is a false vision. Americans have sent men to the moon, but our citizens continue to be sent by the cemetery from starvation and preventable diseases, men and women have found unlivable lives, families have been rent by interpersonal distress, war has been globalized and corporatized, and rage-filled boredom has washed o'er the fruited plains. How could such a technologically sophisticated people produce such a wondrously harmful and inept social reality, where corporations evade nearly all prosecution, millionaire idiots spew obvious propaganda and racist drivel, and the good folks sit and shovel it all in to their bilious maws?

LWSS 2 -   **FREE MARKET PROGRESS?**

In argument against the tSS, the likely foundation is the "Invisible Hand" theory of "free markets," which asks humanity to trust its innate goodness, its natural drives and unregulated outcomes. Look at the immensity of the Supersystem, it asks, which has been erected in roughly 200 years after 150,000 of hunter-gatherer bare subsistence. How can we gainsay the Great Leap Forward from eating maggot meat and pushing sticks into game to gold sinks for truck drivers, all in a recent evolutionary eyeblink? I only ask that we apprise out social reality, measure its dimensions much more accurately, and begin to start distributing the riches of a technological masterworld with new standards of relative fairness. How can we have fallen so far behind this requirement, when the TV and the AM radio promised such a sweet and winnable world right after the helicopters fled Saigon? Who could have foreseen such a train wreck of an empire when the girls were so beautiful, the nights so long, the demands so trivial?

LWSS 3 -   TRUTH

What we think strongly today may evaporate tomorrow, though this truism is also what provides the enduring strength of the supersystem, its durability in its immensity. Thankfully for the human species, we act only rarely on the dictates of our consciences, or else every wrong by another would be met with the canceling seriousness of violence. As humans, we do retain some faith in the power of our minds to arrive at universal truths and rational purpose, despite the terrifying power of historical forces to deny rights and hopes for suffering others. Abortion, for example, has kept its passionate defenders and tenuous viability in a society in love with its non-existent ideals of "respect for life." The supersystem, with its protection for "biblical teachings" and various other fictions, has caused poor women to sacrifice their sexual freedoms, their chances for economic improvement, their health, their minds, for the sake of an illusory "sanctity of life," yet many women also have overcome their lack of access to birth control to have safe and respectable abortions.

LWSS 4-   REVOLUTION?

No critic of the supersystem can call for immediate wholesale change in the form of the purifying specter of revolution, since such social change has brought calamity and genocide much more than   liberation. From the French Revolution to the Cuban Revolution to Bolshevism, rapid social evolution has been enforced with mass murder rather than tolerant re-adjustment. Can you really say you know how a better social reality will function, across the similar breadth to the religion-and-fear dominated supersystem? You have enough trouble dealing with the absurdities of your own personal familial lives – can you imagine how you might reorder the individual lives of an entire swath of your inherited society?

LWSS 5-   WAR AND ANGER

The impenetrability of the supersystem causes social rage. Grown men and women have suffered from a diffuse anti-social anger throughout human history, even while sitting on baubles and riches, but the removal of social supports and constraints has engendered a new level of consummate antipathy.. Intense inner explosions of focused hatred, of the kind that can issue fatwas towards public targets in e-mails, or stoke road rage, or animate bar fights, or fuel money battles, or push men towards suicide, or blow pulmonary gaskets, or let loose bizarre waves of personal workplace animus, don't generally tend to be well-received by proximate loved ones. The task of every human mind is to find 1) reservoirs of personal reliance and 2) rivers of happiness. The pollution promulgated by the supersystem will befoul these two purposeful waters, will have the multitudes pursuing noxious and pathetic means for escape.   Others may see others' avenues of release as cheap, meretricious, or lame, but I am prepared at any moment to give them, the pornographic, sexual, pop cultural, country gentlemanly, televisual, sports, metaphysical, or sub-cultural enthusiasm, an intellectual defense. The supersystem is killing untold numbers of people, destroying the planet, hurting the box office of performance art plate jugglers, and keeping us from appointment TV with "King of Queens" reruns unto perpetuity, but we settle for manufactured consensual non-debate. Embittered solons spittle out hardened antipathies for the approval of their subalterns, who repeat versions in turn to their own sub-subalterns. For all of the talk and the chatter, we began bombing back in World War I, and have not risen from this primordial social violence.

LWSS 6 -   EDUCATION

Butts have been planted for far too long in America's classrooms. They have been attached to chairs for lectures, bolted to support cushions for monotone speeches, anchored to plastic cupping devices for "training," an adult workplace re-enactment of the somnambulant play of kindergarten. . From nursery school through all the grades, into college, and then into graduate school, and then into work, it is a puritanical way of sitting and holding , holding urinary urges, holding the demons at bay, while the accursed the Other holds forth. The alternative is not every fool spouting off with his or her own version of hermetical spewage, but *interaction*, amplification as revolutionary as the electronics of popular music.   If every social institution can be proved to be irretrievably corrupted and functionally deleterious, why do we chase reform rather than dissolution? Gradualism and amelioration leave the powers that be as the powers that will be, only stronger in their adaptability.

LWSS 7-   SOCIAL ISOLATION

As a major point against this line, it can be fairly argued that prescriptions on why and how to remake the entire known human social world should not come from an individual who has avoided that roiling sea of human intercourse. Because the supersystem was so evidently dominant and impenetrable and devolving to me at an early age, I fell into social isolation early, though there were also a few thousand personal traits and circumstances that contributed to my outward trajectory from birth. Each of us is dedicated a certain slice of social reality, and we make our constrained choices for our individual happiness within those regulated parameters. I could place my body in front of a departing military bomber tomorrow, but either I get run over or I do a jail stretch, and the supersystem rolls on. I could give away all my money, go as green as a salamander, or refuse to pay taxes, or become a Dilaudid addict, and feel all the worries of my petulant life disappear into the pharmacological ether, but the universe has not a single care for any of our complaints. Within the liberal democratic paradigm, powerless individuals are made to feel guilty over their inability to effect momentous social change, with that chastening guilt further dampening the individual's inclinations towards skeptical opposition to elite control. In a political system dominated by corporate swaths of money and disseminated theocratic supineness, the voter is bar-tapping rodent fool, even the "progressive" politicians captives of the diseased imperial fascism. Our great remaining power in the face of the dismal supersystem is *disassociation*, to separate from the enduring yet hollow and corroded institutional structures that will govern us the rest of our lives. American politics is afflicted with a nativist strain of violent and repellent conservatism, which rules the road, invades the classrooms, permits the waging of global militarism, targets homosexuality, denigrates love and sex, and kills nature in its name.

LWSS 8-   EDUCATION AS SOCIAL PANACEA

Because the supersystem obviates meaningful work, the trope of *education* was flung around as a corrective panacea to all our ills. Paleo-conservatives insisted on education as the marker of refinement that would permit them to devour the continents with rapacious imperial capitalism, but liberals force-fed the masses the same simulation of refinement while denying them jobs, homes, legal rights, tax representation, post-natal day- or home-care. A classroom became the storage container for all of post-war America, forcing the unusual, artificial theatrics of seat-bound sublimation to stand in for the dynamism of modern life- promoting idle disengagement, covert disenchantment, rude behavior, autistic overlording, generational distrust, odious entitlement. For all of its "democratic" promise, the American classroom was where liberal hopes for the Great Society met the limits of an economy without work, and produced the criminal strivers of the CEO and hedge fund classes.

LWSS 9-   A NEW HIGHER ED

With the death of "higher" education, fatally compromised at birth by its religious dictates, and overcome after a brief ascendancy in it's 60's youth by its pro-corporate order careerism, a new form of advanced education is demanded:

1.   There are no direct financial or research ties to the Pentagon or major global corporations. There is no endowment invested in stocks connected to these enterprises. All research done by the faculty is self-supporting, or funded by blind research trusts that obligate nothing on the part of the researcher.

2.   There are few tests, contestable grades, and students work and live in community. Entertainment is pursued outside of the course of study, allowing for no credit for art, music, dance, language, or sports.

3.   There is no tolerance for "balance" from nascent ideologues – standards of conduct and thought are minimal, yet enforced. Students or faculty or staff who are in personal crisis or who follow rancid conservatism are dropped, given other venues to chase their errant demons.

4.   The courses of study are determined by the important contemporary needs of society. No honorary degrees are given, minimal applications precede entry, no meetings are mandated for faculty.

LWSS 10 -   WORK

Living within the supersystem dictates a resistance to grandiloquence, self-rapture, veneration of tradition, and a disinterest in work. Those who find a cause, a calling, a valued place in the vaunted demimonde of remunerated obsequy, are to be commended, but since the intra-connections are so strong, only the fundamentals are worth attacking, and you cannot get at them. Every facet of the supersystem is protected by arcane, voluminous, and resilient bonds of deceptive history. And for every necessary change, there are corresponding areas of opposite action that will instantly activate. After the rockstar prominence of the 60's "left," American culture could have become dominated by this enfranchised triumph of humanistic concern, but economic fears and mythic antipathy towards losing station prompted a hugely financed promotion of moral violence. The average lot of the average person has improved in slight terms across this post world-war globe, but the lost hopes of global betterment are numbered in infinitude, in the on-going perpetuation of a global supersystem with such blatant killing of promise. When Ronald Reagan became president, all the bile and enmity and vacuous anti-intellectualism of the republic became terminal. There has not been a moment in America since that terrible reign that has not been tarnished by the effects of his disastrous coronation.

Working with humans has been a necessary compromise since the days of the caves, made worse by the enforced proximity of the workplace. Others have found genuine companionship from these thrown-together assemblages of wage-seeking marvels, but humans are frayed units of aggravation, buried ill-judgments, sinister fantasies, and jealous disturbance - it is a wonder we do not attack and kill each other on sight. In the declining workplace of the modern American exurban corporation, private enmities have been buried as each day's successful negotiation of disparate loathings give way to the pleasures of paycheck niceness.

LWSS 11-   OUR CONTEMPORAY NATURE

Humans of all stripes have become collaborators, informants, back-stabbers, collusionists, bystanders, oppressors, occupiers, fantasists, robbers, racists, dupes, doomed revolutionaries, tyrants, dead civilians, beaten protesters, and deserters, all due to the monumental interplay between human need and fear. Where you find yourself today in that list is irrelevant, because no one is really checking, but the quantity of human suffering engendered by the supersystem is of eternal significance, and today's numbers are bad, and not heading up...

LWSS 12 -   A DIAGRAM

The supersystem is not the clichéd Venn diagram of bad 70's English assignments, because there is no central planning authority, no bunker cabal in constant communication. We can think of our individual institutional systems as circles, not closed, of course, but permeable circles, large and commanding, that are coursed through with amoeba-like common substances. Give these common amoebas a color scheme, and see how each of institutions is infiltrated with invisible but similar structures. This pictorial depiction of power's commands should alert the human race to how little influence rationality and human interest have in the conduct of our affairs. Economic inequality, worldwide poverty, genocide, and bad TV are not unrelated, and have color-coded similar viruses operating in their nuclei. Though this metaphor is from a light backpack, there should be much work on this *color-coded representation of power's invisible logics.*

LWSS 13 -   PURCHASING

The smallness of the consumer life is matched by the daily largeness of the supersystem, where since "everything is related," in the true cliché, nothing adds up. For example, your beer is most likely swillish brine that rummies do their vomit warm-ups with, but its being advertised as cold-filtered means that the chemicalized brew is shot through with cold molecules, near-frozen with blue purity, while their shit is put through a bubbling, mephetic cauterization process. Corporate products can taste mighty fine, always partly due to the naming ritual that permits you, the buyer, to become self- distinguished from the rabble of non-buyers. At the moment of the incorporation of the product into your physical system, you are Coors and not Coors, and thus an activated account, not an atomization. It is your beer, your purchase and your purchase on reality, but you will drink that jetsam extract and then move on too quickly to the next branded moment, so you become an obliterated, overstamped product, unknowable even to yourself. Sometimes a cigar is just a cigar, but without the naming, the molecules all float by, without order, without shape. A corporate logo promises reliability, knowledge, innovation, uplift, the obverse of the kind of confusion engendered by our common nouns of family, brother, loyalty, democracy, hope. Within the supersystem, I am Sony, Amazon, my electricity bill, my social security card, etc., all the infinitesimal disturbments of the global economic grid apparatus that can be said to be mine, caused by me, unlike every other natural or conceptual state or environ that will never betray the sufferance of my presence. in charge of skyscrapers. .

LWSS 14-   NO REGULATION

The economy must be run on regulation, but our constructions of regulation are enfeebled, collapsing, over-run with ineffectualism, or outright criminal Although there is not much fortune in documenting the actual machinations of the institutional elite, reporters and apostates have penetrated to a few inner rings, where the great terrors of our age, Northrup-Grumman, Monsanto, the Supreme Court, Congress, Wal-Mart, AOL, Exxon, Coca-Cola, Philip Morris, Google, and a thousand others have plotted and interpolated. There is no great secret here: many books, well-chosen, have testified to the common deteriorations and corruptions that has hollowed out our social institutions: trade unions, courts, schools, colleges and universities, humanitarian interventions, families, medicine, electoral politics, food, housing. Uniting these "developments" is the relentless drive towards remunerated power slaughtering putative regulation: The prosecutors and auditors, the evaluators and the reviewers, are paid a fraction of their prey, have no abiding social ethic of regulation to stiffen their resolves, are given no charge or honor by a hostile public. These bureaucrats of the governmental slowdown have lives and mortgages that depend on their pro forma performance of their constricted, and predominately enemy-affiliated jobs, but a true reformer or radical would be cashiered soon in the Washington or state capital miasma.

LWSS 15 -   INTERNET FEUDS

In the world of ideas, the belles lettres, Internetic instaneity has allowed all new sorts of obstreperousness to over-erupt. Because of the false comfort the screen provides the sole typist against the imaginary world of real humans, exchanges of opinion soon degenerate into flailing attacks on the interlocutor's person, being so easy to do, and emanating from a presumed command of the heights of selfhood by proprietorship of the keyboard. Edifying immediate recriminations between circling antagonists are occasioned by the laboratory of the comments and forum and listserv domains, made worse by the limited ability to *explain* through the medium of the unedited typed sentence. Boasts of superior knowledge, of pure integrity, of bestial disdain for lessers, of cyclonic hatred, of immensity of social effect, are floating across the cybersphere, aimed at abstractions, screen names, the real unknown.

LWSS 16 -   FEAR

The Supersystem is not a perfect and closed system. It does not interlock precisely, was never designed or fashioned according to blueprints, but has acquired its monumental power through the accretion of human institutional and individual action. Fighting the terrible illogic and inhumanity of the supersystem is doomed because *that which we fear the most is that which we detect as latent in ourselves*. Men fear homosexuality, kill to suppress it. Peaceful folk fear the violence that lies subsumed by the overlay of civilization. Humans fear the death that is but yet to be activated within each of our cells. The rich fear revelation of their base ineptitude. Humans fear entrapment and purposelessness, so deny the structures that encircle them.

LWSS 17 - LIFEBLOOD

An image is needed for this mysterious source of institutional outcomes 1976-2010: the lifeblood, or else the intestine. Central inside the workings of all, this red string of gristle was beating, steadily, engorged, animating the corpus with its commands to seek exceptional individual standing. While others slept, while others prevaricated or dreamed, while the mass of men, women and children followed the available paths to expanding livelihood in their found environs, this dominant neuro-biological length of organic muscle grew and hardened. Go to work, it ordered, buy that car, put on that suit, push that button, follow that blueprint, flatter that boss, elect that simpleton, imagine greater sex, fire that worker; collude, conspire, and die. This is not some poetic flight of fanciful immaterialism: there was cellular, DNA-level instinct afoot during these years, uniting all of these worldwide players in a new game of financialized acquisition. The science of this statement may be suspect: this book is the product of a decidedly sub-standard scientific training. A person can only rise so far above his or her socially determined education, and in the bubble of TV America, science was nowhere on the prime-time schedule. However, operating in the crepuscular doom, we should have seen that this social organism has always been operating during humanity's existence, adapting to and exploiting its developing conditions, now interpenetrating the domains of technowar, psychobabble, inter-psychic distress, capital formation. We will never know a selfhood in which that solid strand of fear-based striving does not throb mightily, but there can very well be fashioned a governing superstructure of authoritative regulation, if only in theory.

LWSS 18 - ENTRAPMENT IN THE CAGE

Criticism of the current social reality should not imply that the critic is not benefiting from it. Far from it: any human being endeavors to maximize his or her experience of pleasure and comfort from extant circumstances. I cannot self-impose an external system of reward and punishment that others are not governed by. I know that my life is not "sustainable," since no one else will live it but me, Liberals have interrogated themselves mightily over their post-war spoils, and may indeed have had dark nights of the soul, but the residual guilt is paid with a donation or two, with the added prize of self-ennoblement. Since we are but tiny balls of protoplasm in the void, destined to burn brightly and die off soon, there is no moral worth to our lives, but there is moral worth to supersystem. With the fallacies of "free markets" and "democracy" and "god" coursing through a highly unequal political economy, we are, as individuals, unable to counteract the false language of the supersystem. The sparks of culture attest to our remaining capacity to sing despite our entrapment in the cage, but we cannot speak to each other of the real political conundrums.

LWSS 19 - PLUSSES

Within the supersystem, there is much that works at a sophisticated, complex, admirable fashion. Products are shipped to buyers with Prussian efficiency. Families re-enact cultural myths to evident satisfaction. Entertainment technology distributes the riches of popular art to increasingly rapt masses. The skyscrapers stand, the worries of yesterday are supplanted by today's supersystemic motions. Individuals of limited technical competency are surrounded and encouraged by extremely reliable technical systems that provide constant electrical stimulation. Good times! Unlike the primitivists of today, I cannot ask us to return to the Garden. The indigenous tribes made their naturo-centric ways according to the social structures that they inherited, but we are a few concrete bucketfuls too late to re-invigorate their basketcraft. Our social reality is measured by the adjustments of now almost tens of billions humans, not by a few radical simplicity devotees. Though there are countless movements against the direction of the supersystem, and speeches in your town tonight and tomorrow inveighing against our destructive modern ways, there is no reason to see *positive social change* in the pipeline.

LWSS 20 -   SUBURBAN AMBITION

You and I have been hot to create, to make art, to be insightful, to be fruitful in the wholesale changeover of this molten planet, but ecause of cruel sexual mores, most likely we wasted a good deal of our youth not having the sex our libidos were capable of enjoying. Though our minds were bursting with interests, society channeled the grand intellectual quest into TV devotions; recherché computer speculation; classroom, and religious duty; sundry annoyances and frustrations. We do not drive, do not consume, do not wear our affordable stylish athletic wear, do not sit in plush carpeted classrooms, do not decry injustice within our circle of friends and family, without the historical process of deceitful mass killing of foreigners. As a species, we are borne of hunt and cowering survival, have raided and appropriated territory without surcease – and now we want a just a peaceful world, all of this sudden? Ah, yeah, we do – none of this amateur sociobiology is necessarily our destiny. We have been relentlessly trounced and marginalized, us allegedly *non-violent* and protected ones, and have no record of institutional command to run on. Some terrible institutions, like war and prisons, may never be run with gentle toleration and integrity, and the recent softening of outright rape and torture to its present more bureaucratically protected operation of steel incarceration is not any great achievement. We have given up fashioning barriers against our more widely documented tendencies of oppression, but are hollowing out further the husks of regulation that remained from the Enlightenment. Why persist further with this approach of positivist "reform" that has so clearly been a failure to gain power?

LWSS 21-   THE BACKWARDS LOOK

Historians can document the real contemporary security that middle-class America derives from humanist struggles – shortened work-weeks, civil rights, secular tolerance, running water, ubiquitous electricity, and cheap entertainment. Yet we do not live in the past, and we as a species do not live in constant appreciation for our relative betterment. America's record may be the great betrayal of democratic ideals, or it may have been off on only a couple of matters like slavery, post-slavery genocidal racism, or imperial militarism while giving working people a dishonest shake otherwise, but history cannot clear the path to righteousness, because it is dead. Horrors have been perpetuated all over this globe, by humans, animals, and plant forms alike, and if you think you have a proper understanding of the full dimensions of all of the depravity, how jaunty is your walk past the garbage dump? Individuals have obligations to learn what lies under their feet, and to conduct their lives hewing to some fairly subtle principles, but feeling pain or embarrassment or frustration is only a predilection, not an imperative. Better to see where the supersystem is heading than to look back at the wake.

LWSS 22 -   **LIFE IN THE DEPTHS**

"Progressives" now write "i-petitions" to rulers who employ a phalanx of lackeys to delete and delete some more. CEO's, managers, and politicos are practiced in the arts of denying outside noise in their psychic sanctum sanctorum, and do not respect the chaste little chastisement from unenfranchised malcontents. Fear, of the elemental kind, is what can move the elite of the supersystem, or else they will persist in obeying the commands of the central lobbies. I too will respond with alacrity to fear, and am incapable of bringing fear to these global masters, so we are left with news made by untouchable functionaries. From reading stalwart historians of the covert American shadow government, I know that there have been covered-up crimes of military aggression and terrorism perpetuated by unreachable conspiracies in the US, like Operation Gladio in reality, Operation Northwoods in design, coups and wars from the Philippines to the Dominican Republic. What you do with such "information" – it wasn't me, it wasn't you, it won't be me, it won't be you, right? Imagine one of us as the lead judge in the Global Truth & Reconciliation hearing: what is to be the punishment? What do we gavel as the new reality? Why were we, alone of the 7 billion, chosen to be the Arbiter of All History? Steeped in ancient wisdom, raised to pantheonic heights by tutelage and obsessive study, we can only aspire to keep our heads down, away from the spotlight, where life clings in tenacity to the shards of light that penetrate the fathoms.

LWSS 23 -   **SETTLING IN**

Hedge fund multimillionaires are unbowed by the great financial collapse of 2007-8, building lakefront mansions in the tens of millions for a couple of weekends of actual inhabitation per year. The super rich are headed for emboldened lives of mutant privilege, abetted by the fealty of the feeder system of fee-charging drones. There are many realities, all conforming more or less to a prevailing support of financial power, but do you want me to give you the lowdown on how to place your life against this enfolding madness? You may have enjoyed some of the money you made, you may cherish the creation of your Jesus children and their on-going embodiment of your ideals, you might sit back in your throne and call your life blessed, and it was as a "celebrant" at a local church that many newly deceased elderly Americans have had their lives eulogized, but you will need to reach your own encrusted self-comfort. Like the last hounds of the night, you will lick your wounds and contemplate tomorrow's next chase, or tomorrow's chase of you, curling your tail around your back paws as you settle into the remaining topsoil – were you predator or prey?

LWSS 24 -   **CI**

"Family? Work? Nihilist Needs Mate – Finds." Within every human life, there is a central irony (CI), at least one huge, highly remarkable, irrefutable contradiction of action and principle, though often surrounded by competing major ironies (MI's). Though our lives may appear dull and insipid, seized by predetermination and listless repetition, they are, to a man or woman, stuffed with flux and action, highly contingent at the individual level, and thus open to cataclysmic splits. History does a very poor job of recording the CI, does a fair job of finding MI's for public figures, and yet leaves us forever convinced of our personal integrity. Since the supersystem is beset by such internal, structural rot, there are no end of CI's and MI's to our time and leaders, but irony is no feast. Shall we castigate our accursed cultural enemies across our libations and drugs at hand to our acquaintances, while these same enemies gather in greater numbers to lob cultural derision at us and all that we represent? Shall we construct bibliographies of all the false theories of our age, and keep stoking the fires of resentment toward eternal human folly?

LWSS 25 -   DENS

In a time of atomization, this stalemate of cultural enmity means that we steep ourselves in what disturbs us. We are not a communal species, have too great a capacity for simmering dislike of our intimates who hunted or gathered too incompetently for our tastes yesterday, yet should not need catastrophes to discover communitarian ecstasy. Adulthood has guaranteed a fortnightly retreat to the den for those great unvarnished and undocumented men and women of the post NBC/CBS suburban corral, as they were taken away, from the massively humdrum of their immediate encirclement. but there may be other venues for your intense distrust of the dimensions of the common western obligatory lucre-chase. What could we be looking for from the beat, the silver screen, the mockumentary, the political expose, the blog post, the sacristy, the incantation, the family dinner, the growing of plants, the walks in the park, the Internet start-up, the departmental meeting, the wakeboarding professionals, the pretty female mathematicians, from the hallowed pastimes and fabled commonplaces of cultural over-ambition? If we have written someone off, why do we keep returning to their cave?

LWSS 26 -   THE BOUNTY

Thirty years, as children, we were given the greatest of all bounty, a popular culture that gave us good times, great oldies, and afternoon specials. The roads were paved, the malls made, the TV signals strong and global, the social nexus of the local high school enfranchised. The beat was on, everywhere, from 409 to pick-up truck to the absurd suburban nirvana of "makin' love in my Chevy van.." A society built on bluenose religion shredded all the lust, fun, laughter, dance, mild ribaldry, ubiquitous party hearty reality in favor of a brittle censoriousness that flirted with the alternative inheritance of licentiousness ? Our social problems have nothing at all to do with our *culture*, which is now precisely what you can make it to be, since it is available at low cost to nearly everyone. Our *culture* is capacious, delimited by the fallacious strictures of advertising and mass taste operations, but a marvel of near ubiquity. Would you rather be a 1643 serf, looking at animal entrails for your night's entertainment? Would you want a 1971 afterschool hour of only The Mike Douglas Show? You, the discerning rebel, the singular receptor of the zeitgeist, will and must find your panoplies amidst the Hollywood excess, and that cultural selectiveness will carry you through the stages of decline and senescence

LWSS 27 -   IN THE CENTER

Poets and artists avoid the supersystem, because it represents something so much greater than their efforts. Politicians and parents fain never to make mention of it, as if it represented the atoned sin of humanity, and political scientists are loathe to see it, since it offers no hope of specialized observation. We have built marvelous cities capable of astounding transportation of continental masses of people, but we have yet to see the superstructure as it operates us. To be alive within it we become a reactive, interrogatory people, who can read and think and opine, but who are mute in the production of honest expression of exasperation at the reigning strictures.

LWSS 28 -   TALK

In the same way that fully domesticated suburban dogs, tens of thousands removed from the primordial savannah, kick dirt back upon their shit in the yard, we humans persist in innumerable unnecessary ancient rituals that have outlived their usefulness by eons. For example, we talk to each other, though we have nothing much greater to say to each other than the humming of toads that either warned of predators or boasted of virility. We as humans, however, stand ready to do, to act, to engage, in ways that can directly assure our common survival, just as we did back in the antediluvian plains. What does the human world need from us? Not small kindnesses, not recessive meekness, not the marks of a well-fed, protected life, but activity to a general purpose greater than recumbent incoherency. And yet the social world will not produce that evident need for social viability of individual human competence unless cataclysm erupts.

LWSS 29 -   LOVE

Companionship does not accrue through choice alone, or even choice primarily, but through workings of enormous and great unfathomable happenstance. You may find it, somehow, through irretrievable and minute meanderings and real, brave leaps, and then it will be yours, never in total, always tenuous, but more than sufficient to make all else seem empty or less. Once in love, that state is yours forever, whether in memory or in deepening, hand-in-hand, side-by-side stroll through the descents of the modern era.

LWSS 30 -   POPULAR ART

Sitting, listening, watching, and not objecting are the default condition of western civilization. I know that I cannot undue all the ignorance that I excused within myself, from the ridiculous worries about missing church that would result in bad events, to the unearned faith in my native country's native goodness. After the consolidation of mass culture in 1971, I took a ride on the American fun express, watching pro-war anti-war Hollywood/Boulder movies, reading spiritless liberal histories of American innate inevitability, all strained through my particular limitations, imposed or self-generated. In earlier works contending with the awesome command of the supersystem, I cataloged the bits of pop particulate, the actual, downloadable, pop concoctions of the moment, but that minor critical rack-jobbing is not a serious contribution, just mere reportage that could be easily flipped past for the real celebrity drug lowdown. Beyond-grown men and women persist in fashioning novels, screenplays, book and movie reviews, class assignments for the mediocre junior high school that can never be escaped. Made in the U.S.A., the quadrillionth production of a package of mass produced art, open to the air for an instant before it flows back into the overburdened, toxic landfill. There is good, there is great, there is bad, there is you, there is that elixir that can get you through the existential pain, there is that which you can feast upon and turn into your own MacArthur Prize, or millions, or tenure, there is that emphatic newness that you cannot imagine living without, but in being the product of an assembly process in a manufactured world, there is obsolescence and insubstance in every last one. Of course, all this oxygenation applies to this, but no matter, with the supersystem the only salient project is *what's next*.

LWSS 31 -   **TV**

Whatever your life, if above the bare subsistence level, you can find explosions, encounters, or explorations of epochal transcendence each and every night. No one should pay attention to your little nightly pleasures, nor think too deeply about the significance of your celebrity heroes, but you will be able to reject the enormity of existential despair quite easily. There may be a lack of money that keeps you from the next great entertainment purchase, but keep at it, that glorious state of visual techno-saturation should someday be yours. You have every right to surround yourself with the bathos of ritual entertainment, as it will accompany you as you age, the soundtrack and TV listing of your life unto your death. We will be the first cradle-to-grave television generation, knowing so little about our fellow humans compared to our constantly reinvigorated affinity for animated characters. In our last moments, we will reach for the clicker -or the nano-sized last version of it - with our gnarled fingers, finally unable to complete the last switch to our last hope for escape from the awful boredom of the communicated egos of our familiar humans. The screen will go on, unswitched.

LWSS 32 -   **SENSE**

Did you make sense of the strips of printed bytes of information that came your way today? A thousand clicks; a thousand different routes for investigation; a cornucopia of books, magazines, and newspapers; an onslaught of e-mail, text messages, chats, and phone numbers; but one decision away from you, every second of your non-working or non-observed life. You may narrow this deluge to several hardened paths that conform to your neural grooves, but you will always be on the hunt, yet always not know what to do with the incoming messages, be forever overtaxed by the task of turning your hesitant understandings into productive engagement. You will likely see confirmations of the supersystem's expansive reach and intransigence, now, as the latest news of the day slips through your personalized transom. That improvement in your cognitive operation will not, however, directly translate into ideas for new actions for your life. What should you join, protest, disdain, invoke, or turn towards? If you are American, *you will not have the time*, you will tell yourself. You have assignments, you have obligations, you must prepare for the next demand, you have too much to do, the next hour is spoken for, the kids need to be picked up, the house is a mess, what does the world want from me, I can only do so much, the economy s getting tight, the boss is a jerk, nobody understands me anyway, who is this clown to think he is better than me. In the meantime, the institutional players are refining their concrete aspirations. The corporations are discarding competitive fissures around them as you sink into your easy chair. Prayer cells are meeting; lawyers are arranging further codifications to the avenue to greater profit. If the sun sets on one gang of elite thieves and genocidal delusionists, lower-order cabals are forming in the pressurized vents of the evermore polluted ocean of global commerce. The young become the old.

LWSS 33 -   **BEAUTY**

Didn't the exaltation of beauty preoccupy the Romantic poets, the Impressionists, and the bards of the wilder West? Did we drive that notion into the ground of our American asphalt, smother it with soft-focus mocking depictions of natural wonder in suppository TV commercials? Where in our commuting after work to snowed-in mall parking lots do we see beauty? In the freezing-rain slowed highway of the North, drink and familial complaint seem the season's bounty. Not all life can express precoital rapture, but there are some happy party folks swaying in a seaside cabana, laughing at the sunset and toasting the joy of impending sexual congress. Our modern sensibilities are too refined to be bought off with televisual images of "The World's Greatest Hotels and Beaches," as empty waiting rooms for tanning salons in skid-row northeast cities testify to the dyspeptic condition of the snowbound working class. All of us, miser to pedant to petulant moron, need to have the world's known beauty made more plentiful, given accord, and integrated into a fully modern digital lifestyle. A more pressing issue is to finally get some purchase on an ethical supersystem, but a far likelier outcome is for a Happy Meal for tomorrow's diabetic.

LWSS 34 -   PORNOGRAPHY

Have there been advanced thinking humans who have swum with unalloyed purpose in the pure sea of their own cognitive pleasure? A section of my brain expects to sit in front of the afterschool TV, see the pathos of *The Courtship of Eddie's Father,* and anticipate its replication in some nightly familial drama. Once your male brain had been repeatedly excited by the tableau of Adrienne Barbeau, it could not be programmed to prompt salivation at the thought of scholarly submissiveness. Intellectuals now must contend with the fingertip cornucopia of all-every porn, the the hidden forbidden lusts omni-available for the furtive fantasy boulevardier .   The panting, the seated self-assigned walk on the wild side into the private circus of constantly available secret delights, competes with the more sedate and less frequent desire to read intensively. The prior dystopia of censorious centralized discouragement was a frustration to active imagination, but the current version is throwing all it can at the socially inept. Athletic nudity and boundaries-shredding sex are an incredible bounty for all concerned, but the rest of entertainment needs to shed its inhibitions just to command a look. Frivolous, enraging, boring, supercilious, or pathetic, political philosophy must be drained of its jargon and placed back on the conversational agenda.

LWSS 35 -   AMERICAN ARHCETYPES

The cycles of obedience, rebellion, and profit-chasing have worn grooves into post-WWII America, familiar male archetypes always getting their decade's updating: the hippie, the NASCAR shitkicker, the Fu-Manchu'd sports working guy, the well-heeled gardener, the Village People of basic sociology. Not one of these folks gets a morning briefing from Command Central in their piezoelectric cochlear implant, outlining the conspiracy of action and inaction that predetermines the conduct of our minor-ring fellows. Instead, from birth to senility, ego, ambition, and fear drive recumbent tinypants into socially-available roles. The people of the top, the elite, also are not prone to sinister conspiracies of open diabolical control, but operate much more often with socially promoted impunity. Great disparity comes from the onslaught of commingled instincts and imperatives that promotes those in power, especially the most psychically damaged ones, when countervailing social institutions fail or do not exist. Moral responsibility is just a vacuous abstraction – those whose inner failings prompted business inclinations did incalculable damage, none of which can ever be taken back, repaired, or compensated for.

LWSS 36 -   CONTINUITY

We know the bodies are now dead, disintegrating, or back as atoms of this ceaseless universe. Our beating, well-worn lives are circumscribed by the choices we made, the choices we didn't make, and the choices a collective other have made for us. This or that proposal would make a better world for a great majority of us, but stands no chance in a power-sorting machinery that respects continuity of ideas rather than good ideas. Jobs bring families, mortgages, car payments, and once they go, like in the Christmas season of 2008, the supersystem has no supports to keep those major commitments afloat in the absence of replacement work. We Americans are prepared to lie to keep our economic gains afloat, will fain to smile and joke with loathsome dunderheads just because they come along with the job, will see boredom out to the bitter end if it means the continuance of that paycheck. None of us are covered in glory in what we do for work, even if it is running the most selfless nonprofit, since we are tied in innumerable immediate bonds to the sustaining of dumb, brutal, and horrific institutional practices. When work is taken from us, for what look like impersonal or specious reasons, we see in bold relief the inhumanity of the supersystem, but if work and degree of faint economic security appears, we are in danger of losing the lessons, and shifting our preference to a monstrosity that is shifting to crush untold others. Our adult needs are so dependent on this beast, we forget its chains around our feet, our neck, and around the loved ones around us.

LWSS 37 -   GREEN BUSINESS

How do we fight against that which has proven to be our nature? Green jobs, working with the unjustly disposed to regain their due dignity, building and organizing through sustainable leadership; reforming institutional structures to better reflect and perpetuate humane and ethical transformative practices. Standing on the shoulders of giants to grasp through better technology to reach the promised land of informed stewardship. Creating efficiency and value via the promotion of real-time in-kind dialoguing with clients. The voice to combat this 00's madness is inaudible from the American plantation. Who publicly denigrated the entire masscult of MBA's, hip corporatism, the business-minded imbeciles that steered the American economy right into a wall? A few cranks and gasbags, a couple of basket cases, but outside, in the vast daylight, the billions kept on piling up into the waiting arms of these tyros and mountebanks, your neighbors and mine. The jobs were there, the profit was available, the exploitation of truth and integrity was as easy as preparing Minute Rice in a microwave.

LWSS 38 -   YOUR LIFE

Where are the legal initiatives? Where is there a political policy of note? Why will we have avalanches of books about the Bush years, and the "economic crisis of 2008," and 750 other common issues of the day, but not a single lasting accomplishment of the directors of the supersystem? Not a single reform in the 00's? All of us are engaged in epic time-wasting, making an unnecessary life have some semblance of coherence and vitality, fashioned according to no plan, hewing to no required philosophy, establishing no ground. Of course there are great and bountiful accomplishments to any life, such as a work of art or commerce or children or a deep relationship or two, but even for a nabob of inter-continental fame, there will have been countless diversions and dubious significance. Will what you chase bring you the pleasure that its evasiveness denied you? The supersystem may yet imply a "yes" to that, since neoliberalism has erected magnificent skyscrapers, hollowed out communist state fascism, generated artificial opulence and shiny toys for ensconced adults. There is no change necessary – the supersystem can provide us the shiny ineffable that will mark us unto our deaths, even as all outside of that orbit burns. You have yours, at least if you have a little extra or are getting cable free, and I have mine. Your choices are insipid, otiose, pusillanimous, reflective of ill consideration, and mine are the stuff of irredeemable brilliance, but that is why we are atomized, each one of us free to click on whatever floats our boat. Since our cartoon days, we in the west have distinguished ourselves from our forebears by our incessant *watching*, observing the cavalcade of culture, selecting sources of information and instruction in a revolution of autodidacticism.

LWSS 39 -   CORPORATIONS

The creation and promotion and then domination of the corporation was the ultimate social virus to infect the human species. There were certainly purposes for the corporation in its early period, and it will continue to survive in the regulatory reformation of the supersystem, albeit in severely curtailed, drastically contained minor form. However, the insidious nature of the profit-driven growth-oriented transnational corporation (TNC) overran political, legal, academic, entertainment, and inter-institutional structures with remorseless capacity. Nation, religion, education, age, gender, product: not a single variable affected the overall conduct of the TNC. No conquering army ever bought the allegiance of so many people through the corporation's purchase of loyalty upon the promise of burgeoning individual wealth. Nothing is wrong with buying and selling, or watching and making, but these are either to be localized vocations or leisure-time hobbies, not the raison d'etre of life. In the metaphor of the virus, however, the host body is destroyed when a virus metastasizes. Humans have been issuing dire catastrophisms at every opportunity since the earliest dawn, and yet we see houses stand and disease averted with each new passing day, so we cannot issue command or judgment without the taking a rejoinder's prescribed medicine.

Americans did not restrain the monster that we created, a hazard that accompanies creative construction. Corporations exploited an opening in the human psyche that rewards the capture of the prey, becoming as elemental in the economy as money. Did you want a job? Did you want a product? Did you want property? Were you looking for a future? Did you need a bigger weapon? Did you want have others join you in your quests for riches? For all of these desires, only the corporation consolidated the answers connected to fulfillment. The barriers to the ascension of the post-war corporate economic order fell as if ordained, as research reports of pollution were steamrolled into the asphal; laws were bent to fictions to give personhood; doctors' rooms became invaded by new drugs and insurance controls; politicians and entertainment were papered over with corporate logos; every corner of the social world became colonized by the corporate need to find new or burgeoning revenue sources. Yet this was a protean dominance: there was plenty of room for liberal co-optation, minor defiance, arenas for "personal freedom," jeans-only Fridays, recycling drives, a surrounding mythos of self-hood that kept the workers from looking outside their protective pods. All within know the seductions, the allures, the tough days, the fortitude, the shiny rewards of luxurious personal electronic goods that made for the bluest skies and the whitest whites. The corporate state became humanity's molecular bath, and once entered into, the relationship is uneradicable: the water surrounds, the subject reclines, the bonds of authority can never be reversed.

LWSS 40 - **THE CDI**

The Corporate Dominance Index (CDI) stands at .731 in the US out of a perfect 1.00 of Perfect Fascism, but this is an intimidating threshold, one that demands a full popular mobilization against all extant institutions to rescue humanity. Due to mass propaganda events ranging from college graduations to Super Bowls to Supreme Court decisions, the CDI is forecast to reach the .791 level that presages an enveloping political boredom. The issues of the day, all of them, are deep and complex and deeply entrenched in the corporate supersystem, and demand vast amounts of research to find the conflicts of interests, the governing interests in exacerbating conflicts, the overlapping histories, the vain self-glorifications among the major actors, the secret conspiracies, the relevant statistics, the qualifications, and the sure-to-be-ignored suggested solutions. Attach a CDI gauge to your name-brand sweatshirt as you perambulate your day: it will register red-stage warnings at work, before your TV, from your cellphone, near the stores, as you breathe, when you issue your bureaucratic indecisions, when you retire for the night, near the sleepy eyes of your children.

LWSS 41 - **BIRDS**

The chattering of the pseudonymous horde will accompany the descent into social policy stasis. Moderns humans are increasingly taught that private opinions are necessarily public, as in comments about the worth of teachers, the worth of parents/spouses/kids, the problems of sexual dysfunction, the proper technological approach to 3rd-and-10, what is wrong with the known world despite not having read a book last year. If these public airings of private antipathy are challenged, in any way, the dispenser of instant and *unqualified* criticism reaches for the revolver. Soliloquy has been the preferred mode of the domesticated human songbird, but the songs are not calls for reciprocation, but displays of sexual status.

LWSS 42 - **OLD BATTLES**

Old battles should never be fought, least of all by new soldiers. Against the perpetration of foreign war deaths and internal dissolution of the United States into corporate districts, the chattering classes ask for seriousness, high-minded insider-slinging and ten-point plans for civic betterment. Calamitous economic and ecological destruction could produce actual reformation of the American social order, but in the interregnum, and most likely through the long and brutish lead-up, there is no outlet for dedicated constructivism. Of course there are more legitimate endeavors than others, but the contortions of avowal that are demanded to find steady and paying work in the non-profit sector militate against all but a few trust-funded few. A return towards the local, an upwelling of participatory economics, diets of rutabagas and winter parsnips, or fellowships in community brick-oven making, do not cause the exempted mind from knowing that the masses of humans, and the awful hordes of defenseless animals, are fated to find the social effects of post-industrial humanity bringing them to collapse. As frightened hominids, we are conditioned to step past the dying and the dead, but unlike in earlier times, we can now never imagine a future that does not wake to this dystopian landscape. In 2009, kangaroos returned to their horrifically singed territory in Australia, compelled towards a terrible form of suicide through instinctive territoriality. We humans give whatever exists as socially real extra dimensions of power for simply having acquired the status of superseding all that could have come to be but did not, so that traditional nonsense infests and disturbs and suffocates long after its properties of destruction have been identified.

LWSS 43 -   CHANGE IN THE ELITE

Does a gilded fortune retreat to the sea when the paterfamilias dies, or does the product of crime and graft provide the headwinds for lifetimes of privilege? There is no poetry that ennobles the inarticulate workings from power to more power, that uses metaphor and classical imagery to glorify the upward adjustments of the elites. These are precise psychological states, as judges, politicians, and fixers accommodate the contours of inherited social policy to their individual lusts, ambitions, and interpersonal dislikes. Not a single action of the supersystemic elite is fashioned out of "evil," that fictitious imputation of demonhood to humans, but is always rational, responsive to amalgams of adequate understanding, gross instincts, and status enhancement. The elites, however, are marked by a steady refusal to allow the motivations, dilemmas, frustrations, and depressions of others to diminish their ill-considered depredations. Change that person in the role, and the role would remain. Change the color, the gender, the identities and the training, and still the much larger social forces shape the role selectee into power's handmaiden.

LWSS 44 -   CONFLICTS OF INTEREST

In its daily operation, the supersystem is continually reinvigorated by the countless ways in which the interests of the supersystem are shot directly into the brain of the individual. Neuroscience may have documented the highlighted areas of the amygdala firing when a doctor accepts an invitation to dine with a pharmaceutical company, but the immediate calculations and inclinations of the individual are not even clear to himself. They cannot be mapped. How far can art go to portray all the variables of thought, emotion, instinct and psychic adjustment that go into keeping us in our places? We can see the appearance of these dramatic venues, either on the silver screen or in less Technicolor reality, but we have only the most superficial insight into the tortured cranial electrical grids of the human actors. We can, however, detect the practical effects upon social action by the supersystem, its restrains upon trade and liberal intervention. Under the guise of "free speech," liberal magazines accepted laundered and targeted money from tobacco companies. Lawyers, doctors, and researchers insinuated the corporate plundering apparatus into every new untapped corner, always "just doing a job," unseen and without censure by colleagues or family. There never be could be a "conflict of interest," for all of the educated liberals and their lesser idiot cousins the conservatives, because they were just one cog in the wheel, and numbers in bank accounts never betray their sources. These apparatchiks of empire could point to the real villains, the ones who had no conscience-rescuing charity donations, to the ex-spouses who cashed their checks, to the Jesus or the mommy or the bottle that absorbed and absolved all of their chasings of a buck. They were "professionals," conversant in the technical jargon of their sub-specialties, but sub-ethical. Who was going to call them on their egregious contributions to inhumane social practice - the family dog?

LWSS 45 -   TOXICS

Under the rubric of "freedom," an Orwellian tag extrapolated from laissez-faire economics by corporate propagandists, the promulgation of toxic drugs and pernicious feedstuffs has spread disease, death, and obesity across the susceptible public, those with the generic genetic and environmental combination that draws moths to flames. Yet the right in its unbridled corporatism and the left in its infantile libertarianism united to permit the spread of these marvelous poisons across the supersystemic globe. Harms should have been identified and marginalized, placed in the nether regions of the social environment where addicts go to cop, not on Front Street where Sis and Junior start in the crib on the road to diabetes, chemo, and Prozac. Scientists identify great disasters racing towards us, another great extinction to match the Great Permian Mass Extinction, but refuse to consider the "politics" of what that knowledge may portend for us. Do we eat less or more tonight? Do we drive to work tomorrow aware that this apocalypse is not coming or not coming from the sky, but is accruing due to our very efforts as "sustaining" a social livelihood? This ultimate dilemma awareness is not going to improve due to asceticism, renunciation, reform, or technological invention – humans do not move away from social reality, but towards it, towards its devastating conclusions.

LWSS 46 -   **FINES**

Technology will exact more and more cost from American workers, as we get corralled into our multimedia dens, afraid to drink and drive; afraid to drive a mile too fast for the radar guns and village guns; afraid to have children whose every action becomes the parent's legal responsibility; afraid to be out in public and thus subject to arrest and then loss of job; afraid to make an impolitic remark amongst strangers; afraid to be cut down to size by jealous co-workers. The police are going to pay for their high-tech toys with enormous fines exacted upon their victims, with judges and politicians colluding in pushing bottom-line justice. Countries will refuse entrance to all but the most clean of travelers, those whose passport IDs reveal a life of chastened obedience to rules of finance, social comportment, and public utterance. The misdemeanor convicted will still have their own multi-media dens, after all, where they can marinate in their official opprobrium behind closed shades until they grow a new legal identity, defined as having the money to erase all latent signs of legal stigma, staying alive until old and gray, or dying from poverty-associated disease. By setting video-cameras and speed-activated sensors throughout the remnants of the public venues, social control will grow as the supersystem matures in its capability to dispense near-instant dispensation of rule-enforcement. Just try not to worry about the dangers of being caught – it is all in your best interest, to protect your life and the lives of those you love. Of course, this dystopia has miles to go, and we are as yet in the adolescence of information enforcement, those of us not in China, but there is no strong constituency for free expression

Surely this can be faulted as overwrought leftist agitate – no bullets in the back of our heads, no lock-ups for vaguely scruffy Internet mice, timid cops, a vast babble of fearful First Worlders. Who were we, the dissatisfied beneficiaries of continents of corporate extraction, a threat to? There were great numbers of prisoners and dead attached to workings of our systemic opponents, but the police state was held for us if we strayed into overt violence, tax evasion, or property destruction – too much work for college-educated adults.

LWSS 47 -   **UNDER OUR FEET**

The global corporate order will not give its encircling power back to any other force, nor will it produce spectacular gains that usher in a green social utopia. For every stripe of crisis, the forces of reactionary devolution will have as great an opening as the positivists of liberal reform. No future crisis will ever be "solved" unless it results in an epic confrontation with global corporate capital, but calamities and revolutions have brought only recalibrations of concentrated power. My country had fashioned a dish liquid that could smell sweeter than any fruit juice, inviting the dishwasher to contemplate the righteous olfactory ingestion of Palmolive Mountain Breeze Berry Fruitopia dishwashing liquid, and we know how to adjudge that oversupply, have made it so far through the madness of corporate suburban living by placing fear around all matter and experience. Reformers of the corporate supersystem never allude to the quantity of plastic the industrial wing produced over its years, a fantastical amount of polymer hardening and softening to cover every known inch of this fragile planet over many times. We are going to roll back that commercial process that girdled the blue orb in bright urea and supple inorganic material? The factories have been working overtime through each and every night, and the supertankers have successfully navigated every storm and channel, to bring each and every one of us a supply of packaged plastic structures, and there are billions across the globe who in no way have gotten their due share of that factory-specific plastic consumer partake. Fantasies of prelapsarian solar goodness cannot diminish the eternal glow from that plasticine penumbra. What lies beneath our historical feet? A mountain of plastic, ringed by rivers of plastic, surrounded by banks of concrete, steel, and iron.

LWSS 48 - TALK

The entry point into the supersystem will not be obvious, and may never be found. Ameliorists may beckon us through one promising point, such as health care reform or drug war cessation, but the violence of the opposition will collect, either before or after the entry wound. American nativist entitlement is a fearsome beast once excited, as when gas station mechanics put aside illiteracy to promote schoolteacher and school administrator firings, or workers demand drug testing of unemployed "welfare" recipients. Social uplift is never a pretty sight, bringing out the petulant misery of the advantaged boor who travels in packs of sniping, spittling aggravation-cretins. Trying to recalibrate the human mind, through education or legislation or drugs, is a losing proposition, since there is such ample room for the human intellect to go so far astray on the disseminated idiocies. Perfectly sane, upright folk may conduct an agreeable conversation on four topics, then hit that next one where the what-the-hell cognitive realization whipsaws all that communal regard.

LWSS 49 - THE CORPORATE PATTERN

The regulatory apparatus of the American empire is the sad side of the street, where minuscule and selective prosecution meets the vastness of institutional corruption. Elites in positions of direct power (as distinct from merely super-rich layabouts) are always responsible to imperatives and constituencies far greater than one or two levels. This is self-evident sociology, and the mapping of the workings of power should be our foremost sport, but the money is all gone from journalism, exposes, and anti-corporate boycotts. Public relations, lawyers, and mega-profits have killed the language of dispensational responsibility. Humans apply well-honed evaluation patterns to new-seeming re-occurrences, regenerating the process of decay that is built into every institutional charter – and conditioning new institutions to arrive there in due time.

LWSS 50 -   INDIVIDUAL SELVES

Within the mind of each of us, an outsized, ego-driven cardboard figure of a superstar ego stands propped up next to the no-account mistake-prone secondary self . Self-aggrandizement produces the faith-based coping mechanisms that sustain even the most depressed brooders, and though age may temper the visions of worldwide acclaim, the perspective of the under-appreciated self is an unquenchable human constant. You know that there is a better you that others do not always pay homage to, but you have a general sense of the magnificent self that a series of fortuitous meshing events may yet bring to the front of the stage. With the diminishment of social interactions, contemporary society yields life-long dreamers who have not had the number of failed tests of an idealized self that earlier societies produced.

LWSS 51 -   THE SOURCE OF JOBS

This late stage of the supersystem founders on a stunning contradiction between its aims for comprehensive sufficiency and its "free market" obtuseness over the preferred source and ownership of "jobs." Transnational corporate business chases Profits, slashing payrolls, workforces, wages, and benefits with bureaucratic efficiency. Jobs were historically attached to this sector because of its domineering ascendancy, but shareholder and stakeholder profit is its motivation, not a well-compensated and secure dependent labor force. The government could in theory and in the New Deal reality serve as an employer of last resort, but without a massive redirection of corporate profit towards the funding of public works employment, the government will lose its backing for tax-supported employment. A people which sees the government as the primary thief of labor compensation and primary cause of unemployment is not going to look for that very government to rescue it from its corporate-enforced doldrums. There could be a Corps of privatized CCC workers, drawn equally from the adrift liberal arts college graduate class and the unneeded factory worker castoff class who would be paid from charity drawn from the accounts of the overlord class, but our robber barons don not like social obligations that impose on-going complications on them, such as having to manage the housing and private insurance needs of the lower classes.

LWSS 52 -   CALLS

The theory of the Superysystem (tSS) is predicated on the suppleness and minor shifting of the elite purveyors of social control. The continuities are much stronger than the deviations, ever since the corporate ascension during the Gilded Age, so liberal hopefulness can be easily overdone. With the change of a tone, a new emphasis, or simply a new angle on a common subject, totalitarians can keep the landscape freshened, when no new planting has occurred. Gone will be the old boss, with his radical preoccupations, and in comes the new boss, earning huzzahs for the merest of command alterations that fall far, far short of distinction. As the Obama con smoothed its way through its new verdant fields of power, it was the beneficiary of the glory of having displaced a disgraced despot, but the lies and evasions and religious toadyism meant only a new phase for the Supersystem. Fruitless calls for this or that reform peppered the "progressive" landscape, yet the suits were not in jail, the soup kitchens were not visited by the Food network, the tide did not turn, the land was not purified, the lay of the land is yet with the profiteers and not the resistors. How many unheeded calls are needed to prove social nullity?

LWSS 53 -   THE INTELLECTUAL HUMAN
The most difficult principle to contend with in human social reality is that *to everyone, everything they do and every idea they hold makes intuitive, real, psychological, emotional, and rational sense, to them and thus by extension others.* Humans produce no reality that is not conditioned by the forces around them. All of our enemies, all of our antagonists, every unfathomable foreign culture, all the violence and all the peace, are bathed in social forces that equally produce them as us. We can (or rather, *could*) seek to argue for differing moral outcomes for any common issue, and can find some basis of philosophic triumph, but our opponents will not become our worldview. Human beings respond to the electrical impulses of their individuated brain, which in each and every case, from madman to savant, has been hardened by experience and repeated judgments. Humans can learn and find fault within themselves, can recognize superior argument and restrain anti-social action, but not generally, and look out when the conditions devolve. If debate and verbal contest were to mark contemporary life, we could see greater political enactment of secular humanism, but in our mass-mediated product advertising culture, parking lots are built while ecosystems and ideals die. People hear the repetitive humming of their minds and its reinforced preoccupations, not the beneficial strife of intellectual challenge.

LWSS 54 -   THE ELITES
Every person of power in the supersystem maneuvers behind an overlay of public relations ethical morality, which is very rarely uncovered, and much less torn by regulators. Every night they face the terrors of their deeds hitting their conscience, but most have intact belief systems of excuse and strategic justification, and few have the ethical alternative to their depredations available full strength in their minds. The reward against their lies and sell-outs and is omnipresent in their wealth or status, if not maintained in the excitement of violence or effective duplicity. Take down one supersystem star, and another two or three are ready to go instantly. In the early days of the supersystem, investigative reporters, whistle-blowers, and investigative political commissions used to provide a superficial policing, but now the cover-ups and disregard and inevitable retrenchments and heightened firewalls have protected all but the most unfortunate or egregious of decisive society. The felony class of overlords are destined for a rich yet troubled reign, minus a handful of scandal-assigned mountebanks.

LWSS 55 -   THE QUESTIONABLE SELF
Behind the American military-industrial empire lays the smoldering ruins of the multicultural democratic republic of fable and myth. The United States Congress is elected by the best public relations and monumental organized corporate pressure money and its obligations can buy, religious nonsense troubles the sleep of the mighty high and the vast low, and yet our resistance was always futile to this concerted totalitarian arrangement, since it has ownership in so many ways large and hidden. The little reservoirs of opposition inside the brain soup hermetically encased by our skulls are also under threat. We shall be judged by our actions, but if we retreat to the inviolability of our resistant minds, we need to determine if we are as pure in thought as we wish to be. What is the state of our self-administered pharmacology? Can our brain waves remain resolute against the loss of brainpower through aging and environmental toxicity, and, down the ragged line, can we

vouchsafe that we are the independent creators of our ideas and concepts? From the beginnings of humanity, our selves have been part social creations through culture and honed instinct, but what of the moment when advertising, incarceration, corporations, police, technology, and medicine have us doubting the provenance of even our innermost cognitive rejections? Where will be the "self" that we must rely on then?

LWSS 56 -   RECRIMINATION

Blame runs in the human psyche. Who didn't pull the weight when we tried to bag that mastodon? How come my father doesn't approve of me? Why haven't I written my masterpiece? Why are the kids in such bad shape? Why didn't I make more money? How come I am not as I wish to be? The theory of the Supersystem puts a good deal of blame on incontrovertible reality, away from the inelasticity of the marked self. Crimes and prizes, skyscrapers and corroding beer cans, families and the networks of our enemies, the sleekest corridors of the mega-cities and the dead zones in our befouled oceans, all generated within and through the matrices of social reality. In navigating this conundrum of the percipient individual versus the omnipresent larger human world, we rely on great solo artists and transcendent culture to supply us with diversionary uplift, but none of us can figure where to place our individual selves. We can gaze at the heavens that were once within our Apollo step, but the days of utopian ambition upward are forever over, since we shall forever know that we have irreparable damaged this blue orb.

LWSS 57 -   STORIES

The stories we have been told have centered on the heroic individual, but social conditions are played out in the aggregate, far above our sights. . The planet is not so affected by the exception, the minority who rise above the pull of their straitened circumstances, but is carried by the actions of the main. There will always be those who are impervious to the damages wrought by deprivations that ensnare the susceptible, who convince us that the solitary human is fated to triumph Sociology has failed to tell people that they are bound by invisible social forces, as the cult of individualism teaches victims to ignore the supremacy of their unearned impositions of desperation, vanity, gun violence, adult despair, ill health, lack of safe creative practice, or variations of psychic turmoil that bedevil even the Hollywood gliterrati. A story needs a villain, of course, but the villain of the supersystem is too unapproachable to interest the viewer. OK, it's the supersystem – what happens then? You can't arrest everybody, you can't see justice rule the day, you can't see moral growth, you can't find a way to some denouement – so the convenient villains are fashioned, little monsters whose demise or comeuppance will never stop the motions of power. In our time, when the confluence of mass education, affluence, and cowboy mythology led every second college student to imagine a destiny of hierarchical superiority, the perpetuation of a system without an organizing purpose has left suburbs full of frustrated would-be potentates. This psychic eruption of individualist aspiration overflowed every barrier, and can no sooner emerge into a cohesive stream of social action than lava can clean a swimming pool. We are done, with only the blather of unheedful barkers to accompany our demise. If the colors of the world will never fade, what one issue could such a deluded, fantasizing populace gather round - the bonds of our temporal existence?

LWSS 58 -   **THE RIGHT**

A corollary of the theory of the Supersystem is that adults become lost causes, trapped in dyspeptic neurology. The 90's profusion of right-wing hate radio was matched by the eruption of intentionally callous right-wing trolls in the 00's. In the safety of the noninteractional womb of the personal computer, devoted bitterness-nursers gladdened their deformed psyches by issuing bilious smackdowns of the liberalisms that were appearing on their lawns. Others to them were "lunatics," wearing "tin-foil hats," a recapitulation of the 60's anti-hippie American Legion putdowns. A more precise taxonomy of the rabid right of our time can be found by sticking your head out of the window, and just taking in the culture of the moment, and should only be hazarded under competent professional supervision.

LWSS 59 -   **CONTINUITY OR CHANGE?**

In the enduring terminology, there is a "24-7 news cycle," implying that any theory of continuity like the tSS is ahistorical and false. Look at the change, look at the social movements that erupt, look at the constant flow of names in and out, the technologies out in play and those massing on the horizon. Our dreams become our reality, in rapturous and ever-ascending multiplicity. Who could have predicted X? Who could not be expectant of a brave new world? However, the present is redolent with the failed warnings of the past. Environmental warnings of our fervid befoulings have flowered since *Urban Jungle* and *Silent Spring,* now into their fifth generations of heraldic offspring. The continuities are manned by actors held to their practices by the enduring imperatives of saying that which keeps the next paycheck coming. The sound may be crisper, but the beats remain the same. Who is new politician Y but a recombination of past politician Z mixed with past tycoon A? In our modern suburban carpet emporiums, we cannot surmount our punitive distrust of collective responsibility - the wisdom is in the crowds of politically unaware, stupefied, self-lacerating id fantasists. Social reality is always that which is, not that which we imagine it should be.

LWSS 60 -   **THE AMERICAN DREAM**

For all of the vaunted "power of the people," political scientists could not point to a single case of "the people" obtaining "power." Elites of the western "democracies" had conspired to place the onus for responsibility on the lowly drudge, as if the choice of where to shop and who to elect placed the citizen alongside Caesar and Bismarck. The American people had been the marks, the dupes, the circum-surveilled pew-sitters, encased in the glass fiction that they were the righteous, they were the Greatest Generation, they were rightful owners of the American Dream. We, the people, moved in tight circles, from school to work and back to home, surrounded by the blandishments of a hollowing mega-culture. For some, the birthday parties and the family get-togethers and the ballgames and the traffic-laden vacations and the nightly repose were a life well-lived, good fodder for a Legion toast and a town-wide funeral. Aided by the myths of Hollywood and the buying power of a global empire, these post-WWII mothers and fathers never left the bathos of individualist exceptionalism, until old age robbed them of every last purchase, ownership certificate, and gewgaw.

LWSS 61 -   **THE LONELY AND THE LOYAL**

Built on a superstructure of lies and artifice, the supersystem rewards its well-positioned charlatans. They waste no effort in deriving pride and superiority from the current arrangement of benefits, calling themselves "educated," checking their banking accounts for designations of self-worth, invoking a deity that has so richly swung privilege towards them, castigating their lessers for presumed inabilities and diminishment. Sycophants gain enough material uplift from promoting the vanity of these lunatics, so the upper crust and the entitled arrivistes will live, propagate, and intimidate in reflected faith in their own magnificence. For those within the supersystem, there have been moments of great loneliness, when no one was around to occupy the void created by a wealth-hoarding economic superstructure. Love's great promise as the rescue of an individual life can be left behind on the highway, unused, unattached, a torn backpack. Young people stare out an indifferent world, tethered to an unresponsive family. Divorced men and women occupy the apartments of the fractured domestic diaspora, offspring remaining as the living detritus of a misspent connection. The elderly contend with ailments and remembered slights. Workers trudge off to another day of making the motions to suffice to keep the boss away from the detonator. The technological marvels of the machine age, the skyscrapers and instant communication devices, cannot draw forth the awe of the benighted solitary outcast. Humans need connective social tissue, but connective tissue that is damaged causes more injury than restoration. Yet the human capacity for endurance over-weighs most all social circumstances, even in times of war, permitting all manner of social violation to pass through while the verities of individual solace shine: a friend, a loyal family member, a sense of self-mastery in the single life's accommodations, an animal, or a reliable drug. Life's indignities harden the resolve of the adult to accept traditions as positive, no matter how injurious they may be, cowing any populace into authoritarian acquiescence.

LWSS 62 -   THE MILITARY

The supersystem must be assaulted at all of its superstructures. Of course, this wholesale renewal has never occurred in human history. There never is a full starting over, nor a complete re-atomization of all matter. Although there are fundamental holes in the supersystem, causing great and enduring suffering in all superstructures, there are no revolutions that have not been transmuted into black holes. Gradual change can accrue through systemic accretion, but that is no blueprint for human betterment. The present supersystem, unlike its earlier theocratic incarnations, protects its secular power with ownership of the periodic table. No initiative in any political or social arena can succeed without a redrawing of our basic myths and foundational assumptions, but where do we go to get our conception of social fairness back? Generals and their civilian Eichmanns do not answer for following their inherited imperatives towards sanctioned marauding and killing, and are not likely to in a culture of bounded, virtual militarism, where a million faraway people can die through the inaction of a people taxed for their wages, not their blood. America's bases, and its weapons sales, and its injured-for-life soldiers, and its corporate military supply profits, and its corporate military technology, are built and operated to last, to never go away.

LWSS 63 -   THE ECONOMY

The American economy is functionally a bloodstream of innumerable commercial transactions, enormous and flowing, governed by typologies and common desires, none of which are guaranteed to be positive in any wider social sense. Personal accumulation of wealth attaches itself through this sinisterium of global clicking and signings, condemning vast land sheets of others to indenture and doomed obsolescence. We have no language for, nor any command over, this, the largest institution of the supersystem. Economics is violence, the routinization of effort and pain into numbers, products, hierarchy, and denial of access. Words fail when the brain is contending with physical assault; so too are we incoherent as money and work and finance hits. How can the "economic system" said to be "governed" when 23,000 people are murdered in Juarez, Mexico, during a recent three-year period of calm sleep and beatific investment portfolios for the next-door North of the US? Would you like to answer the worries of a deservedly anxious people? How can the forces of obscene wealth have become so insistent in arrogating world-historical levels of public dispossession to themselves? There is no answer for this, no tidy social theory that places a "context" to this horrific theft, so why should readers seek one?

LWSS 64 -   ROBBERY

Previous political actors have faded into corruption once they have become devoted to strategic alliances and craven associations. Of course, no human exists in a world populated by copies of him- or her-self, and decisions are always compromises between ideals and necessities, but political ideology must become as principled as it is practical. If there is no social power that can be called "democratic" or "sustainable," it is fiction to promulgate calls for a "better world." In between the extremes of ruin/collapse and totalitarian control, the supersystem absorbs all social criticism, as yet unbowed from any singular political development, any competing paradigm. With enough evidence now in from failed neo-Marxist or proto-socialist states, power can never be left to ideology – not any yet developed. Elements from the past can be remixed, underlain with synthesized bass, samples juxtaposed to comment in upon themselves, filling up headspace and the dancefloor, but then the lights will turn on, and where will we be? The robbery is still going on, now into obscene amounts of social capital, and we have made no attempt, none, to stop the thieves. Turn it up , drown out the sounds.

LWSS 65 -   ROLLING ON

Continuity is the watchword of the Supersystem. How do the parts fit together? How is the present a logical, close outgrowth of the past? What factors are predominate, which ones operate to dominate, where are the outlines of our social reality? Protests are now anticipated by a massive surveillance bureaucracy, all run on the obedience of its enforcers to the requirements of performing a job, abetted by some hallucinatory sadism. Do you think you will enjoy running afoul of the global security apparatus, with its black Ninja front-line police, willing collaborator prosecutors and judges, computer-record enforcement of fines and punishments, all heading toward a final concrete correctional destination if you wish to push the issue? Sound like a fun ride? Good for old bank account? Will that path go over well with the family, the boss, the next job interviewer? Do you think the glory of a righteous integrity will draw the aspirants who see their jobs somewhere in the high tech, omnipresent authoritative supervisory state? The basic continuities have only gotten stronger for the cruel demands of the deformational state – fill the slots the machine demands, bend to the prevailing winds of commercial corruption, lose your life in the absurdities of the marketplace, spout bullshit that even you don't believe but is that which the role encodes.

LWSS 66 -   WHAT IS MADE WILL BE USED

We are forever at the mercy of forces far too great to overcome. Our human drive to worship gurus runs into the modern condition of the revelation of at least one whopper per kook-revealed savant. In the dithering fractious Sixties, eons were lost to specious blather about violent archetypes and spiritual claptrap. In our age, again devoted to action-stripped talk, the New Ascetics and the Ivy-climbing Voices proffer rhetoric while the forest burns around them. Men and women are simply inadequate to the task of organizing rational thought. Instead, the post -WWII trillions that have been spent on US weapons and the US military were shown to be combustible, set afire by determined Texans and their sycophants. Now the toxic dump of bombs and tanks and night-scope directed automatic weapons will continue to go off, purchased at such enormous cost and stockpiled so high that the vapors of alcohol alone can touch them off in some faraway desert. Escape the bullets and the bombs in your imperial redoubt, but they pop off elsewhere, providing the sterile soundtrack to films that provide ersatz adrenaline and fake gravitas to a First World escape from responsibility. Deeply-read bloggers and writers *expose* hidden workings of the supersystem, offering the side dishes of *solutions* and minor *plans*, all of which, the positive and the negative, the principled opposition and the junior erector-set instructions, produce only a vanishing paper trail. The wars and the oppressions could have been so much worse – at least we have stopped the beast from complete annihilation of the unfortunate. Think of the villages unburned, the same-sex unions given cultural approval, the solar-powered hot tubs, the hip-hop Palestinians – is that reward enough? As long as the switches work, social reality will be whatever they say it is.

LWSS 67 -   THE RECORD

With all that can be seen, conjured, or re-imagined in supersystem open to monetization, there is not an open area to construct a form of trust. If you were in it for the money, there was no limit to what you angle you would pursue. Wherever profit could be found, that was where you should head. There were going to be endless forays into your economic space to try to take your money from you, and you had very little recourse to limit those incursions, but you would cover yourself at every opportunity by trying to drill into layers of money you could find guarded by others. What would be the barriers of "family," "conscience," or "morality" but so much flimsy concepts against such a commanding imperative? Higher education produced bafflegab specialists bombing Vietnam, bombing Iraq and Afghanistan, advertising obesity burgers and gambling trifles, authoring the sub-prime implosion and the Wall Street Shuffle, an unbroken record of defeat and disgrace from the "best and the brightest." That which has proven itself fatally flawed should be accorded a burial and death, not endless expansion of power and obfuscatory support.

LWSS 68 -   POP CULTURE

Make a chart with all the great, lasting, exciting political actors and political innovations of the past 40 years. Next to that invisible space, start a separate column, considering the genius of American Pop culture, any of your own countless and well-chosen divertissements, and you will see what has shaped social reality. The Sixties gave the world its lifeblood of pop culture, a critical rejectionism by the common man and woman, and the stalwart search for good times – no match for the ownership of the means and ends of production by the elites, but our individual worlds, nonetheless. We are left alone down below to work it out, to sift through the work disappointments and the interpersonal stresses that accompany bills and leaks, while all the while the supersystem governs, shapes, condemns, obliterates. Do we do the proverbial "good job" at any of it? What could we point to to make our case? A devoted dog and a virtual circle of like-minded depressives? Enduring hobbies and a mowed patch?

LWSS 69 -   WORK

In our culture, flim-flam has become the dominant mode of commerce. By the time the victims get wise, the show is out of town, and what recourse do they have then- they only have themselves to blame. In education, the snake oil came under the name "training," with every manner of charlatan peddling dog-and-ponies to helpless rube workers. Using the same fraud blueprint of blithering infantilism and unverifiable "statistics" of accomplishments, traveling "experts" married religious con-artistry with Microsoft techno-idiocy to bamboozle the last of the captive workers, the teachers. Work, in the supersystem, is unrelenting bureaucratic attack designed to *break the will,* a universal growth of superfluous managerialism that has taken the American economy from wide-open industry to beaten lawyers, swamped doctors, morose psychiatrists, artificial non-tenured professors. Notions of bottom-up democracy, workers councils, "input," meetings for "questions and concerns," insincere managerial boosterism, meet-and-greets, suggestion boxes, company parties, perks and bounties, "morale," were steamrolled by the intimidations by the hierarchy and their subalterns. Without unions and any vestige of worker "solidarity," the Koolaid could be put out on the floor at any moment, with the staff becoming management's most effective police and overseer Yet as the economy was hitting the people hard, the workers and the unemployed were surrounded by demands for faith - The job was going to show up, eventually, somehow, in some form, it was all going to work out – it had to. There was no alternative. Nobody had gone to school that long, played by the rules for the most part, had done what society had asked, to end up without stunned and morose. No one could see a growth in work opportunities, no manufacturing was going to be resurrected to darken the already polluted rivers and get actual wages from the bosses, and no one had any good way to steal the rest of the world blind. The job was a piece of shit. No benefits, long tedious hours, no advancement in sight, a job a monkey could do. For now, it paid the bills, barely, but it didn't do anything about the debt, and it was not going to be a future. There were any number of projects and repairs that were so far down the road, but each could represent total disaster if they went south in a hurry. Others had already packed up and left, but that was an all-or-nothing gamble. What was it like to have a real job?

LWSS 70 -   THE WORLD AND ITS INJURIES

By the power of our association, do we stand for the entirety of actions of our employer? What is the cost of loyalty to people and systems you cannot control, did not influence, and must abide by to continue your style and mode of living? As adults, we disassociate by our refusal to enter into protracted contest against injustices great and small, from little comments of surpassing offensiveness that are allowed to waft into the ether to deliberate violence from co-workers or co-religionists or co-inhabitants that is permitted its dry run. Our countenances are legion, beyond the greatest moral code of evaluation, an unbroken string of incapability to detour social derogation or stupidity or remote loss. No moral code can ever be devised to encapsulate the omission of integrity and back-away from cause that daily life entails.. Our thoughts may be true, but our conduct is pure reproach – social truth is always too dangerous to be in plain sight. Retreat from society is always a possibility in view of these dangers, but there will always be a hole where others have found laughter and back-slapping fellowship 'round the pub.

LWSS 71 -   **LOVE & MARRIAGE**

Within the GSI (Grand Social Institution) of Love & Marriage, the ideal is a "happy marriage," as if the two partners are consumed by happiness and nothing else. What about the great occurrences of unhappiness within each day, within each marriage, within each life, where dumb frustration meets the knowledge of its daily repetition? How could a "marriage" be exempt from the experiential vicissitudes that accompany any other human endeavor? Partners can be grateful for the sensational alliance with a like-minded, comely love object, can see the rescue of a formerly forlorn life by the earth-altering act of adult mating, but still be allowed the presence of an "unhappiness" with sets of unshakeable personal and social reality. No two humans establish "happiness" as a constant state of interaction, but they do communicate and co-exist in varying levels of benefit and amity. All of the great institutions construct the social foundation for love or marriage, many people rendered unloved by the deformations of money pressure, societal disintegration, the burdens of financial expectation upon child-rearing, or the destruction of individual opportunity by the criminal corporate megamachine. Only the two people elementally bonded can testify to the dimensions of resistance needed to keep the connections red-hot as the removal of once-common supports of job, house, affordable health care, and future commence in our world.

LWSS 72 -   **REAL PEOPLE**

The stories of people do not need to be collected: the story of life in the supersystem churns over relentlessly fallow ground. This family tragedy blends into this family estrangement into that overcome addiction runs into financial struggle, hits minor accomplishment, abuts new initiative and dreams, staggers through culture and theory, and sits down with more of the same, Studs Terkel or Springsteen, Bonnaroo or UC Santa Cruz, US military or sports team, adolescent drug use or poetry seminars, permaculture or libertarian gun running, rock-climbing or techno-innovation, boredom or anger, America's soliloquies of real life lost to a cold supersystem. The passions of the high culturalists, placing Bach and poetry and dithyrambs and English moor soap operas as *necessary* because of the great judgment of history's intellectuals, is nothing but a salamander's fascination with its miniature world. Against the nihilistic vision of the supersystem deep thinkers posit a "transcendence" to human life, to their lives, that is usually put in the folder of some deity known as "god," or in some revolutionary cause like the working slob or the righteous poor. Nothing in this known world can "transcend" its origins and nature, so if you are looking for mysteries, you are on the wrong planet. Science, so far, and looking down the road, has done a pretty fine job of explaining the natural bases of the beauty of allegedly "transcendent" events like sunsets, babies being born, concertos, love, and cathedrals. Whatever moves you to tears of exaltation or rage can strike another as perfectly banal, conforming to all known laws of physics. The grand tapestries evolution has wrought upon the various forms of life on this planet are wonders to behold, but then there is still a low-intensity dinner to make and the debts to consider. Our tendency toward self-exaltation has us over-valuing our particular circumstances, yet to contend with the consistent pressures of social reality, we must do no less than see ourselves as epic protagonists of the human drama, discounting our late starts at newsworthy endeavors.

LWSS 73 - CELEBRITY

In the Internet age, grandiloquent pronouncements from our overlord gurus still carry the day, but they all occasion pirate commentaries. Every text receives its anti-text, from the hoi polloi or from fellow antagonists on the totem pole, in comments section or rejoining blogs or vicious troll put-downs that established the lonely no-account as the moral worthy rather than the action-figure celebrity. Authors slid low into the cyber-slums to grapple with tormentors, while elderly literati reserved their bon mots for the dinner parties, grateful to not have been exposed as mediocre hecklers during earlier concealed times. How would Melville and Poe and Mailer have done as surfing commenters? Fired off a few choice strafings, only to get dismissals back from territory-guarding simpletons? Every person has now a cyber doppelganger, one who clicks and screen-interrogates with all the sangfroid of an autistic prepubescent, immersed in all the nonsense a wandering imagination can raise. To make a statement, the real writer had to employ a stable of alter egos, link-clicking, insight-exchanging, portal investigating, the useless 24/7 intellectual ferment that would qualify the author to step out of the typing shadows. Humans could forever *lecture* and *postulate* with the certainty of dead abbots, but only as long as the focus was dead ahead, so the conferences and classrooms would fill up with exorbitant-fees-paying penitents, ready to parade inherited family strangeness for a plot or find new ways to package managerial boredom.

LWSS 74 - PASTIMES

Without the means to construct a public self, the distressed individual lapses into the lacerating practices of a trapped animal. Drugs, skateboarding, alcoholism, whittling, poetic reverie, crocheting, video gaming, casino gambling, cell-phone babbling, screen-gazing, khat-chewing, religious prostration, sports-watching – the list of supersystemic diversions is universal and costly. Without a better world to construct, humans chase experience, a form of self-injury when the outcome is so meaningless. Good times await the heedless, but others cannot avert their eyes from the social losses, and inexpressible pain accompanies their fevered wanderings through the inherited culture. The traps around are not some matrix, not some mysterious dark energy, but the very fibers of being that animate our institutions, our practices, our masters. The need to escape entrapment will produce various methods of securing temporary gratification, and those cultural endeavors will constitute the bulk of human purpose, performed now with only minor variation through the decades that constitute life.

LWSS 75 - OpinioNation

The lies promulgated by the present supersystem are too awful and infantile to chronicle. Look around you; check within your family. Who has not turned sideways in the trap? Who has not been infected with undeserved exceptionalism leading to atomized obtuseness? The airways are choked with this year's absurd spectacles of manufactured hostility, oozing like unstoppable pus from the central wound. The left has to chime with patient explanations of the facts and morality that are contrary to the popular mood, while boardrooms are stuffed with guffawing, hands-squeezing profiteers overseeing the carnage. From a little fuse attached to the flimsiest of propaganda delivery figures , the networks and the news stations are set ablaze with dumb persiflage. In OpinioNation, every last human is a reduced to being a microchip of pure opinion, attached by media relays and social capacitors to the grand cosmic motherboard. Nothing matters but the opinion, every member of OpinioNation needs not the slightest experience or rank to proffer commanding judgment, so the content becomes universal. Titled men and women make vapid lies their public face, while the populace issues stern calls at the hardware store and convenience store counter against the "government," that demonic caste known as "politicians," the antithesis to the American conception of the righteous Salt of the Earth known as The People. Almost rarely, about as many times as the Young Communists play the New York Giants, is the stirring populist anger directed at anything as complicated as a "system." The institutional demands placed upon corporate bagmen are not contemplated, nor the far greater culpability of the elite overlords whose interests the rubber-chicken eating pols must safeguard. When gathered around the barbecue, one schmoe never says to the other ten: "You know, if I really knew what I was talking about, I would have run for office. Starting back in second grade."

LWSS 76 -   CYBER-POSITIONING

Enemies become friends of friends, because of one nicety such as a picked-up check or kind log-rolling word or tiny piece of friendship interaction . Heads are forever snapping from side to side – who is on the right side, who do we go with, who is trustworthy right down the line? In the age of the World Wide Web, with so much quick typing about so little, the dizzying speed of temporary assignation creates a marginally malleable self-identity, always subject to in-group re-positioning. What is your view about X? If you say that about X, do you know that Y says this that contradicts what you say about X? This is not just adolescent social chatter, but the average content of intellectual exchange between screen-starers on the finer message boards.   There is a stratified world where having a Name confers supremacy on mundane and superficial Positions, leaving the great unwashed issuing rejoinder opinions in the privacy of their cyber-outhouses. The winds push the rotting corn stalks to and fro, the field a fallow yesterday heading for a frozen destiny.

LWSS 77 -   GLOBAL POVERTY

Poverty is no fun in the rest of the world, not anywhere to close to that in the rotting despair of the Third World, but there is a special intractability to poverty in the world's greatest incubator of billionaires, the United States. Just the basics in America are endlessly complicated and built for capricious frustration: finding shelter, locating food, getting around in some reliable conveyance, finding a job that has more than next week as the horizon. The beckoning vices lurk in constant proximity: drugs such as alcohol and cigarettes, violence from the gun or in intimate relationships, a sense that society expects nothing but riches and glory from the trodden-down. In the Third World, a little money or a temporary helping hand is almost a rescue; in America, poverty is extremely expensive. Living in within the borders of the supersystem is a respite from the early death promised in places such as Mexico and Haiti, but the longer life will bring a life of gross burdens. Improvements have made their way to the poor, but this is is over a long term, sidesteps the enduring provinces of deep misery, and does not explain the endemic and systemic nature of its pervasive continuance.   All the established forces for solving the problems of poverty have failed – animal spirits, gods of all stripes, capitalism, communism, the lottery, education, noblesse oblige, guns or butter, self-reliance, community integrity. Social policy, the actual shaping of economic reward and retaliation, that is our common culprit, and it is a crafty villain, now unreachable.

LWSS 78 -   TV

The   mainstream   culture   of   the   supersystem   is   corporate   piffle   and sanctimonious mush, yet always bright and spirited.   Mocking and abjuring and cataloging its endless retreading of essential lies is a good way to contend with the volume of its shiny drippings, but there are also abiding and dynamic presentations of simulated life. Laughs, ideas, and cognitive stimulation float through the ether along with the barrage of insensate crapola, so as long as the social world has no need for common purposeful exertion from its citizens, the cathode ray is as good as any cultural means to find some version of attachment.   With no end product visible from the ingestion of culture other than personal entrancement, any form of art is a private synthesis, a less-than-transcendent universe of diverse weeds and plants, a generous spot in a contested, demarcated nature.

LWSS 79 -   TALK THROUGHT THE AGES

As the supersystem has built up through the television-corporate years, the nation's social spaces have resounded with the sounds of happy horseshit. Whether on the job, or in the family, or on the nation's airwaves, the fake enthusiasm for the ridiculous or the trite swung through interactions. The computer revolution added one higher dimension of happy horseshit, tricking-up those 18-century pastimes of opinion and celebrity speculation in day-glo colors with frantic clicking noises. Talk news, talk radio, cell-phone conversations about social slights, "holiday" gatherings for staggering families, art installation projects, corporate reports, self-reports to co-workers, substance abuse and also non-abuse, racked by pusillanimous avoidance of the epic mess caused by ungovernable social systems.   In a television-viewer interaction, the viewer maintains the rapt attention that is all but impossible in conversation with other humans,   damning the talking enterprise to intense superficiality.

LWSS 80 -   MONEY

The "corruption" in the body of the supersystem gets its nutrition from the fiber of money. What is not capable of happening through genuine affiliation becomes weighted through the attraction of profit – then is crushed a thousand times over into the finest particles that waft through every institution, insinuating themselves into every crevice. Every monetary advantage is replicated into countless derivations of privilege, some of which become mansions, some of which become expensive cocaine habits.   The   class-based nature of American institutions are obscured by the overlay of absurd myths and co-optations. A punk poetess and a queer novelist are hired by a Catholic college to give "readings" from their edgy works at the student center, grant-funded by the state and the college's student organization. Will the Pope or the cardinals come in for any direct slam from any of these two official voices against oppression? Who can be rude when money is on the line, direct-deposited now or promised in the form of more if all goes well and no tables are overturned in the sacristy? We should refuse to endorse any paper money to our own accounts that is not washed in nature's sweetest purity, but we all accept the "preacher's handshake," opening our palms to the filthy lucre while looking forward, never down.

LWSS 81 -   LIVING WITH DESPAIR

Sober critical histories of the current epoch will never do justice to the complex interplay of insanity and criminal commission that produced such an absurd social reality from such technological abundance. The Bush Terror Years, the Obama Con, the Clinton Charade, the Reagan Horror, the Carter Malaise, the Bush H.W. Debacle, the Nixon Years - all eras of official malfeasance, lying, killing, large-scale and looting, subversions and calumnies, accelerating oil fortunes, a rolling oligarchy of bestial scions and their loony courtiers. Given that the large swamp will end up fetid, dead, our historians will be dishonest if they depict therein animate life and sensible procreation. Who wants to surf a wave of oil? The plastic shine and the bright large screens could distract the observer from the losses that mounted from the workings of the core, but the rottenness was never far from the surface. This is not to single one layer as containing all corruption – the allegedly liberal bastions of American life, such as the Williams and Amherst colleges and MIT and Harvard universities, were to be as mobbed-up in this organized criminal regime as any of their more overtly lawless conservative megaliths. The complicit "environmental" lobbies, the defeated daily newspapers, doctors and accountants, sports and entertainment marketing extravaganzas, tepid documentarians and windy bloggers, tied by their muteness and intellectual obsolescence to the perpetuation of a fraud. Yet few individuals live in daily, close contact with the supersystem – they take whatever on-going joys and electric sustenance from the daily immediacies of their particular lives, so that in the removal of the face of the immense and controlling interlocking system corrupting the fabric of their lives, they feel only twinges of despair. Ideas of acceptance and rejection of greater social damage compete in this assaulted psyche, but the default position is a what-the-hell, permitting a functioning social presence even while larger issues of nihilism obtrude. The trash gets taken out, the dog gets some upside-down-scratch time, the next download is undertaken, even while the ideas of progress burn.

LWSS 82 -   ALLEGIANCES

As the supersystem tightened during the austerity wave, dedicated workers had no end of perfidy and felonious malfeasance erupting within and around the very organizations that signed their checks, but when could they fish and cut bait? The crimes committed by the banks and FoxNews and soda/cigarette manufacturers were easy to abjure, but then the obvious corruption oozed into their own bailiwicks, friends and junior associates got fired, the "downsizing" brought in new and odious owners. The action of disassociation struck these stalwarts of conscience as an even greater violation and capitulation than the evil fascist deeds themselves. Comrades of the cubicle got sent the door on their way to the almshouse, but "concern" meant generic beans when the storm-tossed household needed its income foundation. Principles were warped into deformed hot plastic, even those of mostly voluntary association -   there was a greater set of attractions to staying upright and in the house during the daylight robberies, not confronting the robbers themselves. This is simple truth, of no real concern on a nice temperate day, when the world is overfull of "information" or unremarkable pop analysis of the obvious, which lights up no screen nor augurs quick future riches. "We know this, man" is the rejoinder that places all political works in the remainder aisle.

LWSS 83 -   THE FUTURE OF WORK

As is becoming clear, there is no future of middle-level work for masses of people. Robotics and automation are staffing factories, people are being "educated" for a future of non-work, while the rules and requirements for modern sustenance seem to require last century's employment abundance. The supersystem is not going to permit legions of adults to sit in sybaritic leisure with secure government payments as productive uber-menschen fashion next-gen technology, since humans are wantonly jealous, incapable of resisting imprecations from damaged others, and are resolutely incapable of productive social disengagement. Visions of last century's mostly mythic iconic heights will bedevil the next generation, in this case producing legions of State U grads and their drop-out friends striving for the goodtime happy work in the carpeted cubicles of Acme Corp. In the limited case sample of myself, I became a successful novel-abandoner (In the absence of social meaning, what possible need could be fulfilled by reading fiction, non-stories of non-lives?), then gainfully employed at the most nonsensical of available working tasks, that of a prison "teacher," a laughable and sinister non-job, with benefits. Menial work or skilled craftwork is neither safe nor necessary nor in the cards for the current or future generations of school/technology-raised brooders, whose destinies are in grave balance. The days of "making" money are getting shorter as the fraudulent business of "managing" money envelopes the economy.

LWSS 84 -   FUTURE WAR AND THE MOON

How can a theory of the modern world and its furious descents find a way around the vacuity of terms like "peace"? The word has been spoken and invoked and pursued with the passion of religious zealots across the history of textual humanity, but then there is the working bureaucracy of militarism that promises, in a thousand position papers and factory orders, the weaponization of space. The drones and satellites and super-computers to direct them are already up and running, of course, but China and the US and the rest of the articulated national-corporate world are racing for that next fun frontier. Do you think a comparable force is gathering momentum to establish a global consortium to protect space and the humanity resting beneath it from this predation? Shall we sleep and dream with the protection of certainty that we are headed for the dissolution of our worst forms of virulent aggression? Relative improvement is a chimera if it cannot obviate the greater gathering of institutional forces to effect the next power grab, such as the energy contained in the moon's resources.

LWSS 85 -   NO INHERITORS FROM BELOW

The supersystem can consolidate its gains to greater and greater depths and widths, targeting any area into a neoliberal marketing zone, such as social security or space. The capitulation by what remains of the public commons will not be immediate, nor will the process occur in linear inevitability, but the logic of overthrow through stealth determination by entrenched interests dooms any insurrection. All the fine position papers in favor of liberal humane reform, all the finely detailed whipsawing between what should be and what nonsense is headed our way, none will convince a populace that is conditioned to look for covert "liberal" confiscatory arrogance beneath the rhetoric of fairness. This surge of populist antagonism

145

towards descriptions of social reality is strongest when families and friends gather , making received   wisdom from the contrived bits of corporate "news" and conspiratorial Internet farrago.   Get-togethers transmit this virulence of anti-intellectual chatter through declamatory grumpiness, brassy announcements of peeve, and solidifying disavowals, all the while circulating back to "the government" instead of its true and forever master class, the rich. The amount of spadework necessary to undue a society-wide intellectual hole dug by lunatic rightists and their "centrist" supplicants will last many lifetimes, including a good catastrophe or two.

LWSS 86 -   SEPARATE OR TOGETHER

Looking to artists and writers for profundity to invigorate the ceaselessness of toil and obligation is another off-loading of responsibility, but we are tomorrow's children. In a panocopia (panoply + cornucopia), the choices are too great for any common granting of meaning or purpose. Each individual's mix-tape of life is too stylized and varied to permit appreciative listening. Your life, that is, your private venue of panocopian scanning and selecting, is going to admit the occasional light from others, but the heat will be from your own brain. Your connections to friends and acquaintances and lovers and confidantes may be strong and voluminous, but the sleep will be forever yours alone, the dreams by you only as auteur, and the precision of your thoughts and ideas singular to you. Since we are defined by our cultural choices, not our jobs nor families nor home area nor political affiliation, we face the radical disconnection in our most intimate affairs of separate screens and separate beds, but breakthroughs of determined living happen at the lowest depths of the ocean, at the molecular level of social atomization, through anger and stress, despite all that a massed supersystem can stand in its way. Making human connections under the edict of the supersystem is onerous, fraught with the tensions of fighting the disintegrating effects of razoring power. Loneliness, a terrible condition of finding no usable identity in a destabilizing culture, takes the gift of life and robs it of its natural wealth. The instinct to find alliances with like-minded others, like the pop dreams of the melodic three-minute masterpiece, should not atrophy, but too many of the work, familial, parental, and chore responsibilities devolve into unrewarding blankness. Still, there is logic and passion in every human's performance of his or her day, so the species deserves a special citation for its self-reliance.

LWSS 87 -   THE OPERATING SYSTEM

Western humans have derived great levels of satisfaction with and psychic adherence to the established bureaucracies. From the halls of ivory academe to the VFW hall meet-ups of marines, from the over-arched churches of yester-millennia to the gangs of Greenwich, from the NAPA auto-parts desk to the high-rise corner office of the Mega-Global Corp, entire adult lives are built steeped in the combined organized labor of thoroughly dissimilar corpsmen and -women. Looking behind at the purpose of a life, a family can loom large or small, but the institution that preceded and followed the lonely life of the common fool stands as the human collective aspiration. This magnificent creation, that enduring profit-center of steel and boards of trustees and law-supported bribery and extortionate expansion, headlines the tombstones of prairie and urban honeycomb alike, and has given the supersystem its DNA, looks posed for a marvelous future. . Like urban meccas built on accumulated landfill, these institutions are built upon interflowing streams of bullshit, such as monotheism or bombing helpless Third-Worlders or the inherent godliness of the Sophoclean contemplative life or the beauty of the flavor-enhanced foodstuff, but the history of human inequality is an epic yet to be written. Easy justifications for intense and systematic subjugation of poor people have produced the human institutional default, the layered exacerbation of power. The working conditions for the wretched poor have risen in general terms since the days of imperial slavery and industrial expansion, but that legacy is available for viewing in all the urban diasporas, all the mines and pools and parched landscapes, all the back-water, hinterland, across-the-ocean supply zones of our globalized economic order. Walking on by is human trait, a integral human cognitive capacity to let the crimes of the bordered, delimited self pass through the filter of self-regard. We know how to process all the madness of our variegated social horrors – give them a moment's space, and they dissipate into the vast horizon. Immediate smaller concerns and occupations take over the controls with ease.

LWSS 88 -   CO-WORKERS

Co-workers cannot be made to go away, though you, the modern worker, have chosen neither them nor to be with them. They are not just in the territory, they become the territory, hostile and unforgiving if sufficiently bled of humanity. Work, as a function of nothing in the supersystem, becomes open to all manner of pettifogging nonsense, with only the barest of bureaucratic redress. Job mobility being only for the foolhardy or dragooned, workers are tied to the feet of the mentally dimwitted, the morally defunct, the arrogant busybodies and the louche tricksters, since a chain gang is only as mobile as its slowest member. Cliques and diversions may sustain the lucky worker and have them thinking the work-site an on-going party of friends and associates, but this image of labor bonhomie mostly went the way of the . 99cent gallon of gas and the natural health benefits of smoking.

LWSS 89 -   ARTIFICAL VOICE

The artificial voice is in effect when people must talk to sell, most plainly heard when radio talk-show hosts hawk instead of articulating, but also in the inflections of parents, teachers, bosses, and singers. Each intonation betrays a false self, an alternative being of command, a self-manipulated not-self of voice and stylized knowledge. It's a living, it's a job, it's a role, but it is not true to the internal identity of the normal human. The interactions with fellow humans of the supersystem is quite difficult for seekers of authentic communication of a self – when the social role is so valued in a non-productive culture, personal presentation is fraught with distancing artifice and minute calculation. The person who talks to me - what are they trying to gain, how are their own words reflecting back to them an ulterior version of themselves, how are they calculating the benefit of my responses to them, do they know my assents are more cooperative bleats than real expressions of new understanding, surely they know I am bluffing in so many small ways. This is not agony nor strained intercourse, more an overlay of theater into the quotidian, never to disappear in a social reality of no obvious utility.

LWSS 90 -   ANTI-POLITICS

In a 2010 Gallup poll, 42% of Americans self-identified as "conservative.," 35% as "moderate," and a far lesser 20% as "liberal." Nearly half of all Americans are fascists-in-waiting, a good three-quarters are vacuous of thought, leaving at most 1 or 2 % to identify as some sort of radical outside the three fully discredited political terms. After all these decades of allegedly higher education, after the debacles of

Vietnam and Iraq and the successful campaigns to discredit Nixon, Bush I, and Bush II, after the computer revolution and all the niche-cable coverage of politics a people can stand, after Barnes and Noble and more talk and comment than any people can ever had been subject to, a nation of unawares is the result. A large nation, of 300 million plus, the world's military, home to more professors than any nation in history, the leading per capita purchaser of goods ever to be, and all there is a few odd skeptics of the basic political order, most of this lost tribe wandering in sectarian fever.

LWSS 91 - THE PURCHASE WORLD

Inside the supersystem, cultural and technological riches have been widely dispersed. No social criticism should gainsay the incredible range of hedonic consumer purchasing that suffused the average home with the secular wonders of television, popular music, radio, computer gaming, remote gambling, and reliable refrigeration. No form of expression or technical sophistication was ever hidden for long from the masses of people during this epoch, bringing the joys of art, dance, drug-taking, sexual enjoyment, and communal discussion to every paneled den and carpeted ranch family room across the great suburban expanse. There were hidden costs and overt casualties along this multiply-paved way of big-box hunting and chattering mesmerization, but entire classes and generations of Americans defined their lives by the bounty of produced entertainment. In contradiction to the bleats of high culture ascetic snobs, this was as rich a life of fantasy as humans have ever concocted, disseminated to commoner and banker alike. No Christmas ever saw a bare tree in post-war America, allowing entranced kids and adults alike a cornucopia of treasures, Rock-em Sock-Em Robots to Wii to the newest plastic. Pornography, once the province of counts and pharaohs, became downloadable by the lowliest unemployed serf. This ever-fresh fandom was not the acme of human social achievement, as the ecological, financial, and energy crises that were created and sustained by this international explosion of seated rapture doomed the detailed and magnificent project, but the minimum payment is still being sent in, and the credit limit is still to be reached. Happy Holidays, to one and all, for now and the future.

LWSS 92 - AUTHORITY

To sort out the catastrophes unleashed and fated to be by the actions of the supersystem, humanity must arrive at a global arbitration board to sort out the complex and irreducible claims of knowledge and fact. Interested amateurs are left without a working machete to sort out the incredibly dense thickets of warning and proposal, relying on snatches of received popular wisdom to determine truth from falsehood. Factoids percolate from the established venues of academic or corporate research into the information carafe for the great waiting maw, but science is forever weak brew even for the most mechanical. The Internet has encouraged these amateurs to pronounce themselves experts on every last global or national political happening, but the enormity of the evanescent cyberspace has also reduced intellectual ambition, with every opinion proffered open to complete un-notice, or to petulant derision, or to self-disinterest. Social effect is caused by the actions of fault-ridden political actors of disturbed or defunct ideology, damning advanced and solid intellectual work to spectacular disappearance – though the scientific attempts to break through the ignorant political defenses continue, and some of which do succeed. All of us need help from authority to discern the truth, but authority has proven even more fallible than our own instant judgments.

LWSS 93 - GUNS

Feelings of powerlessness within the supersystem are diverted into the American fantasy of violence through guns. Though the walls of the supersystem may never be breached, being so vast and unknowable, when the authorities do come to make themselves known, the lone gunman thinks himself in possession of an equalizing legal force. However, the authorities do not work through the twirling of the pistoleros themselves; they send in their hired gendarmes, who in turn are supervised by those who are supervised, and on up the chain of diversified command, leaving complex buffers zones between the decisions of power and the delegates who dirty their hands in fulfillment of them. Prior civil wars and revolutions had identifiable targets available in the vicinity, not usually the generals or figureheads in the flesh, but close-enough stand-ins to get the message across. With the bureaucratization of power, wanna-be Panchos and Dons are left to shoot themselves, their ex-wives, or the breeze that wafts through their air-conditioned one bedroom. The small arms can win no more.

LWSS 94 - SPORTS

In the absence of a genuine life , Americans turn generation after generation to the spectatorship of sports matches. Every fan an expert, every game momentous, a lifelong seeking of "victory" through the ritualized exploration of numerical binary contest. Televised 24/7 with the latest technology advancements, corporate sports belie their illicit foundations of performance-enhanced drugs, staggeringly unequal outlays of money to fund teams, practiced physical and mental abuse, the exclusion of poor from any role but gladiatorial, enforcement of jingoism and ethnic exceptionalism, and poor hygiene. Of course, since there are few other acceptable venues for participatory hedonism, even dyed-wool leftists put aside their Trotsky trading cards to cheer on the capitalist running dog team of choice. Opposition to the supersystem too often turned into rancid anti-hedonism, removing happy enjoyment of trifles from the pastimes of sex, drugs, rock ' n roll, and athletic competition. As with all the other straitened and displaced social realms, sports could only offer disturbed and irony-laden spectacle, but there were no competing forms of modern life, none with the packaged, bizarre intensity of the advertising-soaked sports circus, ready to dip.

LWSS 95 - DOLLAR LEFT

The America I know shops at the Dollar Left, in smaller towns, too far from the giant box stores but still able to shop for the latest in plastic effluvia clerked by fellow welfare half-steppers, America's discarded. At Dollar Left, the debit machine is of the highest quality, but the security budget is cut to the bone since stealing the ersatz trinkets would be beside the point. As long as you've got Dollar Left, you've got hope, and as long as you've got hope, you are obliged to turn its way. A good deal might be found, next month, somewhere in the stacks of the unsourced potato chips, so you'll be back. Try not to worry too much about the clanging tie rod or the overdue payments on the way back from Dollar Left, or the Nazi bitch from Probation with the ability to handcuff you for the slightest misstep, or the future.

LWSS 96 -   PAPER AND WASTE

The loss of productive work, both of labor of intellectual-managerial, has led to the imbecilization of the workplace. The dense and the morally atrocious fall upward to the supervisory positions, where they collude in bringing absurd and dehumanizing exercises to the cowed workforce. "Training" exercises, helpfully referring in its title to the appropriate infant stage of life, permit dimwitted autocrats to strut before their victims to enact "trust," "role-playing," call-and-response intimidation, complete with wheelbarrows of instantly shreddable paper. How many educations, how many lives, how much creative potential went down that 80s-90s-00s drain, dramatically changing nothing but the browning of more rust? How many lies does an empire require – first in construction, then in maintenance, and then in propping up the debris as the long slow slide into the toxic ocean continues?

LWSS 97 -   APHASIA

The effect of seeing the supersystem at work is for the observer to become out-of-phase, not in alignment with the dominant ethos. "Aphasic" might be the appropriate term, but this is reserved for people who have suffered brain lesions that prevent them from using words. Advantage will be taken, by those who have the means to do so, so the system of systems will continue its amoral sorting of pleasure and pain. Humans do not turn off their consciences, nor do they refrain from self-examination, but there is no outlet for intense condemnations of wider social dimensions, so the tools at hand are manipulated, chimps using twigs to pull up some ants. In a world of grievous poverty and sensational incapacity to incorporate these horrors into a political shift, the human mind directs itself to light pursuits, an easy sauce right out of the can.

LWSS 98 -   MACHINES WITH US

Technology, in all of its vastness and the vastness of its inter-penetrations, has proven to be greater than any attempts to understand it, even far greater than any attempt to contain it. Primitivists rightly deride technology's decimation of nature, and of the long-gone spirits of "community" and "solidarity," but the human species acts as collective, and the collective has moved past monasticism and bug-catching. There were attempts to analyze the technology of the machine as it grew from industrial production to totalitarian reach, but as it accomplished the latter, intellectual efforts to document the scope seem to have faded, leaving illiterate computer entrepreneurs as the only interested parties. From head to toe, from cradle to grave, humanity is connected to machines, even of the old-fashioned kind like books and monographs, or of the newest cloud cell phone variety. Other humans form bonds with these machine-connected humans, offering some requisite animate warmth, altering the interactions between human and machine with some quotidian to mock-transcendent purpose, but the machines are always in the mix, always at work in the world, interposing reliable banality into the more volatile human-human contest.

Chapter SEVEN
THE ENORMITIES

ENOR 1 -   **THE ROAD**

30 million African dead in the Middle Passage. The tens of millions of native Americans scalped, poisoned, shot, starved, by the European invaders. Last century's millions of dead Iraqis, Vietnamese, Salvadorans, Filipino – were else shall you look and not see deserts covering innocent victims of the American Christian empire? Where did those stark facts fit into your personal version of the manifest journey to enlightenment? Unless there is direct consequence, such breast-beating is neither sustenance nor value. What good are private torments? Who needs any promises of retributive violence when the weapons are farcical? What known world wants protestations of "concern" and "care" that feed no dead infant? Our *policies*, those inchoate distillates being constructed way over yonder in some stale-air conference room by unreachable normal employees, ought to contain the wisdom that there have been murders and genocides and wholesale devastation done to advance American Christian empire, but, with mythos and practice in basic sync, our supersystem has yet seen the American rich fattened themselves to historic proportions. Their tax rates have gone down, their wealth has reached bulbous expansion, and yet they still arrange for more, for greater pity and protection. If ever there was a people less deserving of special concern, less in need of receiving greater spoils from the arranged political economy, it was this generation of rich Americans, and yet, in broad daylight, this was done, by many and all. How do we recalibrate the machinery to introduce some fairness to the competition? How can we answer that, when we have only proven that the opposite tendency, to provide material and supplementary support to the monsters of the productive intent?

ENOR 2 -   **VIOLENCE AND ACTION**

Any social critic must be asked: if you believe so strongly in the evil and criminality of your enemies, why do you then not take up arms and slaughter them? My answer is that we are all common human beings, made disparate by our tabulae of temperament and environment. How could I advocate killing that which could have been me, and could be on a couple of counts be me? I know that our legion of robber barons, and their voluminous coterie of abettors and sycophants, are so damaged by the ill-get of their incredible riches that only another Great Crash will make them into functioning humans. However, they were animated by basic social drives, as we are all, and though they have sponsored calamitous human suffering, are allied with the brute forces of police and prison and genocide, the pages of history are thin with precise reversal, are instead replete with slavery and killings of the poor, reckless luxury for the stupid rich, foreseen decrepitude for the ill-born. Rather than harness the power of the state to kill our enemies, we should harness our social power for controlling our conditions of work, housing, food, health, and leisure, but there are no indications that we as a species are capable of such responsibility. Revolutions are done by wheels, but humans cannot undue their influences nor their propensities to commit violence reprisals, and so have only been sporadic reformists and deluded murderous antagonists.

ENOR 3 -   THE WEIGHT OF CORRUPTION

The sums of money and skullduggery that spread across the intelligentsia have mutated across the years to a new geologic layer of corruption, emanating from the boardrooms, Langley, foundation conference rooms, hotel verandas, high-tech warehouses, and banking offices of the profit centers of power. There can be no apperception of this monumental structure. The layers are too deep, the weight too great, the worldwide sub-stratum of obligation and inclination of the elite structures subsumed under all that earth. From Marxism, through deconstructionism, past the worries of therapeutic psychology, over the carcasses of political debate, and sprinting around the fauna of scientific exactitude, theoretical language is meager against the supersystem, and for those who were tuned into popular culture, the foreign language of academic economic jargon, never learned, separates the onlooker even further.

ENOR 4 -   ANALOGOUES

Global-scale warfare has its sociobiological analogues, its evolutionary precursors. How does a rapist choose his victim? A confluence of opportunity, judgment, secondary justification, and need-driven violence. The schoolyard bully targets the prey at hand, for conflicting, hormonal reasons. Korea, Grenada, Panama, Vietnam, Iraq, and Iraq II – criminal state actions of imperial overreach. Would you like me to entangle their geneses? This involves collecting the ambitions and bloodlust of millions of discrete actors, disentangling the propaganda from the disseminated underground truth, and is fruitless if the military-political alliance is still yet regnant. Are we to see the implementation of a workable structure against imperial invasion? Not in our lifetimes. Corporations of enormous might reap direct profits from worldwide war. Shareholders and CEO's alike are beholden to the exercise of their bought equipment. For every foreign child's unatoned death, the stakes rise on the eruption of the next, more virulent technowar.

ENOR 5 -   ENMESHMENT

We are all enmeshed in determined social institutions that renew themselves each day through the governed actions of compartmentalized humans. Within the very sanctuary of your bed is the supersystem, shaping your sleep, ruling the severity of your nightmares, determining the noise outside your windows, covering your sleeping partner in various throes of economic anxieties and thralls of personal upturns. You are dripping pharmaceuticals from the terribly wasteful American health care system; your day's wants have been excited by a unique combination of propaganda corporate advertising, interpersonal consumerist goading, and sheer need; and yet you believe, correctly, that the sun shines its great munificence on you, and you alone. Your *impact*, your *legacy*, your *value*, your *contribution*, your importance to the known world will be of absolutely no importance to you when you die, momento mori, because all natural phenomena will be beyond the perceptual ability of the little molecules of nitrogen and carbon formerly thriving in your bodily host that will return as pieces of interstellar dust to this universe.

ENOR 6-   LIMITS OF COMMUNICATION

In the meantime before that end of our argument, that precious vale of functioning activity, you will be forced to confront this vision, and see the paucity of your efforts against the real supersystem and the cancellation of it upon your death. There are no talismans that will grant you superiority before this awesome double confrontation, not money, not corporations, not happiness, not books, because the human brain is built on fear, worry, and evanescent self-assuagement. Once we as a species domesticated, gave up the terror of being both hunter and the hunted, we constructed civilizations far beyond our ability to self-govern. Our vaunted capacity for communication, so beloved by us as our greatest distinction from the marmots of the world, served us well in the cave and the jungle, but our last *satisfying* inter-human conversation was most likely alcohol-dependent. Why did post-war America turn away from the scintillating glories of the family dinner table Mom and Pop soliloquy to the tableaux of each person's TV tray table before "Green Acres"? In modern interpersonal dialogue, there are so many layers of power dynamics, hidden agendas, unsaid remonstrance, pregnant pauses, and other-dimensional consideration, that our words become the least of our communication devices.

ENOR 7-   MEDIA

Without the pretense of social regulation, American society became a consumer-satiating power-resource-extraction machine in the 20th century. Those deep within its purview found their needs and impulses for cultural stimulation met by pop geniuses and corporate hucksters, bringing forth the bubblegum classics of the early 70s, after-school teenplays, mass-produced chocolate syrup for pasteurized gallons of milk, a paradise of pop culture for the tetherballing naïf. Nothing so sweet can have been more than illusion. Those with power, and levels of those below them, are bound to perpetuate their positions and advance their interests, through means of evasion, intimidation, disinterest, denial of truth, crime, and arrogance. The secrets of apple-pie corruption poke through these cracks of the mainstream corporate media, but without follow-up, without the intellectual commitment to moral resolution, the tidbits and asides float away in the hosts' high-wire acts to remain somewhat conversant, but ultimately above the fray.

ENOR 8-   AIE AND THE BOTTOM LINE

An entire paragraph can be written only using the clichés of American Individualistic Exceptionalism (AIE) that govern the mind of the ensnared subject about "hopes" related to "a better world." Brought to justice, lawbreakers, sustainability, change, transparency, entrepreneurial spirit, twenty lexicons of patently false constructions of the supersystem, beyond Orwellian in their actual global weight on top of the bound victim. The swath of time that made the current supersystem has been marked by the insidious sublimation of all institutions before the profit statistic imperative. There is no downplaying this - in subjecting all that comes into human interaction to money, to financial governance, the known world becomes a means to this strange power. Business people have infected all American institutions, now non-profits like the Red Cross, a child's possessions, your grandma's health, the schools of your ensnared progeny, national parks, beef jerky, outer space, and DNA. The "bottom line" is a powerful pull, erasing doubt and contemplation, canceling ambiguity and self-restraint, making grown beings into obtuse infants, narrowing all complexity toward the focal point of ultimate financial gain.

ENOR 9 -   EXISTENCE

Real life and its demands will take you away from contemplations of the supersystem. Defeatism and rejectionism are not sure-fire crowd-pleasers, and, besides, we all live in our brains, if we have enough to eat and a durable shelter.

Statistics, however true, cannot pack the dancefloor: sameness of consequence, mired in time. We can know the sweep of history, and then must contend with the overarching fact that we are going to know tomorrow more of the same we see today. What kind of *art* makes us enjoy the location of ourselves as needing to make money, needing to make with the family, needing to make a stab at *being positive* and *making a difference*? Obviously, this kind of rhetorical questioning of blatant conundra is not what grips the active mind of the arriviste public, who desire the new and improved. Who can contend with a entertainment week of ineluctable plethora? There is no story, of any one person, that can mythologize any issue or monstrous social ill, because we are not the humans that came before us, nor the nextgen contenders with greater knowledge and far more spurious claims to innocence. Have you chosen the night's media entertainment well? And the books- debonair, esoteric and eclectic, illuminating in an accessible way hitherto unrevealed truths? You will have exercised; will have not signed any orders to kill innocent civilians; will have maintained your spousal relationship with appropriate encomiums, short and brittle anecdotes, and sundry balm; will have exercised modesty and restraint in alcohol imbibation, discreet pornographic access; and will have followed existential self-questioning down the road but only so far. Is that the very model for proper, moral, dedicated, yet mildly fun-loving life circa the present? Today, you will have been that which you could have not other than that have been.

ENOR 10 -   LEADERS OR MOVEMENTS?

The supersystem is not the product of one or more Leaders acting solo – it does not operate according to the Great Leader theory of history wherein Presidents and dictators become the only humans, the world their plaything. The supersystem is a collective enterprise generated by agglomerated discrete forces of history, institutional traditions, human logics, myths, and supported initiatives. Paradoxically, the great down-surges in political or economic or social reality can be traced to the delusions of mad, powerful "leaders" – from Hitler's Final Solution to the fascist Bush II wars in Iraq to Star Wars defense from the all the recent Presidents. How can we know how power is exercised across such dimensions of time and scope? Since there will be no end to what has only just begun as the Supersystem, and since those who enact history are not given to back-tracking nor to precise measurements of imprecise and hidden power, we will never get the statistics on the back-room dealing. However, we should see all of these events as measurable on this scale, falling between the poles of pure centrally planned conspiracies to singular terrors of top-driven eccentric obsessions. The supersystem was never one person in command, but, unfortunately for us and most especially for the millions of consequent dead, sometimes one central capo can precipitate an avalanche from the miasma of his tortured psyche. . One malevolent idiot, swept into place by concatenations, setting off institutions into death spirals – but it, of course, a measure of the weakness of the institutions that they become abused to these nefarious, moronic ends.

ENOR 11 -   MODELS

The narrow specializations of academia dictate that history is seen not as stasis, but as discrete events lapping into each other. The future is always unknown to the macro-theorists, capable of being fundamentally altered and substantially redesigned. All moments of future time are of course new, all movements directed by the up-to-the-minute calculations of living, variable human actors. Yet when repetition and incumbent power comes to erect barriers to the flow of social change, the supersystem subsumes its constituents, and we get deepening ruts, closed-off paths, transnational pillage. Without a god or gods in charge, we are left to the collective wisdom of humanity, and despite its manifold genius, humanity has given the go-ahead to vigorous plunder of the poor. How much human meanness has the supersystem been responsible for engendering? The dominant social institutions bleed into each other, which is why it has become so hard to escape from the clutches of misery and sourness. The punitive judge is the household tyrant writ large. The petulant student is the caustic state policeman. Humanity only produces varieties upon types.

ENOR 12 -   **CONSPIRACY THEORY**

Conspiracy-mongering can be a fruitless game of speculation without a portfolio to prosecute allegations, but I do admit that I have been conditioned to be naive and credulous, not the worst of traits. Our government/business elites have been proven to have been murderous, complicit in great and varied genocide and pillage, but who has won convictions against them? The verdicts of history do not go to the promise of eventual power, but the actual exercise thereof. JFK/911/vaccine endemic establishment paranoia may be justified, but the supersystem is not going to be slain by the expose of one or two sinister mega-productions. Instead, there has to be a massive hollowing of its accumulated privileges, wealth, and ownership. And that is going to happen how?

ENOR 13 -   **BENEFITS**

The supersystem does have its benefits, favoring production and consumption, the world you can see outside your door in all its skyscraper and clean restaurant glory: good times, great oldies, puppies in the park. If you got it, that is: if you are on the outside looking in, in over your head or simply denied, the picture is not so rosy, not so beer and Skittles. The supersystem funnels its rewards to the birth-advantaged, DNA-enhanced, well-situated, or temporarily insane. You might be one of these, or you might not – though it is certainly not just a matter of perspective.

ENOR 14 -   **NATURAL SHOPPING**

The psychology of consumerism has not produced notable defenders of the human urge to shop for material goods. Critics abound on the left, who scorn the complications of acquisitions, contemplations and fantasies surrounding the buying of things. Voluntary simplicity sages, small-is-beautiful academicians, ascetics of the naturalistic bent, spiritual seekers, the café French, dumpster divers, college rebels, squatters and punks, re-moralists –   a   diverse chorus of condemnation of the wastefulness of a perennially unsatisfied society. Yet none of us in the developed West needed brainwashing to buy – it comes all too naturally, which is why the draining of this glutted cesspool of consumer anxiety will come only with extreme economic worldwide seizure, and nothing less. A natural haven of fawns sipping by the pristine pond will not appear to cleanse our society of its carbon-fueled sins – humans will continue to satisfy their socially dedicated wants as a condition of living. The corporate disgorgement of popular material goods has been the inheritance bequeathed to us, and if that epoch is to be replaced, as it no doubt shall, take the over rather than the under.

155

ENOR 15 -   REWARDING THE RICH

The most salient fact about our economy is that never has a group of people been less deserving of getting more of what they already had and had purloined – the American rich. Boomers and Gen X, Generation Y and the Toys R Us suburban children – no one could have been less in need of grabbing more – yet with the preposterous notion of the Unseen Hand, miraculously to these fair, unborn hands did the riches of the world flow ever higher. From tax chicanery to corporate financial crime to outright confiscation of others' wealth, the supersystem did these few million proud in innumerable ways. The cultural moment had been seized by young liberals daring to march on Washington for rights and a war-free culture, but instead of that terrifying spectacle, all involved became champions of the rights of global finance capitalists. Such a despised minority, these masters of the boardroom and the two-hour martini lunch, an untouchable caste who had to attend prep schools, operate the family crime enterprise, avoid the Vietnam draft, get by on convertibles and an evening at the country club – the 70's and 80's were going to right history's damnation of this supplicant class. The great wealth give-away was not by stealth, but with the active conspiracy of nearly all, in broad daylight, through the great force of ownership of the levers, myths, courts, jobs, political positions, and new products by moneyed elites. Great advantages accrued to these owners, an augmentation of the perquisites of history with the new methods for resource extraction latent in the supersystem. . We had let loose this monster, born of earlier monsters, and we had no idea how to restrain it, tame it, turn it around, or direct it. No one seemed to want to recognize the monster's presence, let alone become its master.

ENOR 16 -   UNTOUCHED BANKERS

What would be the point of delivering chapter and verse on the stupidities and criminalities of the economic branch of the supersystem, when there is no control from below, no opening that admits popular investigation? The investment banks, the commercial banks, the private cartel of the Federal Reserve, Wall Street, the accounting firms, the bond-holders, the entire interlocked economic apparatus – do you think they will collectively admit their power is ill-gotten and deleterious to the common good? Are you expecting to stop the on-going, historical, incalculable looting of the public treasury by these gangs of commandeers, brigands, and lunatics? Why chase illusions of intervention in this marauding stampede?

ENOR 17 -   SPACE AND REACH

A proper *spatial* appreciation of the supersystem is helpful, but not words can do justice to the size and reach of it. We are but one trillion-celled organism, with a limited visual field and perceptive qualities that often have us doing the same thing, with the same people, for the same dismal results. The supersystem, on the other hand, is a military-industrial complex, only at its most murderous leading edge, with this branch's active communications network of that should have the original DARPAnet originators gibbering in fear at what they wrought. How many wires lead into how many laptops and mainframes that govern what circumambient line of bombers, tanks, missile launchers, and bullet repositories? Where is the budget figure for this elevation of destructive manufacture and its salaried operators? Even the beginnings of an accounting for this world-historical military build-up and its attendant coups and conspiracies would not begin to ground the supersystem viewer in the inter-locking, dynamic, globe-straddling, bilge-pumping colossi of the next segment of the supersystem, the corporate-financial industry. Products made, resources extracted, profits laundered, by the fractional second, this is the body of neoliberal control, and its owns every piece of the known world, along with the temporal approximations of the past.

ENOR 18 -   DISCREPANCIES

What could we be looking for from the beat, the silver screen, the mockumentary, the political expose, the blog post, the sacristy, the incantation, the family dinner, the growing of plants, the walks in the park, the Internet start-up, the departmental meeting, the wakeboarding professionals, the pretty female mathematicians, from the hallowed pastimes and fabled commonplaces of cultural over-ambition Behind the screen, the final lament: we, the thoughtful chosen ones, have been so *ineffectual*. The waste, the degradation, the losses, the defeats, the worthless in charge of the power structure, the mountains and oceans of rhetoric and talk and position papers, all leaving us up Shit Creek without a paddle. There can be no undoing of the conspiracy of gross international theft of value perpetrated by the elite. Can you register the bill of attainder against this global malefaction? The money needs to come back, the houses need to be down-sized to a livable space, off-shore companies need to be smashed, the derivatives and commodities robbery needs to be prosecuted to the demolition of the industry, the reins and restraints need to applied, all in the service of containing the destructive impulse of aggrandizement that is all too human and historical. And then we see large pigs flying next to the pies in the sky – oceans of hypocrisy churning, chatter and text coated with oleaginous self-basting rhetoric. Because of the endless permutations of *connection* that all of us have to the supersystem, from clothes to food to culture, our speech and thought is laden with bombast and discrepancy. In the fantasy of the reformer, on comes a new supersystem, with new countenanced evasions and corruptions favoring another powerful elite. The improvements would be monumental, truly to be cherished, with lattes for the indigenous masters and happy singalongs with non-hierarchical seating, but supersystems do not get "overthrown," there are no spacetime ruptures in social reality, we do not all of a sudden get to be in charge of skyscrapers. .

ENOR 19 -   RABBITS

A rabbit, its torn hindquarters covered in blood, prone, in the middle of the dirt road, kicks frantically to try to get up, to remain alive, to move away, but it will, of course, die, within an hour. One human brain has a hundred billion neurons, with synaptic capabilities that stagger into the realms of particulate infinitude. In authoring a materialist, straight-forward social reality theory, I do not concede that all life is reducible, bendable, surmountable. The supersystem will govern us, throughout our diminishments, as the resolute intractability of aging, aching, and losing become sinister companions, but the least we can do is kick as naturally, as instinctively, as the suffering, doomed rabbit. Boomers will lose their aged parents and become ethnic, religious reverters, intoning ancient texts of divine authority as they confront a redrawn personal world, and others will see a more immediate violence of killing in their villages.   Other rabbits will run freely and safely across the highway, emboldened with the gift of life, unconcerned with its attendant conundrums stemming from awareness, finding hidden riches amidst the thickets.

ENOR 20 - **WHAT POINT OF ENTRY?**

And where do we start? Where or when does the rational become the normal? In this era of elite monopoly, the news and the corporate teams and the lecterns and the books are stuffed with the sub-rational, the ethical detritus that money accrues to its being. The recent past has been populated by the dim-witted and the absurd, the elevation of college-degree-bearing conservatives and military dictators, a Lexis roll call of names that have escaped the lips of our network anchors with numbing frequency. Do you want to spend the rest of your life picking apart these UC, Princeton, Harvard dilettantes? This has meant no representation, no country, no court, no contract, no peace for the true and the grounded, the lonely acolytes of social betterment and easy hold on the remote. With the languor of post-suburban plenitude as an inheritance, the American post-60's generations have gone off into the void, unarmed except for their taxes.

ENOR 21 - **PERFECT WORLD**

The dead are owed our commitment to living. The complications of a western life, principally money but very truly commitments to known others, moribund conversations, errant technology, limited achievements, and physical debilitation, are but so much cornsilk in a rich field of abundant stalks. Your life, my life, may be seen as plastic, unserious; whetted by spurious desires, pathetic re-playings of lower-order anxieties; churlish, bacteria-ridden, ego-driven; and absurdly over-privileged, yet the world should be on its feet in appreciation for the humble life well-lived. You held your tongue, you made another human feel loved, you did your chores, you did not give in to the forces of darkness - have a drink. If only you could be the leader of the supersystem, its shining light, its emblem, your life of effacing goodness the dominant ethos, then babies would coo, the birds would sing, the poor would be grateful for society's helping hand, and places of worship would close up shop overnight. The bombers would be abandoned one after another, the lights for the hospitals would be popping on all over the globe, ties would be loosened, mothers would swoon into a mate's arms, the television would create smiles with nary an ad, and schools and colleges would be let out. Sex would lead everyone satisfied and relaxed, if your life of transcendent but unnoticed decency were to become the standard.

ENOR 22 - **JUDGMENT OVERCOME**

Power accelerating, intensifying, occluding the light, disinheriting its progeny, gathering its more secretive, entrenched, mortgaged, rootless tribes, and sweeping across the drought-stricken plains on its way to the fertile crescent where the elite, is the latest chapter in the story of human civilization. American military and economic universalism has spread across every plank of our times, shadowing every move of even the most privileged, suburban apparatchik. Looking into the corporate office, past the government buildings and throughout the land of assisted-living seniors, their tattooed grandchildren, and full-tanked Ford F-150's, should leave the artist/academic exhausted, "spiritually" exhausted, unable to finish the next act. Posterity's judgment should be that only the best American artists had nothing to say, but that the hacks kept on scribbling and brushing in defiance of obvious societal commands to stop. Humans have chosen many means across the centuries to express their continental bafflements of what to do next, what to have done, and what to do with all that intense befuddlement – drinking, drugs, silent suffering, suicide, obsessive cultural attendance, grudge-nursing, and money anxieties. Our governments are born to act not in our stead, but to complete acts of "development," and who do you suppose they have been for? The common democrat imagines a progress, and there are great supersystemic markers of longer age, better meat, and happier technology for the masses, but the roil of antagonism and disparity should convince even the most enluxed Punjab that the ship of plenty sailed long ago.

ENOR 23 -   NEURO-REALITY

What, then, lasts in this world? Entanglements. We act, not of our own accord, but on the basis of conditional, environmental factors. However, we lack the operational, articulate means of identifying those factors – not ahead of time, and very rarely afterward. There are very few humans who must make even a partial, specified accounting of their actions, and of those that do, very few have interrogators who can design comprehensive frameworks for deciphering causality. We know what we do, but we know not why we did what we did.. We do not act on impulse, but respond physically in a delay of electrical charges that formulate seconds ahead in the brain. All acts of violence, all acts of love, all "choices" and ethical decisions, are products of innumerable molecular contestations. Who wants to delineate the precise dimensions of those nuclear reactions? We may still be rational beings, in the sense that we apply of gloss of cognitive reflection to our radical movements, but seldom is this cognitive examination deep, and less is it subject to the kind of debate that is an investment in structural integrity. Indeed, we could scarcely operate as social beings if we did this kind of intensive analysis, as is witnessed by the sorry history of cadres and cooperative Maoist groups. If we can evolve, we humans will find a more effective social means for understanding individual actions in the contexts of societal and psychological truths, but it also may be that we never will get above the delusional muck that constitutes our "free will" ecology.

ENOR 24 -   DESTINY

We cannot affect world events, we cannot disintegrate the coordinates of the supersystem's course, but we can look after our bank accounts and adjudge our interpersonal and intra-familial successes or failures, like ants scurrying over our minor part of the side hill. The poetry of life demands more than this working, commuting and fretting, but a view from space would allow us nothing more than an image of a species falling apart with environmental disturbance and degradation. Yes, I made something of myself, says every sentient being over a certain age, but it was hardly more than doing more of tomorrow what I did yesterday. You want glory, transcendent purpose, resolute companionship at the middle of your life? Are you a titan of industry, an entrepreneur for peace, a scholar for truth, a leader of genders, a clean, green earning machine and beloved Pops? Fine, you are nothing but a *string of accomplishments*, but though gifted with a massive pre-frontal cortex, humans have developed no adequate measures to comfort one another, to provide through their actions or words succor to others. You cannot help destiny.

ENOR 25 -   BOATS ADRIFT

To track the revolutions of the college-drug-delivery system lackeys as they swirl around towards the bottom of the toilet takes anhedonic fascination for the minutiae of one's own chains and oppression, and most of us lost the chance to become tireless researchers into global pain and corruption when we arrived into the televisual orbit. What do we do to approach the intricacies of global capital and global political control? As with most mysteries, we retain a fascination without finding any entry point that constitutes an actual opening into consequential action. Knowledge without action is like a boat in the ocean without a motor or oar – good luck riding out the swells. You'll have a better sense of where you are, what has gotten you there, but you will drift and drift, holding to the smallness of your immediate refuge.

ENOR 26 - SLAVES AND SERFS

You could sink into a conditional malaise, decrying the dead babies, the starving innocenti, the bone-weary over-worked lower classes, the suffering and destruction of so much humanity... yet it can be said of generations, since the plow was exchanged for the typewriter: we could not stem that tide. Human suffering is governed by great, immovable processes woven into the supersystem – and has been the great near-constant in human history, since 80% of the human population was slave or serf in 1800, as Lierre Keith referenced. Our actions, to a man, woman and child, are affected at the societal level, not at the infinitesimal individual level of *feeling*. All human actions should be performed according to a glorious, secular ethic of humane responsibility, but that Valhalla will not be reached by this version of an upright chimpanzee.

ENOR 27 - THE FACING OF TRUTH

Leftist social criticism in the United States must contend with charges with hypocrisy, of course: you folks living in the lap of luxury – what's the matter, five TV's aren't enough? Mad that life isn't peaches and cream below your castle? The earth is blood-slicked with murdered martyrs to the small cause of social justice, from the tortured and killed students and teachers of Chile, to poor workers and trade unionists the world over. State power, in which the police and the courts and government and corporate sponsors unite to kill the innocent, the moral, the true heroes of humanity, is an irreconcilable feature of our common global history. Our American suburbs are not being sacrificed to state murder, our little rebellions are not met with the DINA, the SAVAK, the CIA, the Mossad, the KGB, not in the overt way of the knock on the door. Yet the operators US have bombed incessantly since they discovered twice-removed military killing, and have strewn complex munitions across the valleys and deserts of our far-away circled areas. This is no small, minor historical footnote – but a rejection of all that we may contend exists to protect social order. Do not judge yourself too lightly – you live within a supersystem that has killed untold children, men, and women while small numbers of others have squandered vast reserves of wealth that is soaked in the sacrifice of our fellow unfortunates. This is not a call to remember, nor to forget – we all live with the injustice of the world in our own ways, with our own ingrained patterns of disinterest and avoidant motion. What you *think* about this callous picture of maiming, obliterating, and disintegrating of civilians is idiosyncratic, a product of your culture, but if we do not think about all that controls us, we think about nothing at all.

ENOR 28 - GLOBAL VILLAINY

You want *information*, though, the smoking gun, the inside scoop, on how all this supersystem runs. Who is the arch-villain? Who will never be revealed as the sinister force that precipitates nuclear disaster? Who runs geopolitics? What ultimate plan for world domination are they holding? What's behind each twist in the unseen global world of war, force, and devastation? Though a fantastically nebulous world, this primal arena of duplicity and avarice and killing is real and populated by human actors, so it can be diagrammed and understood, though time is running out, and so is the audience.

ENOR 29 -   WHAT?

The battles have moved from the streets, comrades, and into the color-coded wires, where only the bravest shall tread. Untangle the cables, get it all right with Jesus and his fourteen boatmen, and we can regain the lost sheep. What is wrong with rationalizing futility? If we did not make this world, but contend with obligations to have done so, what good is the mind but for these considerations? We must use our faculty of reason to delimit that which we did not, are not, and cannot do. The supersystem is issuing events and new personalities at the speed of a new commercial, but it all conforms to the dismaying arrangements of myth and lies. The corridors of power are still yet staffed in the night, giving life to the executive's memo, moving capital anew, chasing the implied promotion, occupying the raw molecules of time with deceptive aggrandizement that continues the human vector. Take your every night's trip down contemporary lane, and you will encounter the same scenery that you passed by on your way in. We started out as the hunted out in the savannas, killing to survive in small bands, not a moment's breath guaranteed to us in such fearsome company of the mastodon and the wooly mammoth, so this little status of endemic futility is a minor drawback to an existence of monumental security.

ENOR 30 -   CARING

The reality of power has consigned its efforts to a vacuous sense of *caring*. We care about the poor. We care enough to want to Free Tibet. We care about torture. We care about the suffering. We care about not offending other people. We care about our children, above all else we care about our own pure genetic offspring, we care about women, children, babies, and the elderly dying in American-sponsored warfare. We care about the dying planet. We feel your pain. We care about history's judgment. We care about the concerns of our charges, be they students, clients, customers, or patients. We care about sustainability. We care about AIDS, about Africa, about the plastic in our oceans, about the threatened species, about our sex lives, about anything and everything. We care about having a good time, we care about "relationships," we care about our work, we care about law, God, existence, and our lawns. We can be made to feel crippling guilt if we do not care enough, about Tibet, Somalia, the future, the planet, your mother, a sick bird. We care terribly to not be accused of not caring. However, *caring* is the cheapest of "feelings." Caring is at best a precursor, at worst an arrogance of superior morality that masks futile inaction. If I am suffering, I will reject your caring, and ask instead that we work together to stop or burden that which is directly causing my suffering, such as the knife you are twisting into my side. Even the enemy of caring, the uncaring, can be of help, if they can be directed to remove the causes of my pain, my hunger, my imminent death. We need not to *care* about "alleviating" global hunger, global economic inequality; global ecosystem devastation, global civilian death – we need to place blocks upon the systems that cause them.

ENOR 31 -   ONE LIFE

Our lives are but variants of others'. Creative artists and top-rank professors have lived on the upper reaches of sanity, pursuing their maniacal quests past when the less directed have given in to lassitude. Sports, home, music, hiking, raw and puerile anger, road rage, obsessive love, sexual desire, withering but fragrant boredom: one life, one supersystem. You also: one life, one supersystem. I know that each description of a life is diminution, and that there is no universality to any of our adventures. We will have left a lot on the table, and should desire no one's inspection of our achievements.

ENOR 32 - THE ENDGAME

None of the post-Nixon governmental machinations can be approached as minor aberrations, nor as glitches in a machine being fine-tuned. There was a full-scale takeover of the supersystem in the daylight, with everything not nailed down taken and removed for appropriation by wanton plutocrats. As a greater truth, this period was also the death of the social institutions that could not provide any check or counterweight to these disasters. For all the righteous bombast, the books and the bumper-stickers, the intense loathing and the animadversions upon the uncouth corporatists, the ground upon which these critics stood was forlorn hinterland. We should have never trusted ourselves or our social institutions again, should never have permitted the institutions to roll on as if temporarily errant – there was murder, and genocide, and far bigger mansions, all so hideously pointless. Yet, of course, no society gathers shames around its shoulders, so without its forceful imposition, none accrued. Those same desiccated institutions of the papers and the courts, the classroom and the NGOs, the publishing houses and the Internet chat rooms, the ballot organizations and the animal husbandry, kept their payrolls and charity campaigns, and so we stand today. How will this turn out? That is always the judgment. After the journey, the points, the work, the process, the mighty labor, none of which can ever match the finality of the outcome. What will be the endgame of this? Where will we arrive? The youth will be gone. The accomplishments will fade the monetary triumphs over in a heartbeat – so what is the ultimate score? The problem is that the supersystem will never be in its final state. Others can see order in its upper reaches, but that is a work of anticipatory deceit. The burdens of humanity act upon us in our social roles, so we move over the trials with the stumbles of the last days' drunk. The sheriff's deputy writes out the speeding fine for $126 in a pitch-black raining night, commiserating with well-worn rue about the demands of his job and the opening of deer-hunting season. Young mothers face low-wage work with unaffordable child care. The social toll can be found in any family, any small city, defying art and now analysis, because who can see the denouement as being anything but more cruel lottery morality?

ENOR 33- MORAL JUSTICE

What justice should the elite of the supersystem face? Were they little Eichmanns, or normal soccer dads, or brazen thieves, or conscience-less drones, or technocratic nobodies? What justice should be meted by the poor or starving of the world towards the gas-guzzling, military –tax –paying, wage slaves, most including me and you? Should there be a guillotine, a swift death for first world sins, an enforced revolution to bring the meek to the command of judgment's sword? The simply cry of "circumstance" should not permit us to retain our ill-gotten surpluses, but the knowledge of the cruel power of environment should stop the executioner's rage - please? When the supersystem begins to incorporate a moral accounting arm into its daily operations, then we can start to fear the reaper, but for now, these are times of no consequence. Turn the channel, rely on the insulation. Who are we relying on to wash away the blood of human corruption?

ENOR 34 -   LEGAL ARENA

Large-scale enterprises like the supersystem demand large-scale interpolations. Courts have a shameful history of upholding dispossession, militarism, and punitive incarceration, updated with a clerkish stupidity in the late globalizing 00's. On each and every issue, there are nuances and backgrounds and histories that predate and supersede mere declaiming against the Authorities, but we have run out of time. Will informed masters provide revealing information that will obviate claims against them, casting doubts on lower-order rectitude? The connections between the decisions of those emplaced powers are the evidence that proves the grand scale of collusive, reinforcing action, but there is no court in the world ready to indict the supersystem, let alone its active myrmidons.

ENOR 35 -   SMALLNESS

Every age recapitulates its essential myths of supremacy in its essential supersystem failures. In our earlier incarnations as hunter-gatherers, we humans conducted every day's quest for survival as group members, attuned and responsive to group dynamics above all else. In our much later age, we are atomized individuals, circling the nightly entertainment as solo hawks. Our resultant blindness is to the worthlessness of the individual in relation to the known mass worlds of circumscribed institutional action. We write, speak, think, vote, argue, dream, work, and chastise ourselves and others as if we were powerful agents of enormous social consequence *on our own selves*. Though we have relative degrees of standing and effect as unequal economic actors, none of us are irreplaceable, none of us are much, none of us are history's darling. Measured against the universe, we as individuals are below nothing. Nearly all of us are anonyemes, while the big cheeses among us are ready to disintegrate under the pressures of gross ego inflation. Shout and rage with spittle as we might, crank up the amp past the blood-inducing number, we still are mere mortals, leaving trails behind us only in metaphor.

ENOR 36 -   CURRENT STATE

Human beings, without work to do, end up devouring themselves. Unless a war or a collective economic enterprise comes along to focus the energies, humans fall back into competitive destruction – drugs, family strife, overeating, robbery, business duplicity, aimless hatreds and lunatic religions. Once primordial man had hunted and gathered, the next phase was up in the air, and so often a degeneration into cave-befouling screamfests. Where do we turn when our bloodlusts remain unsated? No one knows, though the idea of dissolute artistic creativity excites a few, with a little gardening and children-shepherding thrown in to stay the forces of ennui. So bring the war home, or reduce us to pre-industrial savages clearing land and slaughtering animals, and then we can make this humanity enterprise work, but failing that, we look at our psychic displacements and blame those at hand for what we could not become.

ENOR 37 -   CONFIRMATIONS

The confirmations for the tSS come all the time, through the transom in newspaper articles, on-line, in magazines, in books. Placing all these pieces of evidence in an order is a Herculean task, and there is no glory in selfless monasticism. This was not an epoch for the shaking of the head, nor could outrage be directed towards a useful protest. What was new or *news* about the sinister, limitless takeover of social institutions by superior interlocked forces of profit and corruption? No amount of informed reading, no grasp of a meta-conceptual framework, no theoretical command of Engels and Friedman coupled with graduate-level neuroscience knowledge, could prepare the critical ground for the tSS. Hopelessness, however, is not a good sell at the State Fair. Other histories could testify, with great professionalism, to some of the Hidden Facts, but if the great point was pointlessness, how could the masses come aboard? Humans have lived and died in arrangements of stupefying violence and incalculable social defilement across dozens of generations and throughout all cultures and continents, burning lonesome anger into heirs who fall into new graves of avoidable construction. What good comes from bemoaning the human misfortune, when unearned privilege can be enjoyed for the price of a withdrawn conscience?

ENOR 38 -   **BLAME**

Where should we direct our honed scorn? Should the individual be *blamed* for actions done by his or her government? *Blame* is a concept only, not a nightly show. There is not a blame board in the sky, and precious few opportunities for any human actions to receive formal censure. Who blames, who carries out the blame decision, who gets the blame benefit outside of the specious arena of the courtroom? If the supersystem functions to deny power and control to its vast municipalities of lower subjects, then the hypothetical blame must be forwarded to the elites, who in turn are operating by the established logic of the supersystem. In no case does any of this intellectual morality matter, since human society continues to produce real and mortal effects day after day, from death to undeserved riches, all under human purview and control. Social science can tell us how the work is going, yet if the signs continue to stun the notion of radical improvement, where do we turn but to impotent castigation of the conditioned subjects known as "the people"? These folks may benefit mightily from political economies, yet how have they acted but in their own self-interests derived from the arranged particulars of their collective institutions of far superior control?

ENOR 39 -   **THE FUTURE OF THE INTERNET**

Say you take this radical recalcitrance to heart, pick your favorites, and adopt the urged worldview: what then? As currently designated, there are no mass movements for systemic reinvention that meet the high standard of the tSS. The Internet , another long line of cultural artifacts now the servant of industry, is harassed by polluting ads, editorial control of absurdly named "administrators," a pestilence of trivial engorgements, and a morose future; without the direction of committed democrats like Tim Bernars-Lee, who wants to wager on a product of such corrupt ownership groups? Little snippets of ego-driven calumny – where is the genius in participatorial clubhouse apologetics? Who got off on typing clicks to a backlit screen?

ENOR 40 -   **THE TOTALITY**

The supersystem will not be adjusted by the centrist political panaceas of "bipartisanship," or "nudging" social policy, or tax cuts, or the World Trade Organization, or by Interfaith Councils. Parents cannot be expected to "raise" their children inside the supersystem, nor can teachers "teach," nor shall the meek inherit the beauteous fortune of the earth. Our great faculties of speech an text and art are not matched by any evident propensity for social organization, so we are seeing Great Failures in all the formerly venerated traditions of liberal democracy, consciousness raising, barn raising, knitting circles, monasticism, surly drinking binges, catafalques, and ermine ranching. Against the breadth of the supersystem, the "liberal" or "radical" practices *selective compassion* (SC), directing withering anger at injustice towards, not a totality, not a system of systems, but at narrowed obsessions. Each issue or cause or even venue may be fully in need of reform, but the full package dwarfs any of the gains, to say nothing of the risks of death, prison, or penury. Eco-warriors save tortured trees and martens while puffing on American Spirit cigarettes, swilling Anheuser-Busch, and leaving the world to starve its human babies. Genocide in one continent occasions a worldwide boycott while genocide in another land evades the selfsame movement's pure righteous opposition in theory. Bombers fuel up while surveilled marchers take to the paved streets of first-world dictatorships of the elites. Living green becomes the motivation for conference attendees to fly and drive to an urban oasis while a pipeline leaks leaking effluent into a Nigerian delta. What one area of systemic oppression demands sacrifice while others are accorded a pass? Who could see overall success when not one facet or sub-facet of any institution is governed by entrenched power subservient to standards of fairness?

The night could be studded with position papers from some of our finest scientists, sociologists, futurists, metaphysicians, and lords of the manor, but proposals and diagnoses are in the billions since the Enlightenment, and where are we now? Instead of Nobel-level ten-point plans, and rather than the magisterial histories of our recent past, and substituting for overviews of the onrushing calamities that will scare the pajamas off the cat, why not demand of tomorrow the full redress. No leader will come forth to brighten the darkening skies, but there could be the terror of a storm. In opposition to the supersystem, there has been only *talk*. Without the reins to power, without portfolio, without political consequence, without jails or supertankers, the opposition has issued, in sum total and covering all, the chirpings of books + speeches. The putative opposition were alive, had families, read and wrote, but they inevitably failed as the purity of declamatory rhetoric met the corrosiveness of institutional corruption. Anarchist philosophers wrote narcing letters to the police. Level-headed naturalists mutated into spiritualist gurus. Anti-corporatists wore corporate shoes. Humanists were awful parents. Male leftists were beastly to their mates. How did any of us baby boomers equipped with a mind do as a rounded human being in the face of such statutory pitfalls? Down the checklist of purely cultural integrity (CI) each of us can go, minus points for being Bob Dylan fans, plus for shopping at Trader Joes, minus for...

ENOR 41 -   **ANOTHER cliché**

In every great crisis there is, paradoxically, great opportunity, great opportunity for the reigning forces of the supersystem to consolidate and superimpose further exacerbation of crisis. Humanitarian intervention in war-ravaged or genocide-visited areas has been proven to be disturbed, ineffective, or dangerous, and so the great liberal fiction of bringing relief through American-led military/scientific invasion has been killed. The UN lives on in tatters, grossly underfunded and without the backing that could ameliorate the economic ruination of billions. When pessimists are called idealists, and idealists are graduated alongside their antithetical corporate antagonists, the only product is interpersonal sniping on the job, on the blogs, or in our large sporting arenas. The deformations caused by the vectors of monotheism, neoclassical traditionalism, munitions, and corporate reinforcement hardens the mass mediascape into crude re-enactments – those 57 channels not worth noting or combating, but if they get some segment of the masses through the day with smiles and excitement, then they are worth their social weight in Ivy degrees.

ENOR 42 -   SOCIAL SCIENCE AND PURPOSE

Social science held such post-war promise to bring rational intervention to society, and in fairness there have been towering professionals on the margins constructing our social reality. These marvels of bureaucratic integrity are mavericks, able to shepherd their projects through the mazes of funding, professional obstructions, and real world dissemination. However, the supersystem does not respect the accomplishments of those in corners, but moves with violent power across large dimensions. In each of our working lives, we certainly could have done more to be of benefit, though we acted in accordance with the directives of our self and social mores. Were were underutilized by our society? Did our best intentions and greater talents get thrown away in the chase after a buck? Shall we look back with an admixture of pride and regret upon the path destiny guided us through? Only if the sun smiled us alone and pushed us into the locus of power, because, in the supersystem, there was nothing for us to *do*. Wherever we traveled in that great ordered plain, we established no frontiers, but lay our light burden upon an arranged bathoscape.

ENOR 43 -   THE ENTIRETY

The supersystem is capable of many horrific conspiracies, ones that started wars or funded corporate domination, but the evidence has been post hoc, when we live in a pre-hoc world. The power will reside with the players, and if none of us are players, how we are to claim greater competence? Those of us on the sidelines have the unsullied integrity, yet the world does not run on the fumes of verbal righteousness, but on the effects of true, crushing decisions and inactions. Imagine trying to unearth the perfidy of the global corporate/military complex, through all its secret, covert, cross-planetary alliances and operations, resolving all the motivations, triple-crosses, money laundering, drug trading, weapons procurement, genocidal science, and subtle academic and journalistic flatterings and corruptions, and then trying to enjoy the sunset. This stream of war and military killing would become an unstoppable flood, overrunning any hold on a sane world. The glassed-off world of high-tech state murder will forever be the netherworld, where all becomes blood, deception, and social hatred. A human resolution of our drive towards the purchase of remote harm upon destructible others is not forthcoming. Everyday violence that has been the lot of humanity since its emergence from the sea can make any sentence a pale exercise in aversion, and in an age of technowar and mass incarceration, dead babies and massacred villagers, no prescriptions for a halcyon world should have the lead.

ENOR 44 -   MONEY

Money in the supersystem lows in epic coursing from its original accumulation outward through and over and around the flimsy or low-level social levees.. The obligations are never without jealousy or machination, but the money is in every form of energy, from liquid to rock, from gas to blood, and defines social reality through its absence, through its constant dispersion into though and action, through its unknowable dimensions, and through its inherent distortions and limitations. Money could from nothing, it could come from writing, it could come from being a computer genius, it could come from the trust fund, or from working for the Man, from basic plunder and corruption, but the lack of money did far more damage than the possession of money gave happiness – unless the item bought was a bargain and worked.

ENOR 45 -   **THE SCORE**

A life will be measured against the supersystem. Who are you, what have you done, in the face of such a monster? Were you a part, an outside element, and how much of your destiny did you control? How did you get along with your significant other, and how did you make yourself happy? Were the good times yours, or did they pass too fast?   What fraction was worry and anxiety to what part unconcerned purpose? No one can answer that, since no other person can be an accurate judge of the honesty of the response. The larger reality of the movements of the entire mass of humanity, and of the domesticated animals and performance animals that join in the dance of planetary life, constitute the standard. Upward and beyond we view, never knowing that most elusive reality: *the score.* Pop psychology rushes into that brink, offering every approximation of moral judgment, thrown at the porous brain from every media angle and cell-phone harangue from a semi-friend, but the life passes as a sequence of 1's and 0's with no record kept nor label affixed.

ENOR 46 -   **BEASTS**

The wayside is littered with works of seriousness. Others have not given up on the mapping of the wayward dimensions of the supersystem, evidence that when properly focused and supported, the human mind can produce professional monographs. The world can be told, for instance, that American's top 1% of taxpayers paid a 33.13% tax rate in 1986, and 22.79% tax rate in 2006, and that the same top 1% of taxpayers made 11.3% of the total income in 1986, and 22.1% of the total income in 2006. Why not then throw out all of the country's degrees, all of the country's books, all of the country's managerial class, along with all the yachts and loafers, into the eutrophic miasma if these statistics stand? Not a single moment needs to be spent in justification or in amelioration of these perfectly unjust, dismal facts. The country's rich, built on structures of family fortunes tied to every capitalist exploitation imaginable yet buttressed by the collected aspirations of upwardly striving manager-bureaucrats, became the beneficiaries of economic charity from the entire world below them. So then we are to cry in our beer, deride our intellectual enemies as vermin, and embitter ourselves to an infirm old age? What constitutes a real support beam in living atop the superstructure? Expressions of fatigue will not last, since our lives are always built upon the marvels of inherited construction that allow us to see ourselves as the greatest beings the known world has ever produced. Every facet of our social reality has been formed by the wondrous collective of blind human industry, far too great and disparate for any consideration but our own appreciation. Other generations of humanity spent their adult capital on passions of progress, which we know has been conclusively determined to be a false vision. Beasts like the American health care debacle, the American corporate advertising horror, the American military establishment, the American car monopoly, the American higher education colossus, will not be "reformed," any more than any beast of the field became small and docile. Instead, they either continue as great and awful beasts, or another beast causes a fight into extinction. Bet on the former.

ENOR 47 -   **CONTINUITY**

Having foreknowledge of global calamity is not the same experience as being in one. Heedless rejections of sour contemplation will become existential marvels as the lights grow dim, the lines grow long, and the young and old see no jobs ever coming their way. In an uncaring, life/death cycle universe of finite experience, we will adjust our sights as we see truths both radiant and horrific deepen. Tenured poets kill themselves, and while the sunshine is still bright, others point to the looming darkness. Apologists for the supersystem are merited in their condemnation of gloom-wallowing beneficiaries, who feel better when they try to feel bad for those who have it bad. A significant element of the thinking classes professes consternation over the horror associated with the supersystem, but they are loathe to detect the processes of damage and decay will accompany all our earthly exertions. Our efforts at redress and re-balance are far too late, doomed to only minor effect against epochal forces. Of course, as humans who always live in a limited place and time, we will confabulate a cognitive existence out of the available sources of light and optimism, damning the majority to the wayside while the lucky and the driven pass around the destruction.

ENOR 48 -   **CCLA**

The great danger in another clarion call of the looming apocalypse (CCLA) book is the lugubriousness of the solitary herald. Impassioned by his or her own imagined perspicacity, the savant hears the grandiose notes while others bleat and clamber. Down go the facts towards the abyss of recitation, the accompanying philosophy stripped of rejoinders, imprecations, self-rejections. Pessimism need not be such a sad business, but a grand and good-humored celebration of verity's cold security. Science promises great reversal of physical reality in the future, cooking versions of incredible change that will, alas, not reach the mass of humanity in time. Teleportation and eternal human life may be a human's birthright in a few odd generations, but will any fantastical advancement represent liberation of humanity's collective needs? The track record for the transformative morality of all of science's concoctions is not good: we live in a majority of longer, but not better. Though we are in the rule of social turmoil and devolution, the auguries are for increased social mismanagement, not collapse. Humans do not tend to give up spoils, gathering the booty as if won by rewarded exertion, not conditional placement, giving the social burden to unseen others as a natural law. None of us can change it all, so we persist in changing very little.

ENOR 49 -   **THE CMP**

The planet and humanity alike are under multiple and dire threats, and only a dedicated team of reformniks without portfolio (the Crisis Management Party (CMP)).can organize humanity back to a semblance of proper functioning. Coming to the scene with light baggage and under no corporate control, the CMP can alert the mass of humanity to the need for a *Mission: Impossible* approach to the criminal, dispiriting, overwhelming, seemingly intractable array of metastasizing social problems. Sponsored by the monied class, who will fund this rather than face the updated guillotine, the CMP will develop a Civilian Corps (cc) of unemployed, underemployed, and disaffected workers who will build, fix, design and construct parks and community centers, day care operations, high speed rails, and pony ride carousels. The rich have profited obscenely and beyond measure in the post-Vietnam neoliberal supersystem, yet they will feel happy to be alive, in some possession of a fraction of their stolen spoils, but with more direction on where their taxed wealth can go than down the "governmental" rabbit hole of military hardware and surveillance technology. However, the vested interests will not accede to a diffused anti-power, one that claims no objective but social reform, and there is not likely to be a competing uber-mythology to capitalist profit that humanity can produce, once its communal arrangements have been breached. Humanity is well aware of poverty and economic inequity and the horrible deaths of civilians in protracted wars of empire, but it cannot move from this initial stage of awareness to a forestalling action – the available designs for civic improvement are historical failures.

ENOR 50 -   NAZI GERMANY TO THE US

Cheering like Germans, professing patriotism like the Germans, valorizing hard work and naturalistic leisure like Germans, permitting intrusive corporate and political advertising like Germans, organizing personal life around communal mass media like Germans, sending deluded young men off to technowar like Germans, we Americans are, like Germans, caught in the totalitarian power of a irresponsible supersystem. There are yet the "Untermenschen" in corporate diversity America, those who are not in the crematoria, but who are less than worthy, our "asocials," who should not imagine an equality of humanity because of their sexuality, their economic status, their racial assignation. Europe's virus of anti-Semitic eliminationism has mutated into the American corporate governmental endorsement of disequal economic practice that casts communities as virulent, abnormal, or pestilent. Mass death may not erupt in this version from political bullets and gas, but there is death, there is dismal suffering, there is arrogance, enormous waste, and intense boredom. The fallacy of historical equivalency absolves the present of commensurate guilt, and there are massive differences between the times, but in the laboratory of human social engineering, we are being manipulated by some of the same variables, none of which need to have continued to be of such enduring power. Good – now let's go out and party!

ENOR 51 -   ONCE IN, AFFIXED

If there are gaps and stretches and exacerbations and off-kilter arrangements in our social economics, we have to shovel in enmity, myth, violence, conspiracy, and propaganda. Multiply our problems by the weight of all history, and then factor in the exponential value of discordant social institutions, and we will still be galaxies short of the numerical representation of our social economic inefficiency. Can we block all the social imperatives that keep the supersystem destroying its very foundations of ecological plenitude and human initiative? Not today, not tomorrow – and the prospects for righting social injustice are yet made greater by the co-optation of lifestyle liberalism into the corporate supersystem, so gay marriage gains its acceptance from the central powers as it shaped into another mainstream force producing gay corporate couples, LBGT corporate assimilation, conservative-friendly religious gay culture, LBGT bombers. The supersystem is the dominant force, allowing token pockets of deluded resistance as it makes private profit out of whatever was temporarily public. Making what has been privatized back into a public good, such as was proposed in single payer health and net neutrality and higher education and corporate law and campaign finance reform, has proven to be impossible – once affixed, the forces of profit are symbiotically locked upon their area of predation.

ENOR 52 -   **ART AND SHOPPING**

Prolixity funds its own demise against the supersystem. Burners-on-high fictionists and never-hesitate philosophers release streams of fast consciousness, outpourings of observation and consideration and research that is as worthy as any other human act such as breathing or staring, except that those are virtually involuntary necessities, and printing verbiage is an attempted statement of rationality. Little ink marks on a flat sheet are one way to swirl around the given chaos of a human world, but no one should mistake desperation for transgression. A human goes into the wild and scream imprecations ceaselessly unto the void, for hours and then days, and would be adjudged a lunatic. A writer clicks out hermetic sentences without surcease, without interjection from challengers, hell-bent on fantastical self-explication, and is safe enough to be a parent and store household toxins. Forget the ironies, just go shopping, says the modern world.

ENOR 53 -   **SELF-CONVICTION**

Those who chose the corporate path must live by it. Others, who can claim they made no overt move toward the corporate reward, must still face their concessions and associations with the beast. Buying products, flicking the switch, cashing the check, sitting through the annoying advertisement, easing the children in front of the friendly monster, listening blankly to the rock-climbing pitch for the Marines – our living space is now a supersystem colony. There are many, many ways in which we will not live as pure, righteous, soul-enriching, virtuous, world-changing, nature-protecting saint-visionaries. There is no giant tote board in the sky, tabulating all of a person's eco-friendly missionary work on a column next to the purchases of eco-killings, nor is anyone going to save the earth through exhortation or advice, or through leftist I-piss-golden-genius nectar-and-shit-parabolas-of-fresh-God-earth-dirt blogswoggle. You are as *guilty*, as I am likely to be, and as *innocent*, call it a cosmic wash for just being born, absolving none and yet absolving all, since each of our collective social measures has been determined by unchangeable mass errors of private car culture, territorial robbery, religion-based discrimination, military dominance of governmental budgets, historical injustices that multiply and then renew in different forms.

ENOR 54 -   **BACKSLIDING**

In the supersystem, there is always the danger of backsliding. The consumer goes to Wal-Mart for a cheaper tire. A big Mac for the way home. A bigger car for crash protection on the freeway. A job working for the Man. In innumerable ways, the forward-thinking progressive lets the Cause down, sooner or later, in ways big and small, mostly due to entering the slipstream of of profit-centered private purchasing and ethics-less employment. What you buy tomorrow, who you vote for, where your energy comes from, how much indulgence you permit yourself, is conditioned and governed by the supersystem, which has been under strange and epileptic and harmful ownership since humanity survived the supervolcano 73,000 years ago. Given that we have supervolcanos to the left and right of us, are hurtling through an asteroidal space, have armed opposing armies with humanity-extinction weapons, are staggering toward incredible climate destruction, are invaded by replicating lethal viruses, and are being entangled in ungoverned computer complexity, we should enjoy the heroic survival of our species thus far. Despite all of the obstacles, both in nature and in our own nature, despite the fragility of our delicate constitutions and the havoc we often unintentionally wreak on the means of our subsistence, we have not overcompromised the communal generational project of dreaming, thinking, acting, and sleeping. In many ways a grand failure, humanity still laughs off its harm-causing predilections and finds its disturbed way to blunder through.

ENOR 55 -   SOCIAL ENGINEERING

Pentagon academics pursue nuclear primacy and construct world wars according to sinister but palpable ideology, and a housewife buys Palmolive on sale because of an offshoot of that very ideology. The overarching absurdities of global disequity through neoconservative think-tank covert strategy have been the epitaph for so many victims, and they yet continue, bureaucratic imperatives now writ across space, cyberspace, dead territories of Third-World oil nexus, and the corridors of extractive corporations. We all sleep under this supersystemic shadow, some in precisely climate-controlled luxury, many with dreams of private gain, not bad for a species that erupts in organized mass murder every so often. The consumer shopper-world of upgradable labor-saving gizmos was a far less threatening model to human life than the Nazi forerunner, but it will prove utterly destructive to the natural world that supplies its materials. If the machine is evidently working, it requires no thought to turn it on again to produce its observable work, even if that work will destroy the very ground beneath the machine and its human operator. You will like what you have, or think it can be improved with some new product, providing all the forward momentum from below that the supersystem requires. Our remonstrations will do no good: a total system redesign, only in theory possible, would involve the deaths of vast numbers of our fellow humans, as corporations violently disintegrated, social reality collapsed into overnight cultural warring, food distribution became problematic in a week, energy and power systems trembled into chaos, the violent urges of the envious human species became overt and widespread in rolling waves of mass deprivation.   Better to paper over the problems of a rotten, ill-designed, badly managed building, and hope that the lights continue to turn on.

ENOR 56 -   THE AUGURIES

The sun set upon an ungenerous age. Oldies rock could be played unto the nursing home, but there was going to be no safety net that would support the fall of the spectators in the cheap seats. Gone were the defined benefit pensions, the unions, the affordable rents, the low-cost health care, the manageable tuitions for the confused children, the happy teachers, "good" wars, honorable professions, the community centers, the $10 tickets to the game or the show, the bank loans, the New Deal, naive optimism in a space race or a technology fix. In their place, or in the place of the illusion of social progress their ideals represented, the culture could provide a mediated reuptake of calamity-voyeur immiseration. There was no "living organism"at work, no fanciful woo "Gaia," no predestined steady state, but a complex system of systems built and operating on faulty principles encapsulated in myths and mythos, as capable of heading towards collectively-generated disaster as towards halcyon "sustainability." No outcome was foreordained, so humans had the eternal task of assessing the auguries while trying to adapt to the massed verities.

ENOR 57 -   THE FUTURE WITHOUT OIL

The post-WWII American empire was based on the the mass industrial exploitation of cheap hydrocarbons, from oil to coal to natural gas, burned in innumerable scientific processes from car fuel to plastics to global transportation to agricultural fertilizer. The world's population of humans grew commensurately with this exponential development and release of this 500-million year store of fossilized solar energy. There were great disparities in the application of this planetary employment of the energy produced by these extracted hydrocarbons, but these massive global inequities will be dwarfed by the looming resource depletion of these same hydrocarbon energy sources. There is nothing in the pipeline to replace these past-peak sources of both human energy usage and planetary pollution, nothing at all capable of lighting the way for the planet's arriving 7-8 billion. No social or economic forces exist to distribute the remaining hydrocarbons from the earth's interior reaches that will forestall war, mass deprivation, or starvation. How would we replace human blood if it were endangered? Technical solutions have arrived in human history, but not at scale, and not because of conscious social cooperation. We have made electrons jump and aggregate to satisfy commercial interests, but we have never arrived at working social organization. Run-of-the-mill apocalyptarian soothsaying has become endemic to the self-styled "opposition," portraying the issuer as living with future certainty, when the basics of life and death and human communication are forever vexatious. Whatever we "know" will not bring back to life those lost to death, nor secure to us a sense of who we are. As global political events assure us that there is no positive element in charge, we can look to each other for confirmation of that truth, and then take it from there.

The screws have been turned so many times across the centuries that they have become incapable of engaging with the durable wood – yet every new intellectual attempt must be a *new style of approach*, not just another turn of the common implement. Ample evidence exists to confirm that humans can adjust and continue in the face of mass death, terrible inequality, horrific devastation – so there is a human future, after all. The planet will heat and kill a now-forlorn concept of a "better world for all," as humans entertain the reality of a dystopia that was their own doing, and they will find ways of rationalizing the fractious divides that will seep from ecological crisis. Although this will obviate the moronic 18th century phrase of "happiness," a state of non-consideration of others, human communication will produce more consonant attempts to provide a cover story, with suitable advertising tag lines. Science and technology will prove wholly unequal to the new set of global problems, as we computer-chart our way precisely to series of terrible "developments." The global security and surveillance industries will place their lids on insurrections that threaten to spill over from the great slums of our doomed Third World mega-cities, creating invisible walls between empires and their colonies. Collapse or stasis, more downward-facing inequality or momentous ecological desertification – our eyes will remain blinking, our self-generated comfort still an electrical impulse away. Until our screens become unlit, culture will absorb the ringing political realities, but those "in charge" will still be a few hundred Venn diagrams from those that know *how things work, and how they can be made better*. So many will suffer from this disconnect, but elite ascendancy is always awaiting a sub-selection of mostly basket-case middle-rung strivers.

ENOR 58 -   HUMANS

The human brain is prone to enormous private psychic pain, maelstroms of recrimination, self-disparagement, worry, antipathy, repetitive frustration, repressed fury, ineradicable disappointment, and that is on a good day. Yet, judging by public utterance, all is smooth harmony and frolicsome bonhomie, nary a thought passing through the sunny skies of a life well led and surrounded by generous friends and joyous family. Why the discrepancy, which is evident according to the levels of anti-depression medications, therapeutic interventions, drug-taking, physical unhealthiness, public obstreperousness? Humans cannot let the guard of propriety down amongst others, not generally, since the air becomes befouled with unearned pitiableness and unresolvable angst, and status competition mitigates against finding support from the common miseries. To see humans contending with their minor yet voluminous burdens with a traveler's determination is to see how others see you- vaguely pitiable, possessed of limited self-awareness, not quite young.

ENOR 59 -   THE RICH

In this parched and denuded intellectual landscape, the American rich come in for staggeringly low levels of opprobrium. Who could be an easier target than these harrumphing, money-engorged, self-besotted incompetents? Surrounded by the tinsel trappings of a anti-meritocracy, kept at bejeweled arms-length from any of their lessers, the modern rich hear very little of the criticism of their opulent, charmless vagrant lives. From cradle to grave, the bureaucratic imperatives of oligarchy have supplied both the material and mythic support to their arrogation of cascades of money – private school, "elite" higher education, access to large credit , incredible legal and political undergirding of their massive failures, fawning service at gated hotels, a social conspiracy to supply voluminous entitlement to every thought and action. After the scare of World War II, wherein the rich were liable to die on front lines as soldiers and pilots, the young rich could walk on the clouds of privilege, showing up for beckoning non-strenuous classrooms, partaking of the cultural pleasures of the burgeoning sixties, falling into tech booms and investment graft with the ease of practiced mountebanks. With every institution bending in silent homage, the scions and debutantes saw comfort and rescue, invitation and growth. Churches and classrooms, boardrooms and tax shelters, far-away bombing sites and cobalt mines, sewers and satellites, all in service of the never-satisfied or responsible well-born. Social mobility having halted in America after the grand upsurge in industrial wage development, the rich see themselves as winners in the world's only democratic meritocracy, a fantastic lie on all its counts. All human lives are built on the infinite, unknowable, historic, inexpressable exertions of others to sustain their places in the grand drama of advantage, yet the American mythos promotes the fictional "self-made man." When will the bill come due for the American rich? What process could begin the calculation of what is owed for so much accrual? If I am, you are, the product of so much suffering by others, yet there will never be an accounting, nor a rectification, do we need to write a check?

ENOR 60 -   POST-CAPITALISM

Are we to see the demise of this oligarchic rule – the "postcapitalism" that all righteous folk have so longed for since the antediluvian demarcation into the propertied and the property-less? With machines taking over the human need for human labor, can we get to that state of health and happiness that a well-fed yet engaged animal seems to exude? Can we put our human talents for analysis and technological co-operation together to fashion a self-correcting societal matrix of plenitude and enforced restraint? Sure – that should be no problem from now on. We know our errors now – we know what is to be discarded , what is to be introduced. Shall we all join hands and commence the redo? Where do we start? How do we get agreement from a fatally disputatious species? How does entrenched and overwhelming and enormously variegated power let its death grip slacken -because some good folks demand a world of bounteous purity to reflect the enormous self-regard they cherish? The known world never was place of abundant sweet social harmony, not even in the America of Jeffersonian yeomen and farmers exchanging hardscrabble recipes and Elizabethan scat-verse. Instead, humans have invented psychic melodrama to cope with the immovable largeness of time and disturbed outside movement, and so it shall it be – informed self-analysis.

ENOR 61 -   **THIS WORLD**

Towards the source we incline – where is that animating control for the social reality within which we are entrapped? Since a god or gods is so obviously long dead, we ask for a political system of systems, determining overt policy through debate, elections, and competing policy papers. Yet the more talk about "change," the more social reality doubles back upon itself for tiresome mocking of sweet desire. Americans by a growing majority understand fully that voting is a superfluous act when large corporate entities determine the scope and theater of the political game. Honest brokers give up on the possibility of adult romance, going to sleep alone after another night of televisual non-sexual entertainment. Authors give up on book projects, give up on being an author, as musicians abandon the band and athletes retire. The supersystem specializes in providing dreamers the adult knowledge that they will not "overcome." There are fully realized aspirations, of course, beautiful products of relentless preparation and risk that place their architects in great and exalted superiority, but these are exceptions, quite minor in number, that testify to the totemic nature of human frustration and loss. The best of times is no match for the times that the best is gotten of us – yet that is just pure fact, to be fought by the glories of this, the best and most salutary world we shall ever know.

ENOR 62 -   **OVERVIEW**

During the course of writing this book, the fortunes of those at the elite level of the supersystem, that 1% or so, have grown fattened beyond understanding. The money, the yachts, the numerous unlived-in mansions, the plastic surgery, the private educations for their unbrilliant children, the investments and degrees of regulatory control, the wars and the wars of want and suffering imposed upon the poor and badly-situated, have increased by astounding degrees, all moving in concert to that great assumption of power across the globe. After the writing of this book, those indices will grow and mutate further, all expositions of human social reality, not some metaphor or literary conceit. The outcome of unveiling this supersystem should be a momentary near-unity. Look anew upon this magnificent beast – but then we must find, after our nods of in-commonality, some mutual defense plans. How do we look upon the now-inherent silliness of our lives in dramatic appreciation? All of us have differential standings within the supersystem: some are pharoahically rich, some are determined to wrest financial riches no matter what, some will benefit in undue ways until they die from massed forces of inherited or ill-obtained financial capital. Your precise position in the supersystemic hierarchy is always affected by major and minor social tremors, is affected by fears and anxieties both real and imagined, and is often wholly misperceived. How can you fight a massively superior force when you do not even know where you stand? As much as we may steel ourselves that we can "fight" this monster "together," when the lights come back on, we must scurry back to our variably sized, variably provisioned holes. There is no "people"s revolution" coming, no nobility from "fighting the good fight," no looming "singularity," no "progress" that will not have come at enormous cost borne by our fellow, though doomed, humans. The gulf between our aspirations and our accomplishments, between our achievements and our failings, between individual flight and collective grounding, between the purity of happiness and the gloom of suffering, will widen in both reality and in the realm of perception, yet this the gulf that all humans have encountered. Our lives will not have been the "end" of anything, nor the culmination, nor the beginning, but the enactment of large, ineffable social realities.

Since, according to the work of Tim Garrett, the world is heading inexorably for 1000 ppm by the end of the century, we, each of us, are one of humanity's declining generations. The line will come to end as the planet heats too much for human life, thought the next generation will be the one to inherit the burgeoning cataclysms that accompany climate devastation. If we try to geoengineer or decarbonize our energy systems, human civilization will go through massive die-off. With human population passing the 6 billion mark on it way to 9 billion, the fossil fuel systems of food production and fertilization will be necessary so that mass starvation does not occur, but that mode of production will hasten the climate catastrophes headed straight for us. All our worries for mundane "reform" and existential improvement are but weeds before this howling wind. The pseudo-science of doom-and-gloom may have had its mistaken calls of imminent apocalypse, but where are the papers that can blend economics, sociology, psychology, and atmospheric science to show humanity able to alter its global course away from an uninhabitable earth? Can we only look back at the temperate Holocene as it begins to recede that fatal retreat from view?

ENOR 63 -   DESTINY

All we can do is what we are impelled to do, though listening to the wise or challenging words of others is a good practice on the way to the grave. We are significantly driven by the particularities of our circumstances, for which we have but slight control, though we can sometimes surprise ourselves with our out-of-character swings. Within these parameters of defined but permeable social happenstance, we can see the improvement that comes from being rational and expansive in our private choices, and should imagine ourselves and our worlds capable of genuine uplift through great fortuity – but the reality of the social future appears its antithesis. The abiding diamond pleasures of our individual lives are to be enjoyed without neurotic guilt, since they will disappear as the various interlocking sections of our brain issues their last cranial electricity, but until then, we have the right to attempt to document the actual operations of the large domains of the wider world as well as history, future as well as past. Most likely each of us has a better or true "calling" we missed a few thousands of turns ago, but there are not enough slots of merit that a society could ever produce, leaving trails and wakes of frustration for the masses.

What can be used for free expression of contrary views can be monitored and utilized for direct dissemination of controlling counter-views. A witless democratic viewpoint never accounts for the inevitability of massed authority intervening in the balance through superior organization, staying power, financial incentives, and punitive capabilities. What theory of radical change through direct action sees the weighting disparity properly?

ENOR 64 -   AGAINST THE NIGHTLY TELE-COMA

Real scholarship, and voluminous essaying, has marked the left of the Education phase. Blog sites, books, still some professorships, entire swaths of Hollywood, a few fine speeches on the killing floors of the houses of Congress – a cornucopia of writing, decades after the zenith of left cultural influence, now reduced to nestless peeping. Capitalism as far as the eye can see, even as its tenets are as discredited as an Edsel manual. Disbelief in one system of lies should not lead to equally specious belief in the imminent resurrection of a somewhat competing, completely theoretical system of unknown nature. Who will save the tedious punk rockers and the politically thoughtless doctors? Only the practicing nihilist rises above the miasma of credulous flattery. Should a micro-movement of pure rebellious honesty sneak around above the colossus to come your way, you are of course permitted to be its adherent spokesmodel, and the civil disobedience you will engage in is certainly a step above the nightly tele-coma, but in the warm bath of the western culturology, there is no direct stimulation to leave – what alternative temperature is there? Cold, like Siberia, or hot, like Africa? For all of the individual complaint, the existence of observable, measurable entities like bank account numbers and pine tables makes the known world unlikely to be substantially altered. Our routines of thought and avoidance are of concern to us only, subject to an enormous waste of intrapsychic remonstrance and evaluation – what will we watch tonight, what did he think of what I said, what will bring the problem to a head, where are my socks, how clean is my living room, what will it be like when we get what we want. Higher level thought, such as in structuring world peace or producing a rock 'n roll live spectacular, is as destined for the cancellation by time's relentless march, so why not.

ENOR 65 -   INCONSEQUENCE

Easy corruption has followed the performance of the American government-corporate empire during its century of hegemony. . Any protestation of the present being a new era for the regeneration of these institutions ignores the systemic damage that has been wrought upon every facet of these enterprises. Successive generations of captains and stewards of these ships enter with often benign intentions, only to steer into the prevailing winds of theft and extortion. This voyage is not an exception, nor a failing of moral fortitude, nor a lamentable aberration, but how social conditioning has worked. Those operating the tills can claim the superior knowledge of practice: this is how things are done, this is where the balance of real power leads, at the top there is to time for rhetorical naivete or liberal fantasy. The ships need to get in the water, the voyage proceeds according to wind and weather and the vagaries of competition, who can claim any other reality? The judgment of history may weigh against public figures left, right, and center, but during the time of living power, when decisions cause wars and fortunes and mass suffering alike, there is only the realm of social action, not speculative morality. We, as individuals, will stand in awesome insignificance as holders of only social inconsequence.

What stands as the the threat to the continued rule of the Supersystem?

1.   **Street Protest** (*Current Rating 2.0; Ultimate Rating 3.0*) In other parts of the world, traditions and conditions encourage strong forms of street protest, but not in the US, where the police are armed, equipped, and ready to be hired to incarcerate every variety of protestor, from Black Bloc property damager to labor marcher to simple attendee. The threat and practice of police killings of demonstrators is certainly higher in the Third World, but this history of mass murder raises the stakes and potential effectiveness only there. In the United States, hundreds of thousands may march under the solicitous care of polite police, and listen dutifully to tenured opposition via high-tech speaker systems, but there is no anticipation of any result other than efficient booking and unfavorable media coverage.

2.   **Political Reform** (*Current Rating 0.5; Ultimate Rating 1.5*)   Seas of print, thought, and comment, plus a stratosphere of cyber-wrangling, and there is only the meekest of threat of actual political development. Centrism, even liberalism, may make an occasional ascension to actual governance, ameliorating the harshest consequences of the neoliberal order, but these victories are no match for the debased discourse, the earnest piety of "hope" on all sides, the attention given to intellectual nonentities, the rampages of empire, the latest chapter in this absurd dystopian novel of political deceit. To achieve some forward position in some better age, the Supreme Court must be dissolved, elections financed through equitable public shares, swords turned into ploughshares, and pigs as the national airline. The vaunted "democracy" of the American political system has always been a fiction, capable only in the most dire and conditional of economic times for even remotely allowing for anti-elite rule. There is too much financial advantage for the ruling class to permit political inroads upon their ownership of varied means of social power. The off-shoring of jobs and the forced disintegration of the laboring class into competing factions of unrepresented strivers has marked the decades of wage stagnation and demand pressure, and will continue.

2.   **Cultural Shift** (Current Rating 1.5; Ultimate Rating 3.5) The arc of history was bought in open government sale by Altria Worldwide in 2004,and bends in the vicinity of Davos, Switzerland 30 degrees toward the leeward side. Humane and liberal institutions have been constructed, painstakingly, since the Enlightenment, from mental health teams to atheist websites to dance clubs to solar installers to power pop resurrecters, but they are a collective howl against the prevailing winds of sanctioned obfuscation. Humanity has a beastly record of further oppression of its disadvantaged poor, abusing its defenseless children and defenseless slum dwellers and "weaker" women and girls since the advent of industrial civilization. That legacy of religion-supported, official perfidy periodically returns to cause the recurrent gusts of blame-the-poor and bomb-the-brown hate-pate (antagonistic patriotism) of the American center. Unctuous yuppies vie with viper upper management to staff the forward cabin of the massive ocean liner, using the advertising propaganda of earlier ages to set the party theme. Recurrent news items serve to highlight only the "budgetary" failures of the neoliberal order – lunatic young male shooters, rabid hero rightists, killer cops, dead poor, infrastructure in the dust, open Treasury thievery. If there is to be "Progress," it cannot come at the expense of the degradation of the masses, for that will not be Progress at all, but the amplification of the separation of the human species into two.

Distemper and superficially-buried annoyance and dull grievance mark the outlook of a people who have no firm purchase on a sense if life's bounty. Mental illness, nursed negative ambitions, finely-honed sense of innate individual superiority, reduced empathy, an alternating focus on trivial slights and grandiose destiny mark the modern damaged male in this supersystem, where sexual anxiety and hierarchy anxiety mix with a societal encouragement of self-directed obsession to send the lovelorn fantasist into violence or psychosis. Positive understanding and healthy social awareness are certainly attainable in this consumer wonderworld, but without a viable outlet for a normal adult enjoyment, what can define a "well-adjusted" psyche? Saying not-weird things on the Internet? Being thought all-right by the maddening crowd? Having a clear driving record? Not being under indictment? Having a firm sense of the absurd, but being sufficiently engaged in the mundane tasks of family and work to fake it as an upright citizen? Never looking down, or back, or up, and too closely?

3.   Rationality – (Current Rating 2.0; Ultimate Rating 2.5) The existence of the Supersystem explains the persistence and supremacy of irrational, functionally nonsensical, ahistorical, moronic effluvia like Republican tax cuts for the wealthy, invasive wars in extremely poor Third World countries, Fox News, Grateful Dead reunion tours, TV advertising, legal semi-automatics, In God We Trust invocations, SUVs, any day's events. Placing political efforts in local political elections in a de-growth stealth infiltration campaign cannot supply rationality to the diverse systems – no local interest groups or radical city alderpeople are capable of canceling the combined oppression of the dominant growth criminal syndicates. Natural crises may precipitate new configurations of power, but none of these horrors will be welcome or salutary for their victims, and these mass deaths or widespread sufferings from enforced deprivation may cause further ratcheting up of state control to further the cause of the wealthy, rather than openings for a few hip folks on a drug mission.

Within the supersystem, accepting and retreating are fine and rational options. Life situations are far too nervously balanced by large forces to permit fake tough guy stands and martyr climbs. Animals adjust to their roles within a hierarchy, and become the role that is assigned to them by this combination of innate disposition, genetic predetermination, conditional shaping, and mild role exploration and occasional role rebellion. Humans push against this on-going arrangement of destiny, searching for that extra biscuit or that necessary display of submission from subordinates. Within the political arena, non-actors blame elected representatives for not performing as any rational humane person should, but in order to get and maintain that political position, the elected representative must acquire anti-humane and supra-rational characteristics in operation. The grand sweep of history suggests flux and fraught social negotiation of operating power, with wars and territories and identities shifting in epochal battles of war and peace, but the destruction of natural human habitat has grown too widespread to permit a resumption of the Ages of Exploration and Empire and Expansion.

The supersystem is a global crisis today, not some theoretical construct down the winding road. We are within its great and omnifaceted operation, not seeing its reach nor its daily insidious command. This is not an extinction event, this global order, not yet, but it is an endangerment, and the signs are not good. We can persist in this odious economic inequality, twirl in our climate befoulings, drive our basic resources towards unmerciful ends, watch our great inheritance of rational information evaporate, and this may take some lifetimes to end with humans unfurling the last sail to bake in the Antarctic heat. Independent public action may well up through the interstices of the governing superstructure, relocalizing portions of the economy to grow rutabagas in the sidewalk cracks and re-purpose technological detritus, but the main areas are too strongly welded by myth and delusion and conniving practice to permit restructuring.

The conclusion is too dire for many to entertain. The great story of usurpation of nature by the industrial colossus is a reigning myth, one that sustained corporations, invaders, prospectors, willing workers, politicians, judges and now neoliberal intellectuals – humanity on laudable quests for expansion and utilization of its environmental riches, only now the obverse consequences of unchecked ambition are supremely evident. The rules of rationality dictate that the bill for heedlessness will eventually come due. However, that process of discovery of destructive by-products takes place long after the first signs of devastation ahead appear, sweeping up societies in absurd cargo cults that discount any skepticism. The oceans of plastic, beheaded mountains, dammed or dry rivers, extinct species, offloaded problems on the Third World, are all the evidence we should need to question the religious notion that mankind has a divine right and divine guidance in its economic affairs, but the attempt to clean-up, let alone re-organize, has been comical in its feebleness and bullied timidity.

The ghosts of battles lost and ground once held and now corrupted float above the opposition. Old goats and young whippersnappers intone and propound and expatiate like the world belongs to them and the revolution is nigh in their house tonight. The Internet adds the instant chorus of a thousand self-appointed experts upon topics both big and small, furthering prying the opening in the mind to its breaking. Vicious turf and alliance battles, the hallmarks of any work site, become the preoccupation of the margins that have no recourse to more important considerations of actual power. Who said what about whom? stands as the concern of the age, from homeless barrel fire to exalted Bilderberg conference soiree, enmity crackling the cell-phone towers and fiber-optic cables as adults turn upon each other in the absence of true work or inter-personal solidarity. And this is just within families and allegedly like-minded sites and groups, let alone the sect vs. sect battles too hateful for more than a few disconsolate psychopaths to stomach.

ENOR 66 -   **INTERNATIONAL**

Positive developments! Unrest and uprisings and protests and non-violent restraint breaking out, in the Middle East, soon to be in the Second World, then the First. Who cannot be heartened by the spontaneous will of the people exercised against oppressive rulers? Down with the old, in the with the new? Shall the supersystem perish in our lifetimes? There is, however, a great distance between Third World poverty under authoritarian rule and the lives of middle class Americans, and an even greater gulf between the authoritarian rule of the transnational capital and local terror of America-friendly autocrats. The structures of rule and control vary in their horrors across the globe, and if one or two malign forms are overturned by long-suffering peoples, this does not constitute an overthrow of the entire supersystem, which is Job One for the human race. Political power within the supersystem requires extremely complex adjustments of rhetoric to the omni-

179

directional axes of existing social power, damning all protest movements to subsequent deformations in the real conduct of business and security and law. Street and revolutionary military victories have occurred in small global venues, but the large sweep of global social history is defiant in its preference for large-scale disintegration. Popular attention may go to the unusual, to the martyrs and street marches and the selfless political arrestees, but social reality is a record of dutiful conduct, the flattening of ambition, the long flat plane of dominant adherence.

ENOR 67 -   ANALYSIS

Boredom, ennui, anger, and loath-filled anxiety are hazards in trying to analyze the scope and operation of the supersystem. Tales of banking intrigue, though central to the story of the looting of the global economy by the elite pillagers, can cause cognitive paralysis. How many scholarly exegeses, of what we know to be the murder of all that could be good, can we stand in their formal, correctly referenced APA prose? How much bloodlessness is allowed in contending with the bloodletting of the public weal? The rise of popular culture in the west, disseminated now and forever in ever-more available and effective forms, should mean that theoretical political tomes have to get as radically technological as the competition, with accompanying music, multimedia presentations, free trade T-shirts, interactive cell-phone ringtones, and website forums for crowdsourcing audiences. However, that all takes money as well as the certainty that the supersystem can be hacked or attacked, and neither means is currently in play. The supersystem gets to play in all its futuristic technological wizardry, while its opposition has only 16th century gray text, plus some sharp social networking sites bound for sophisticated monitoring suppression.

ENOR 67 -   UP AND DOWN

Humanity is on track to use 47% more energy by the year 2030, 87% of that new total in the form of fossil fuels. The atmosphere is already at 390 ppm, with extreme weather due to climate change having already made its permanent entrance. Population rise, and the need to feed and and house and electrify those imminent masses, is incontrovertible. There are no mitigating factors – this is our inheritance. Cheap fossil fuels powered humanity's ascendancy from the huddled and running hunters and gatherers, yet that extraction-and-use technological achievement is now placing its natural environment, as well as its own social civilization, on its road to spectacular demise. We who rode the apex of this curve will wake up to some blue skies, some placid oceans, non-glowing fish for dinner, money in the bank and electrons juicing our nights, but we know the truth, that others are busy perishing because of our insatiable collective needs.   Death will eventually relieve of us of responsibility and concern for this dichotomy between our exploitations of economic opportunities and our desires for pure sweet natural harmony, but until that individual end point, humans will tell themselves many, many lies about how good it is, how good it could be, how much we can fight this determined sentence. The logic of this minor closed system is stark – more people, more energy, more fossil fuel energy, more destruction, the boredom of inescapable destiny – but the promise of querulous intellectual wrangling over the particulars will be sure to keep the role of the institutions intact. The question is one of preparation – will the advanced world create structures of comprehensive worldwide enforcement to permanently and completely divest itself of its supersystem, and create structures of comprehensive worldwide enforcement to prevent the second and third world from entering into wholesale adoption of the advanced stages of its economic structures? Sure, it will get right on those matters, fortwith – no problem on either end. Wait for the "reply." End of message. Engineers and other specialty scientists can focus on possible thermondynamic systems, but they are uniformly woeful when entering sociological dimensions. How will human societies react to the variables of energy use, cultural doctrine, psychological distress, economic inequality, mass deprivation, off-loaded economic drudgery? . In the immediate global human predicament, first-world luxuries will be the precipitant of third -world poverty that will travel into the very homes of the decadent American rich, more as a function of historical truth than climate catastrophe, for all the talk of children and grandchildren. The big delay could also occur, as institutions right their ships for the moment, with temporary adjustments, enough suffering human ballast below for the time being.

ENOR 68 -   **VERITIES**

Throughout this period of the evolution of the human psycho-social brain, humans have stepped over or on other suffering and dying and dead humans on their way to engorgement. The immoral rich now have more buffers of inter-continental distance and community gates and systemic enforcement of spatial separation to enjoy their trivial wealthy lives, and their brains now specialize in the latest form of outward-directed avoidance. I am worthy of what I have, these rich think in common, and will stand to profit even as others who cannot be me face their deaths, as other economic and political forces larger and greater than me do their mysterious work. This avoidance is not much cognitive work – nature has placed easy grooves in each human brain for acceptance of both unearned gain and unearned demise. The coming epoch does have new opportunities for direct engagement with the expressive immorality of the hideously self-protective rich who have had centuries of beneficial social myth, but because humans abide their social systems if they do not believe that they are at the true bottom of them, inside will remain inside. In the supersystem, wealth and position are built on phantasms and insubstantiality, allowing the worst and the most untalented to rise or stay atop, as self-deception continues its victory run through the firing human psyche.

ENOR 69 -   **FUTUROLOGY**

Corporate futurologists at multinational behemoths like Shell have issued dire and detailed warnings about likely futures of rampant social unrest and instability, using informed computer models to depict enormous gaps between population growth impositions and resource availability. In earlier times, humans could have narrowed visions and still see themselves as social luminaries, but in today's opened-up perspective, no amount of personal accomplishment can provide the dramatic vista of global supersystemic change that is necessary for a sense of contentment. An estancia of a thousand acres and seaside homes in five continents – will that sufficiently obscure the views of world-wide crisis? A Nobel in Literature and royalties to last seven generations – will that remove the social conscience that comprehends a disconsolate human majority seeing its social superstructure break at the seams and in the interiors?

ENOR 70 - DOWN THE ROAD

Prognostication should be our national pastime, but the Information Age has yet to turn research into insight. Despite our production of knowledge and statistical certainty, we falter when processing this into realistic anticipation of our collective future. For every expression of optimism, that mankind can work out the ecological/economic/political conundrum of more growth leading to corrupt pro-growth anti-politics leading to ecological collapse, there needs to be a specific mapping of antecedents. Where or when have elites ever given up on their advantages? When has self-interest ever handed its perquisites over to long-term concerns for unrelated others? How many endless fascinations with the "young," with the trappings of "a new world," are allowed to dissipate through the continuities of power before the project of injecting the synthetic drug of liberal optimism into every upwelling of popular discontent is discontinued? The ship of globalization has sailed, and the Happy Meals are tightly wrapped and secure below-decks, headed for every far corner of the globe. Water and fire, insect and large mammal, trinket and job, family and fun, headed for series of rolling crises that will envelop all social institutions – only not yet, not for you, not while the systems of commerce are guarded and sheltered.

ENOR 71 - ATOMIZATION

The costs to the atomization of culture and society were nevertheless evident on many levels, from the individual to the family to workplaces to politics and culture. Masses of people were left to contend with the ravages of loneliness, as other humans and other endeavors lost their flavor in comparison to the single enclosed abode with the self-chosen entertainments. Depression and suicide attached to the host cells when the real world was no match for inner turmoil. The vagaries of a sedated and sedentary life in the privileged West mutated into animated flicking of keys and channels, as the inter-tribal connections that permeated ancestral life became lost to the digitized ether. The question of which life was better was irrelevant, since people can only live in their own times, a limitation of time and place that makes nostalgia a curse. Free in theory to choose their destinies, humans in practice are pushed in the back by strong social hands towards similar places, but when feelings of self-importance and -accomplishment are so fleeting, herded people turn their displeasure at their bare meadow inward upon themselves. Despairing of finding that elusive non-annoying friend, people have check-listed themselves into a solitary corner, but this is as much a function of the supersystem as any deficiency within the human social skill. What is the precise set of social competencies that will provide an emotionally secure psyche in this insecure age? How much rage, outer and inner, is admitted to that demarcated level? Who should feel that they will have done well with the intensely variable-driven life – truly *satisfactory* people, or only those with higher than average self-evaluation?

ENOR 72 - ADVANTAGE WILL BE TAKEN

One by one, the vaunted solutions offered by the neoliberal state supersystem are revealed as hoaxes, blights, frauds, black holes, budgetary nightmares, mafia extortion campaigns, endless roundelays of deceit and cover-up, but the supersystem does not lose any steam. Those who perpetuate the wars and the corporate hegemon are in prime places to guarantee the next round of distorted management and governance. Bad news and staged interventions to subdue the victims dominate the day, but no human wants to see the world in that stultifying, morose sense. Advantage will be taken, by humans, no matter what the conditions, and with only tenuous bonds to the people and animals involved. Cooperation and reciprocity and bounteous self-disregard are within our human capacities, and they can often flourish, but not within the configurations of the present supersystem. Friendship and love are rare and extravagant defenses against the intrusions of the modern corporate state, but do they generate profits and safe ecosystems, happy families and functional societies? Can the world be traveled and the work-day be done on enclosed shared understandings of a social anti-reality? The post-war years of official exploitation of the idealism of well-intentioned liberals are revealed as propaganda, with sanctioned exacerbation of cruel social disparity at play in the Roundup fields. Yet our social reality will not be a dystopia, but simply a long degradation of sad and vicious "tragedies," all due to the official failures that are mandated from the stupendous distortions wrought by the power imbalances. Catastrophes are thought by radicals to be fertile ground for reformation and solidarity, but even this rosy fantasia is contradicted by the ever-present ability of the established churches, the protean militaries, and the shape-shifting trans-national corporations to sweep into scenes of great death and emerge with new blueprints for conquest. What force ever willingly gives up advantage?

ENOR 73 -   HATE

Social criticism is a mug's game, suitable for bachelor cranks and obsessive autonomists. Surely a solution or two would help, or a reference to the good old days when Americans were one intact family of shopkeepers and tow-headed kids and all the racism a religion could buys. Why all this "hate" for prayer, for America the Land of the Free, for elite academia, for politicians, for old folks and for young folks, for nice good liberals and We Shall Overcome, for the future and the past, for books and for speeches and for technology and for computers and for dinner parties and for the artist as savant, and for the written word and tabulated research monograph, for hope and optimism and good times with good people? "Hate" implies violence and malevolence, in a package of righteous fury that avenges all the wrongs that emanates from the evil-doer – so there is not "hate" in the theory of the supersystem. Who could try to right that much damage? Injustice can be "hated," of course, but the long view of humanity's course indicates a high probability of more injustice, spread even further to cover the newly erupting cracks. The condition of perception can be delimited with any verb, but the world is made of action, and our perceptions shall forever remain our own, resplendent for the indifferent world, fated to remain inside.

Deep within the bonds of social reality, there can seem no way out. Unlike the comforts of history and accepted science, there is no guarantee how any of this works out in the end. The motoring landscape of America, where so much of postwar America has been lived, features the dextrous coordination of stop-lights, the parking lots of megastores, low-wage fast-food snackfood dispensaries, precision-made foreign automobiles, and locked-in beasts of suburban pasts. Birth, school, peer sorting, more school, semi-work, and the chance to pass that stupendous legacy to another round of screen-dependent progeny marks our asphalt'd version of life. Try to contend with these imposed social conventions, through some application of the latent powers of artistic alteration or original political formulation, and you risk being lost in baleful discontent, shamed by any constituency that defends its social turf, however doleful or bereft From this glass house, all the humans appear stupid and manipulated, and the stones can be thrown in any direction, catching the dumb robots upside their gibbering mouths, but who wants live constantly searching for rocks? Who wants to maintain the upkeep on all those shine-needing windows?

There is no rationalism or secularism that can support a benign view of our social reality, since we are implicated in countless ways in species extinction, intense global poverty, mass hunger, preventable deaths, all of the boilerplate litany that causes our fellow alert humans such boredom to be confronted with, yet again. Life itself is not sustainable, since its chemical energy causes its own habitat destruction – some version of the second law of thermodynamics of states of order tending towards entropy, and then dissolution. For the good of the cause of all humanity, we should attend to the task of the clinical observation of this bizarre occurence, closely and with unalloyed good humor, though only for a few hours a day – there's high times and new complications awaiting the resolute.

www.ingramcontent.com/pod-product-compliance
Lightning Source LLC
Chambersburg PA
CBHW060301290526
45789CB00001B/376